THE HISTORY OF COUNSELING PSYCHOLOGY

THE BROOKS/COLE SERIES IN COUNSELING PSYCHOLOGY
John M. Whiteley, University of California at Irvine
Arthur Resnikoff, University of California at Irvine
Series Editors

Helene K. Hollingsworth
Editorial Assistant

APPROACHES TO ASSERTION TRAINING
Editors: John M. Whiteley, University of California at Irvine
John V. Flowers, University of California at Irvine
THE BEHAVIOR THERAPIST
Editor: Carl E. Thoresen, Stanford University
CAREER COUNSELING
Editors: John M. Whiteley, University of California at Irvine
Arthur Resnikoff, University of California at Irvine
COUNSELING ADULTS
Editors: Nancy K. Schlossberg, University of Maryland
Alan D. Entine, State University of New York at Stony Brook
COUNSELING MEN
Editors: Thomas M. Skovholt, University of Minnesota
Paul G. Schauble, University of Florida at Gainesville
Richard Davis, Northwestern Community Mental Health Center
COUNSELING WOMEN
Editors: Lenore W. Harmon, University of Wisconsin-Milwaukee
Janice M. Birk, University of Maryland
Laurine E. Fitzgerald, University of Wisconsin-Oshkosh
Mary Faith Tanney, University of Maryland
DEVELOPMENTAL COUNSELING AND TEACHING
Editors: V. Lois Erickson, University of Minnesota
John M. Whiteley, University of California at Irvine
THE HISTORY OF COUNSELING PSYCHOLOGY
Editor: John M. Whiteley, University of California at Irvine
THE PRESENT AND FUTURE OF COUNSELING PSYCHOLOGY
Editors: John M. Whiteley, University of California at Irvine
Bruce R. Fretz, University of Maryland
THEORETICAL AND EMPIRICAL FOUNDATIONS OF
RATIONAL-EMOTIVE THERAPY
Editors: Albert Ellis, Institute for Rational-Emotive Therapy
John M. Whiteley, University of California at Irvine

THE HISTORY OF COUNSELING PSYCHOLOGY

EDITED BY

JOHN M. WHITELEY
UNIVERSITY OF CALIFORNIA AT IRVINE

BROOKS/COLE PUBLISHING COMPANY
Monterey, California

A Division of Wadsworth, Inc.

Acquisition Editor: *Claire Verduin*
Production Editor: *Stacey C. Sawyer*
Interior Design: *Laurie Cook*
Cover Design: *Sharon Marie Bird*
Typesetting: *Instant Type, Monterey, California*

Printed in the United States of America

10 9 8 7 6 5 4 3 2 1

Much of the material in this book originally appeared in *The Counseling
Psychologist*, the official publication of the Division of Counseling
Psychology of the American Psychological Association.

Library of Congress Cataloging in Publication Data

Main entry under title:

The History of counseling psychology.

(The Brooks/Cole series in counseling psychology)
Includes index.
1. Counseling—History.   2. Psychology—History.
I.   Whiteley, John M.
BF637.C6H56   158   79-23441
ISBN 0-8185-0370-X

To Rita Milhollin Whiteley

SERIES FOREWORD

The books in the Brooks/Cole Series in Counseling Psychology reflect the significant developments that have occurred in the counseling field over the past several decades. No longer is it possible for a single author to cover the complexity and scope of counseling as it is practiced today. Our approach has been to incorporate within the Brooks/Cole Series the viewpoints of different authors having quite diverse training and perspectives.

Over the past decades, too, the counseling field has expanded its theoretical basis, the problems of human living to which it addresses itself, the methods it uses to advance scientifically, and the range of persons who practice it successfully—from competent and skillful paraprofessionals to doctoral-level practitioners in counseling, psychology, education, social work, and psychiatry.

The books in the Brooks/Cole Series are intended for instructors and both graduate and undergraduate students alike who want the most stimulating in current thinking. Each volume may be used independently as a text to focus in detail on an individual topic, or the books may be used in combination to highlight the growth and breadth of the profession. However they are used, the books explore the many new skills that are available to counselors as they struggle to help people learn to change their behavior and gain self-understanding. Single volumes also lend themselves as background reading for workshops or in-service training, as well as in regular semester or quarter classes.

The intent of all the books in the Brooks/Cole Series is to stimulate the reader's thinking about the field, about the assumptions made regarding the basic nature of people, about the normal course of human development and the progressive growth tasks that everyone faces, about how behavior is acquired, and about what different approaches to counseling postulate concerning how human beings can help one another.

John M. Whiteley
Arthur Resnikoff

PREFACE

This book entitled *The History of Counseling Psychology* is the first of two volumes addressing the past, present, and future of the profession. The companion volume, edited by John M. Whiteley and Bruce Fretz and also published by Brooks/Cole, is entitled *The Present and Future of Counseling Psychology*. Together they constitute the most comprehensive treatment of all aspects of the profession and its development that is available.

The books in the Brooks/Cole Series in Counseling Psychology normally reflect the significant developments that have occurred in counseling psychology over a brief span of time and on a specific topic.

This two-volume work departs from that tradition, addressing the history and growth of the entire profession for over half a century including projections of role and function to the year 2000 A.D.

The intent of all books in the Brooks/Cole series is to stimulate the reader's thinking about the field and its basic assumptions. This two-volume set extends that intent to include the role of standard reference work on the profession. As such, it is intended for the permanent collections of libraries and professionals, as well as for use in training programs for instructors and both graduate and undergraduate students. Each volume may be used independently as a text, or incorporated together as a source book for studying and understanding the counseling psychology profession — where it came from, where it is now, and where it is expected to go in the future.

I offer my thanks to a number of individuals and groups for their help in the preparation of *The History of Counseling Psychology:*

The American Psychological Association and the individual authors for permission to reprint the articles credited to them in the text;

Teachers College Press, the individual authors, and the good offices of Roger Myers for permission to reprint the articles credited to them in the text;

The Counseling Psychologist and Allen E. Ivey for permission to reprint his article;

C. Gilbert Wrenn for taking the time to carefully review his files and give me access to pertinent documents;

C. Winfield Scott for accessing his set of *Counseling News and Views* to look up information I needed;

Irwin A. Berg, Harold B. Pepinsky, Edward J. Shoben, Leona Tyler, David Tiedeman, C. Gilbert Wrenn, and C. Winfield Scott for their permission to publish their previously unpublished manuscripts;

Helene K. Hollingsworth for her diligent editorial assistance on all aspects of this project.

John M. Whiteley

CONTENTS

INTRODUCTION 1

Chapter 1
The Historical Development of
Counseling Psychology:
An Introduction

JOHN M. WHITELEY

I. INTRODUCTION

The history of counseling psychology reflects a number of important influences: the hard work of visionary professionals; the development of a research base for applied psychology; institutions, particularly universities, schools, and the Veterans Administration; publications like the *Journal of Counseling Psychology* and *The Counseling Psychologist;* psychological interest and aptitude testing companies; and developments in society that have permitted the enhancement of individuality.

The organization of this volume reflects the intent of presenting these formative influences and historical developments of counseling psychology, since these antecedents have had and continue to have a profound influence on the profession as it is practiced today and as it is projected into the future— at least for the balance of the 20th century.

The book is organized into six sections. Section 1 consists of this chapter, which attempts to highlight what is significant in each chapter and, where appropriate, to put the chapter in proper historical context. Section 2 is four chapters tracing the main chronological events in the development of counseling psychology. Section 3 presents the inaugural definitions of the profession that appeared between 1952 and 1956. Section 4 includes a number of previously unpublished chapters written between 1954 and 1962, each reflecting the diversity of opinion that accompanied the growth of the profession.

Section 5 reprints portions of the proceedings of the Greyston Conference that have been out of print. This conference, focusing on the professional preparation of counseling psychologists, provided an important stimulus for rethinking where the profession was heading and what were its central tenets.

Section 6, chapters on conceptions of counseling psychology in 1968 and in 1976, reflect the continuing differences of opinion on the proper emphasis for counseling psychology. Section 6 sets the stage for the second volume in this series (Whiteley & Fretz, 1980), which focuses on the present and future of counseling and psychology.

II. HISTORICAL DEVELOPMENTS

Section 2 of the book presents a selection of historical articles that chronicle major events. Super (1955) in Chapter 2 explores the origins of counseling psychology, particularly those stemming from vocational guidance with its emphasis on exploratory experiences in guidance and on the use of psychological tests as a basis for vocational counseling. Psychotherapeutic procedures based on Rogers' (1942) work, which provided a focus on the person in counseling rather than on isolated problems, led to numerous research and theory-building efforts by many members of the profession. As Super (1955) summarized the early developments:

> the movement which started as vocational guidance in the United States, first with an emphasis on vocational orientation activities and then with a parallel and eventually merging emphasis on aptitude testing, both leading to placement, recently also assimilated a psychotherapeutic approach and has emerged as the "new" field of counseling psychology [p. 4].

Super reviews the debate on the distinctiveness and definition of counseling psychology, particularly in its relationship to other professions. For him, counseling psychology is concerned with the "normalities even of abnormal persons" (p. 4) and with helping individuals make the most of their "personal and social resources and adaptive tendencies" (p. 4). The variety of settings are noted in which counseling psychologists work, including schools, hospitals, universities, social welfare and rehabilitation agencies, and government, business, and industry. This diversity of location of employment continues to the present day, with a trend away from recent doctoral-level graduates of counseling psychology programs going to work in university settings (see Whiteley & Fretz, 1980).

The focus of Scott's (1979) contribution, Chapter 3, is on the seminal developments surrounding the initiation of Division 17 in the period 1945–1963. His paper was commissioned originally at the 1954 meeting of the Executive Committee of Division 17 held in conjunction with the annual American Psychological Association Convention. The minutes of executive committee meetings and a complete file of *Counseling News and Views* (an early publication of Division 17) were the most important sources of data.

From the long-standing conflict between theoretical researchers and applied psychologists (which continues to the present) and the psychological service demands that accompanied World War II, Scott traces both the reorganization of the American Psychological Association and the birth of Division 17. Division 17's official records began with the first annual business meeting held in September, 1946, in Philadelphia, Pennsylvania. Edmund G. Williamson and John G. Darley are credited with significant roles in the founding. Darley, in a 1956 letter to Scott, indicates that Division 17 sought organizational status to "protect the integrity of the field of counseling as a legitimate applied specialty within the new APA organization."

In what is a particularly valuable historical contribution undertaken in 1962, Scott asked the past presidents of Division 17 through that year to submit their "opinions on the most important achievements" and the "gravest issues" the Division had faced. Excerpts from the responses serve as the closing section of Chapter 3.

The subject of Chapters 4 and 5 is the *Journal of Counseling Psychology*, the history of which is inseparably intertwined with that of Division 17. Wrenn (1966), a past president of Division 17 and the founding editor of the *Journal of Counseling Psychology*, reports that the idea for the journal was conceived in 1952 and initiated in 1954 with the appearance of Volume I, No. 1. The creators are identified as Milton E. Hahn, Harold G. Seashore, Donald E. Super, and Wrenn.

In Chapter 5, Pepinsky, who is also someone long active in both Division 17 as past president and in the journal itself, focuses with his writing colleagues (Pepinsky, Hill-Frederick, and Epperson, 1978) on the journal from the perspective of policy development. It was written as a 25th anniversary tribute with special reference to the social and political circumstances influencing its development over the course of its first quarter century. The Pepinsky et al. (1978) chapter is a valuable supplement to the Scott (1979) early history. Pepinsky et al. amplify the events of the "baptismal years" (around 1945–1946) and what they call the "accompaniment (1951–1956) and aftermath (1958–1965) of the landmark years." One focus of this treatment is the relation between the Division of Counseling Psychology and the American Psychological Association. The authors comment upon Division 17's actions and inactions with respect to the American Psychological Association.

An additional publication has been influential in shaping the intellectual dialogue within counseling psychology—*The Counseling Psychologist.* The basic idea for this was germinated in discussions between Ralph Mosher, Norman Sprinthall, and the present writer during the period 1963-65. We were unsuccessful at the time in getting support for a research-oriented monograph which would allow greater depth in reporting methodology.

In 1968, during the presidency of John McGowan, the decision was made by the Executive Committee to discontinue *Counseling News and Views* and put expanded resources into what was to be called *The Counseling Psychologist.* The present writer was named founding editor, Arthur Resnikoff was in turn named managing editor, and the initial editorial board included Thomas W. Allen, Ralph L. Mosher, Cecil H. Patterson, Thomas Magoon, and Carl Thoresen. Hazel Sprandel served for a number of years as assistant managing editor working on the myriad problems of production and circulation.

The design of the cover was by Barbara Jaeger, then a student in the School of Fine Arts at Washington University. Since the first issue, composing and typesetting have been by Fred Faust, proprietor of Just Your Type in St. Louis. The editor is both editor and publisher, as details of both content and production are sources of concern.

In the inaugural issue of *The Counseling Psychologist,* its purpose was described as twofold: (1) to serve as a vehicle for critical analysis and commentary on major professional problems; and (2) to offer a forum for communication of matters of professional concern to the membership of Division 17.

Each issue of *The Counseling Psychologist* has a different topic of concern. The specific format for the consideration of the major issues of necessity varies with the topic. The usual format, however, involves a major treatise on a problem followed by critical analysis by eight or so prominent scholars or practitioners; the author of the treatise is then accorded the opportunity for a rejoinder. This format has proven so popular that when it is departed from for a specific issue, there are usually letters urging a return to the traditional dialogue. Through Volume VII, the topics covered have included:

Volume I   No. 1 Vocational Development Theory, 1969
           No. 2 Client-Centered Therapy, 1969
           No. 3 Student Unrest, 1969
           No. 4 Behavior Counseling, 1969
Volume II No. 1 Black Students in Higher Education, 1970
           No. 2 Encounter Groups, 1970
           No. 3 Existential Counseling, 1971
           No. 4 Deliberate Psychological Education, 1971
Volume III No. 1 Individual Psychology, 1971
           No. 2 Integrity Group Therapy, 1972

	No. 3	New Directions in Training, Part I, 1972
	No. 4	New Directions in Training, Part II, 1972
Volume IV	No. 1	Counseling Women, 1973
	No. 2	The Healthy Personality, 1973
	No. 3	Career Counseling, 1974
	No. 4	Gestalt Therapy, 1974
Volume V	No. 1	Sex Counseling, 1975
	No. 2	Carl Rogers on Empathy, 1975
	No. 3	Marriage and Family Counseling, 1975
	No. 4	Assertion Training, 1975
Volume VI	No. 1	Counseling Adults, 1976
	No. 2	Counseling Women II, 1976
	No. 3	Career Counseling II, 1976
	No. 4	Developmental Counseling Psychology, 1977
Volume VII	No. 1	Rational-Emotive Psychotherapy, 1977
	No. 2	Professional Identity, 1977
	No. 3	The Behavior Therapies—Circa 1978, 1978
	No. 4	Counseling Men, 1978

III. INAUGURAL DEFINITIONS OF A PROFESSION: 1952-1956

Section 3 of the book, focusing on inaugural definitions of the counseling psychology profession, begins with two chapters (6 and 7) on standards for the profession by the Committee on Counselor Training of what was in 1951 still called the Division of Counseling and Guidance of APA. The development of these chapters, according to Super's (1955) article, preceded the Northwestern Conference of August 29–30, 1951, which had been called by C. Gilbert Wrenn. These two chapters and the Northwestern Conference, according to Super (1955):

> crystallized current thinking and standardized terminology, giving birth to the term *counseling psychology* and creating an awareness among psychologists of some of the important differences between this and the related fields of applied psychology [p. 3].

Edward S. Bordin of the University of Michigan chaired the committee that produced Chapter 6 on standards for training psychologists at the doctoral level (APA, 1952b). Donald E. Super was chair of the committee producing Chapter 7, the recommendations on practicum training (APA, 1952a).

The final chapter in this section, Chapter 8 (APA, 1956), provides the first of a series of definitions of the status, scope, and emphases of the specialty of counseling psychology. Harold B. Pepinsky was chairman of the committee which produced the statement.

The version of counseling psychology's emergence presented in Chapter

8 is the union of personality development, psychometrics, and vocational guidance. For the authors (APA, 1956), there was a balance among emphases upon:

> contributions to a) the development of an individual's inner life . . . , b) the individual's achievement of harmony with his environment . . . , and c) the influencing of society to recognize individual differences and to encourage the fullest development of all persons within it [p. 283].

The thrust of the work of a counseling psychologist is presented as helping individuals toward "overcoming obstacles to their personal growth" and "achieving optimum development of their personal resources."

IV. THE DIFFERING VIEWS ON A DEVELOPING PROFESSION: 1954-1962

Section 4 chronicles the continuing debate over who are counseling psychologists. Chapter 9 by Hahn (1955) is his presidential address to the division in 1954. He observes that various professional groups are "stacking out zones of influence in unclaimed territory" and claiming functions traditionally considered the province of other groups. Counseling and clinical psychology as well as psychiatry and social work are seen as "competing for status, legal sanction, and advantage." Hahn's (1955) paper is a proposal to establish counseling psychology as a "functionally unique pattern of practice." The basis for patterns is the type of client, objectives, work situation, and professional training.

He begins by offering a series of hypotheses on how counseling psychologists differ from clinical psychologists; then he expands the discussion to include observed differences and closes with a summarization of what he considers a "relatively unique" pattern of eight functions for the profession. The concern is with clients, not patients. Employment is not under other professionals. Practice is based more on normative approaches than is true for other disciplines. Clients are helped to change attitudes and values, not personality. The anxiety dealt with in clients is frustrating, not disabling. Counseling is not complete until there is client-accepted planning for future action. Finally, there is a stress on psychological strength as opposed to psychopathology.

The Hahn (1955) statement, in the context of the work of the Committee on Counselor Training (APA, 1952a and 1952b) and the Northwestern Conference in 1951, provides definitional statements for counseling psychology.

The next phase in the development of the profession was occasioned by an unpublished controversial paper by Berg, Pepinsky, and Shoben (1960) which was commissioned in 1959. This books marks its first appearance in print. It may be the most influential unpublished (until now) paper in the history of the Division! What it did was initiate a concerted dialogue on the *status* of counseling psychology (Tyler, Tiedeman, & Wrenn, 1961; Tiedeman, 1962; Tiedeman & Mastroianni, 1961) and on alternative roads for the development of the profession (Berg, 1962).

The paper by Berg, Pepinsky, and Shoben (1960) was commissioned by the APA Education and Training Board in 1959. The charge was to "examine, review, and prepare a general report concerning the status of counseling psychology as a professional specialty." The authors characterize their commissioners as believing that counseling psychology had "lagged behind" other specialty areas. Where it had been prestigeful several decades before, it now "appears to be in some ways on the wane."

The balance of the article articulates the viewpoint of Berg, Pepinsky, and Shoben after their study. A lead sentence proclaims that "There is clear evidence that counseling psychology is declining." One source of their evidence is a report (Goodstein, Buchheimer, Crites, & Muthard, 1959) on behalf of the Scientific Status of Counseling Psychology Committee that the scientific status was "far from satisfactory" with a dearth of integrated and systematized empirical research.

Counseling psychology is portrayed by Berg, Pepinsky, and Shoben (1960) as not having had the "burgeoning development" attributed to clinical psychology. Alternative solutions are offered that include a fusion of clinical and counseling training at the doctoral level. This would lead to changes in both clinical psychology and counseling psychology. Clinical psychology would acquire, for both its scientific and service roles, a "greater scope and greater usefulness." Counseling psychology would become an "identifiable and highly contributive emphasis *within* the more developed clinical specialty."

Another alternative that the authors identify is the development of "counselors first and psychologists second" (Danskin, 1959). This would yield a number of potential identities for counseling psychologists. A third general area of possibility presented is the "educational process with a special concern for pupil personnel services, particularly at the college level." A final alternative offered is counseling psychology as essentially an M.A. specialty with a technician-level set of competencies including that of guidance and personnel workers and vocational appraisers.

Berg, Pepinsky, and Shoben (1960) close by indicating that they have represented "either ways of increasing the identity and distinctiveness" of counseling psychology or making its "contributions and helpful characteristics more available to other specialties." In contrast to the conclusions of Hahn (1955), Berg, Pepinsky, and Shoben (1960) see counseling psychology to have:

> developed more in the way of affinities with other areas of specialization, especially clinical psychology, than a distinctive identity of service functions or training patterns [p. 13].

Their conclusions and observations were not well received. The paper remained unpublished until now, though it was frequently cited.

Tyler, Tiedeman, and Wrenn (1961) were asked by the Executive Committee of the Division of Counseling Psychology to "draft a statement on the current status of counseling psychology as a field of study and work." Tyler et al. (1961) indicate that the opinions expressed in the Berg et al. (1960) study were not considered by the 1960 Executive Committee as reflecting the "variety of interests of the members of the Division" nor did it "adequately marshal the factual evidence concerning the current status of counseling psychology" (p. 1). The charge to Tyler et al. (1961) was not to write a rejoinder but rather a "positive statement deducing conclusions from documented evidence."

The Tyler et al. (1961) contribution is particularly directed to the clarification and re-examination of the components of vocational psychology and vocational counseling. After reviewing the early history of the Division, the authors characterize the membership of the Division, its overlap with the Division of Clinical Psychology (about 25%), and the predominent work-setting location (educational institutions).

The question of what is distinctive about counseling psychology is addressed. Perry's (1955) view is quoted to the effect that although psychotherapy is concerned with intra-personal conflicts, counseling is concerned with role problems such as marriage, vocation, and education. Counseling and clinical psychologists (Brigante, Haefner, & Woodson, 1962) agreed that counseling psychologists characteristically

> work with normal people and people having vocational and educational problems, to use interest and aptitude tests and paper and pencil personality tests rather than projective techniques, and to try to find an environment compatible with a client personality structure rather than to try to change his personality [Tyler et al., 1961, p. 6].

The Tyler et al. (1961) paper was endorsed by both the 1960–61 and 1961–62 Executive Committees of the Division of Counseling Psychology. Their statement summarizing what is important about the specialty, therefore, may be seen as representing a dominant view at the time:

> It focuses on plans individuals must make to play productive roles in their social environments. Whether the person being helped with such planning is sick or well, abnormal or normal, is really irrelevant. The focus is on assets, skills, strengths, possibilities for further development. Personality difficulties are dealt with only when they constitute obstacles to the individual's forward progress [pp. 6–7].

In a section on furthering the development of counseling psychology, the authors focus on two alternative directions training could take. One direction is the merger of clinical and counseling training, with counseling as a subspecialty within the clinical area. The other direction is the increase of the distinctiveness of counseling psychology training. The roots of counseling psychology are seen to be in social psychology, personality theory, developmental psychology, the psychology of learning and of individual differences, as well as in abnormal psychology.

Citing the progress in developing a concept of role and function, the authors conclude with the observation that the emphasis on development, assessment, plan, and role contributes to a concept of role and function that is "broader than vocational guidance but different from clinical psychology. . . ."

Tiedeman and Mastroianni (1961) found that "the old 'Personnel-types' in the Division have proven able to accommodate the influx of both the 'Therapy-types' and the 'Rehabilitation-types' that occurred from 1952–60." Their basic conclusion is as follows:

> Since 1953, the composition of the areas of professional investments of those affiliating with the Division has remained amazingly constant from year to year. This finding of the seeming dynamism of the waters of professional self-interests as they spread across the Division as a whole over the period studied is at odds with the opinion that the Division has lost its vitality, is not unique, and suffers from identity diffusion [p. 1].

They note the development of a needed theory of vocational development, and they offer the view that, although counseling psychology experienced an identity crisis in the 1950s, there was now (1961) an identity. For these authors, the "militant interest in *psychological development through educational means*" separates counseling from clinical psychology.

Tiedeman (1962), in Chapter 12, addresses the question how to best improve practice in counseling psychology. His previous papers (Tyler, Tiedeman, & Wrenn, 1961; Tiedeman & Mastroianni, 1961) dealt predominantly with the question of what is and whether there should be counseling psychology. Tiedeman (1962) argues that, although successful in the past, counseling psychology in 1962 had only a weak potential for growth because:

> 1. our espousal of "counseling" with the concurrent negation of "guidance" focused us upon a *single* technique without due regard for purpose, setting, and the arousal of motives; and,
> 2. our espousal of a mode of science typical of psychology in general has caused us usually to ignore the essential part of the object of our work, a person "becoming" [p. 3].

The remainder of Tiedeman's (1962) paper is devoted to a consideration of "these dual problems—technique in relation to purpose and setting, and science in relation to goal." As part of this, he presents what he characterizes as a "linguistic frame for guidance in which it is possible to consider purpose, theory, function, and authority simultaneously" (p. 3).

In a paper read at an APA symposium, Berg (1962) takes a very different focus in emphasizing counseling psychology as a psychology specialty much as physiological, clinical, or social psychology are special fields. He makes a true distinction between counseling psychology and counseling as an activity using psychological knowledge. Although the latter is seen as growing in numbers, the former is not.

Berg presents three alternative roads for counseling psychology. The first is a merger with clinical psychology—a fusion creating a new field for the training of professionals to deal with both normal and seriously disturbed persons.

The second alternative is the training of counselors first and psychologists second. This emphasis would produce specially trained counselors capable of focusing on an array of problems from delinquency to job or worker retraining.

The third alternative is a concentration at the M.A. level on the training of vocational appraisers, counselors, and guidance workers. A consequence of this approach, in Berg's view, would be the disappearance of the psychology in counseling psychology.

V. THE GREYSTON CONFERENCE: THE PROFESSIONAL PREPARATION OF COUNSELING PSYCHOLOGISTS: 1964

Section 5 of this book focuses on the work of the Greyston Conference held in 1964. Originally published by Teachers College Press, the papers from the conference have long been out of print. This volume, therefore, makes available to a broad readership some of the most influential writings about the profession during its development.

The conference originated in 1961, a decade after the Northwestern Conference, under the presidency of Harold Seashore. Planning was conducted during the presidencies of Robert Waldrop and Albert Thompson, with the conference actually occurring during the term of office of Irwin Berg. Albert Thompson and Donald Super served as conference planners and editors of the conference proceedings, and they categorized the outcomes of the conference under four rubrics: roles, content of training, organization of training, and unity and diversity (1964). The portions of the conference proceedings selected for this book cover all four basic areas.

Robinson (1964) in Chapter 14 addresses the topic of the growth of counseling psychology since the 1951 Northwestern Conference. After briefly tracing the key historical events that have been treated elsewhere, Robinson shifts to a number of important issues: why counseling psychologists were low in the APA status hierarchy, whether we were attracting nurturant individuals who are good counselors but poor researchers, and whether too small a number of institutions were dominant in the training of counseling psychologists. He also raises the continuing issue of age distribution of persons in influential roles. (Hahn (1953) had previously discussed the danger of an inner circle preventing institutional growth within the profession.)

Robinson's final section focuses on another continuing problem; namely, the interdepartmental (within a university) and interdisciplinary (between education and psychology) rivalries that persist in complicating genuine debate about training and certification. In the past, these rivalries have also had the potential for spawning a nonpsychologically based orientation to counseling.

Samler (1964) in Chapter 15 addresses the question of where counseling psychologists work, what they do, and what they should do. As he phrases it in the introduction:

> When, finally, we create our long sought-for identity, soul-searching will deserve an honorable place in it. In this almost constant self-questioning enough data have emerged on where we work and perhaps on what we do to lead to acceptable inferences on who we are [p. 43].

The balance of his contribution details what he learned about the questions he posed. Most counseling psychologists work in higher education; however, regardless of setting, there is a commonly held view of function. The central themes, which form a classic definition of the role of a counseling psychologist, are as follows:

> The counselor assists people to grow and develop. Clients may be well or ill, within the so-called normal range or not. Client anxiety is dealt with at the frustrating and interfering level rather than when it is incapacitating. Client strength rather than weakness is stressed. The client is helped to increase his resources for coping with the environment. The counselor must therefore know community resources for meeting various client needs and play a role in influencing the environment. He utilizes various assessment devices in appraising client traits for educational, vocational, and social functioning. The counselor is a direct participant, a resource person, or a researcher [p. 54].

Samler also reviews Super's (1955) "hygiology" formulation and a number of other "unofficial" reports on role and function. He summarizes the common methodological core as embracing a

> two person relationship, supplemented by: group methods; the utilization of assessment devices peculiarly appropriate for the study of vocational potential; assumption of a measure of responsibility by the counselor for the client; involvement with the client's environment (family, school, work); and considerable activity by the counselor on behalf of his client outside of counseling sessions [p. 61].

The definitions by Samler (1964) of the role and methodology of counseling psychology have been highly influential in the sense that they reflect a consensual assessment of the dominant opinion of the time and that they are an articulate statement of what had been achieved in the early years of the growth of the profession.

Samler's concluding section covers his view of what counseling psychology should do in the future, including the need for

> a special awareness of the forces that affect and change our society, moving from that awareness to anticipation, and from anticipation to considering what our function as counseling psychologists might be in a changed situation [p. 62].

Two specifics he cites are the changing conceptions of work and the effects of automation on the work force. As might be expected from the above, Samler (1964) sees vocational counseling as the major element in the "unique identity" of counseling psychology.

Darley (1964) addresses the important issue of defining the substantive bases of counseling psychology. He departs from the assumption that psychology should come first and quotes the Committee on Training in Clinical Psychology (APA, 1947), outlining detailed basic training in three areas: general psychology, psychodynamics of behavior, and research. Building on thorough training in basic psychology, Darley sees trainees being given "general minimum competence in the specialty of counseling," then learning on the job and in post-doctoral experiences.

Thompson and Super (1964) summarize the recommendations of the conference. Departing from Darley's (1964) view above, they indicate that a special substance for counseling psychology training

> consists of the educational and vocational, and less distinctively the familial and community environments of the individual, of the psychology of normal development, and of the psychology of the physically, emotionally, and mentally handicapped; the special emphases are on the appraisal and use of assets for furthering individual development in the existing or changing environment [p. 4].

The recommendations, which are worth scrutinizing in detail, address a number of topics including what individuals and the Division should do, what the APA should address, and the implications for trainers and employers.

VI. CONCEPTIONS OF COUNSELING PSYCHOLOGY: *1968-1976*

The final two Chapters by Jordaan, Myers, Layton, and Morgan (1968) and Ivey (1976) are both products of the Division 17 Professional Affairs Committee. They differ sharply on what should be the proper emphasis of primary counseling psychologists' roles: remedial, preventive, or developmental (educative). For Jordaan et al. (1968) the primary order of emphasis is as presented above; namely, remedial, preventive, and developmental. Ivey's (1976) order was different:

> It is believed that the educational/developmental role of the counseling psychologist must now be considered to be primary with the preventive role serving as the secondary function. The traditional remedial and rehabilitative role is not discarded, but it becomes subsumed under a clarified and enlarged definition of counseling psychology [p. 72].

The Jordaan et al. (1968) booklet is intended to help persons outside the profession learn more about it and to help people decide whether or not they wish to pursue a career as a counseling psychologist. The Ivey (1976) paper is the central core of the Division 17 Professional Affairs Committee Report for 1974–76. The Ivey report was not endorsed by the Exe˜utive Committee, and it was and is a controversial position paper. It is beyond the scope of both Jordaan et al. (1968) and Ivey (1976) to explore the training implications of their divergent positions on what should be the primary role, but there are fundamental and basically irreconcilable differences.

Counseling psychology remains a profession in search of an identity. Nearly 30 years after the first national conference at Northwestern University, there remains no consensus. The next volume in this series (Whiteley & Fretz, 1980) chronicles the current debate about professional identity, and it projects ahead to counseling psychology in the year 2000 A.D.

REFERENCES

American Psychological Association. Committee on Training in Clinical Psychology. Recommended graduate training program in clinical psychology. *American Psychologist,* 1947, *2,* 539–558.

American Psychological Association. Division of Counseling and Guidance, Committee on Counselor Training. The practicum training of counseling psychologists. *American Psychologist,* 1952, *7,* 182–188. (Chapter 7 in Whiteley, J. M. (Ed.), *The history of counseling psychology.* Monterey, Ca.: Brooks/Cole, 1980.) (a)

American Psychological Association. Division of Counseling and Guidance, Committee on Counselor Training. Recommended standards for training counseling psychologists at the doctorate level. *American Psychologist,* 1952, *7,* 175–181. (Chapter 6 in Whiteley, J. M. (Ed.), *The history of counseling psychology.* Monterey, Ca.: Brooks/Cole, 1980.) (b)

American Psychological Association. Division of Counseling Psychology, Committee on Definition. Counseling psychology as a specialty. *American Psychologist,* 1956, *11,* 282–285. (Chapter 8 in Whiteley, J. M. (Ed.), *The history of counseling psychology.* Monterey, Ca.: Brooks/Cole, 1980.)

Berg, I. A. *Some alternative ro ds for counseling psychology.* Unpublished paper, 1962. (Chapter 13 in Whiteley, J. M. (Ed.), *The history of counseling psychology.* Monterey, Ca.: Brooks/Cole, 1980.)

Berg, I. A., Pepinsky, H. B., & Shoben, E. J. *The status of counseling psychology.*

Unpublished paper, 1960. (Chapter 10 in Whiteley, J. M. (Ed.), *The history of counseling psychology*. Monterey, Ca.: Brooks/Cole, 1980.)

Brigante, J. R., Haefner, D. P., & Woodson, W. B. Clinical and counseling psychologists' perceptions of their specialties. *Journal of Counseling Psychology*, 1962, *9*, 225-231.

Danskin, D. G. Pavlov, Poe, and Division 17. *Counseling News and Views*, 1959, *12*, 4-6.

Darley, J. G. The substantive bases of counseling psychology. In A. S. Thompson & D. E. Super (Eds.), *The professional preparation of counseling psychologists. Report of the 1964 Greyston Conference*. N.Y.: Bureau of Publications, Teachers College, Columbia University, 1964. (Chapter 16 in Whiteley, J. M. (Ed.), *The history of counseling psychology*. Monterey, Ca.: Brooks/Cole, 1980.)

Goodstein, L., Buchheimer, A., Crites, J., & Muthard, J. *Report of the Ad Hoc Committee on the Scientific Status of Counseling Psychology*. American Psychological Association, Division 17. Unpublished paper, 1959.

Hahn, M. E. Counseling psychology. *American Psychologist*, 1955, *10*, 279-282. (Chapter 9 in Whiteley, J. M. (Ed.), *The history of counseling psychology*. Monterey, Ca.: Brooks/Cole, 1980.)

Ivey, A. E. Counseling psychology, the psychoeducator model, and the future. *The Counseling Psychologist*, 1976, *6*(3), 72-75. (Chapter 19 in Whiteley, J. M. (Ed.), *The history of counseling psychology*. Monterey, Ca.: Brooks/Cole, 1980.)

Jordaan, J. P., Myers, R. A., Layton, W. L., & Morgan, H. H. *The counseling psychologist*. N.Y.: Teachers College Press, 1968. (Chapter 18 in Whiteley, J. M. (Ed.), *The history of counseling psychology*. Monterey, Ca.: Brooks/Cole, 1980.)

Pepinsky, H. B., Hill-Frederick, K., & Epperson, D. L. The *Journal of Counseling Psychology* as a matter of policies. *Journal of Counseling Psychology*, 1978, *25*, 483-498. (Chapter 5 in Whiteley, J. M. (Ed.), *The history of counseling psychology*. Monterey, Ca.: Brooks/Cole, 1980.)

Perry, W. G. The findings of the Commission on Counseling and Guidance. *Annals of the New York Academy of Science*, 1955, *63*, 396-407.

Robinson, F. P. Counseling psychology since the Northwestern Conference. In A. S. Thompson & D. E. Super (Eds.), *The professional preparation of counseling psychologists. Report of the 1964 Greyston Conference*. N.Y.: Bureau of Publications, Teachers College, Columbia University, 1964. (Chapter 14 in Whiteley, J. M. (Ed.), *The history of counseling psychology*. Monterey, Ca.: Brooks/Cole, 1980.)

Rogers, C. R. *Counseling and psychotherapy*. Boston: Houghton Mifflin, 1942.

Samler, J. Where do counseling psychologists work? What do they do? What should they do? In A. S. Thompson & D. E. Super (Eds.), *The professional preparation of counseling psychologists. Report of the 1964 Greyston Conference*. N.Y.: Bureau of Publications, Teachers College, Columbia University, 1964. (Chapter 15 in Whiteley, J. M. (Ed.), *The history of counseling psychology*. Monterey, Ca.: Brooks/Cole, 1980.)

Scott, C. W. *Division 17 emerges: History of the origin, function, achievements, and issues of the Division of Counseling Psychology of the American Psychological Association, 1945-1963*. Unpublished manuscript, 1979. (Chapter 3 in Whiteley, J. M. (Ed.), *The history of counseling psychology*. Monterey, Ca.: Brooks/Cole, 1980.)

Super, D. E. Transition: From vocational guidance to counseling psychology. *Journal of Counseling Psychology,* 1955, *2,* 3–9. (Chapter 2 in Whiteley, J. M. (Ed.), *The history of counseling psychology.* Monterey, Ca.: Brooks/Cole, 1980.)

Thompson, A. S., & Super, D. E. Recommendations of the 1964 Greyston Conference. In A. S. Thompson & D. E. Super (Eds.), *The professional preparation of counseling psychologists. Report of the 1964 Greyston Conference.* N.Y.: Bureau of Publications, Teachers College, Columbia University, 1964. (Chapter 17 in Whiteley, J. M. (Ed.), *The history of counseling psychology.* Monterey, Ca.: Brooks/Cole, 1980.)

Tiedeman, D. V. *Status and prospect in counseling psychology.* Unpublished paper, 1962. (Chapter 12 in Whiteley, J. M. (Ed.), *The history of counseling psychology.* Monterey, Ca.: Brooks/Cole, 1980.)

Tiedeman, D. V., & Mastroianni, W. J. *Scuttle the division of counseling psychology? Nonsense!* Unpublished paper, 1961.

Tyler, L., Tiedeman, D., & Wrenn, C. G. *The current status of counseling psychology.* Unpublished paper, 1961. (Chapter 11 in Whiteley, J. M. (Ed.), *The history of counseling psychology.* Monterey, Ca.: Brooks/Cole, 1980.)

Whiteley, J. M., & Fretz, B. *The present and future of counseling psychology.* Monterey, Ca.: Brooks/Cole, 1980.

Wrenn, C. G. Birth and elderly childhood of a journal. *Journal of Counseling Psychology,* 1966, *13,* 485–488. (Chapter 4 in Whiteley, J. M. (Ed.), *The history of counseling psychology.* Monterey, Ca.: Brooks/Cole, 1980.)

HISTORICAL DEVELOPMENTS

Chapter 2
Transition: From Vocational Guidance to Counseling Psychology

DONALD E. SUPER

In 1951, rather suddenly but not unexpectedly, a new psychological job title came into use in the United States, and a hitherto somewhat amorphous and debatable field of psychology emerged as clearly a field in its own right. The job was that of *counseling psychologist,* the field was that of *counseling psychology.*

These terms were adopted at a meeting which took place at Northwestern University immediately prior to the annual meeting of the American Psychological Association in September, 1951, at a special conference called by C. Gilbert Wrenn of the University of Minnesota, president of what was then called the Division of Counseling and Guidance of the American Psychological Association. The conference was attended by some 60 leading psychologists interested in vocational guidance and in counseling. The way had been paved for this conference by a Committee on Counselor Training headed by Francis P. Robinson of the Ohio State University, and two co-ordinate subcommittees, one on Doctoral Training Programs headed by Edward S. Bordin of the University of Michigan and one

"Transition: From Vocational Guidance to Counseling Psychology," by D. E. Super, *Journal of Counseling Psychology,* 1955, *2,* 3–9. Copyright 1955 by the American Psychological Association. Reprinted by permission.

on the Practicum Training of Counseling Psychologists chaired by the present writer.

The work of these committees and of the Northwestern Conference, published in the June, 1952, issue of the *American Psychologist* (APA, 1952a, 1952b), crystallized current thinking and standardized terminology, giving birth to the term *counseling psychology* and creating an awareness among psychologists of some of the important differences between this and the related fields of applied psychology. It may be of general interest to outline the origins of this new development.

ORIGINS

Vocational guidance began, in the United States, as a movement by philanthropically minded citizens to improve the post-school vocational adjustments of boys and girls (Brewer, 1942). They allied themselves with social agencies such as Civic Service House in Boston and the Young Men's Christian Association in some communities, and with the schools in many cities such as Providence and Grand Rapids, to provide occupational information and orientation for boys and girls leaving school or adrift in the chaotic world of work. This movement was soon joined by psychologists working in the field of psychometrics, for at the very time that Frank Parsons began his vocational guidance work in Boston, Alfred Binet published his intelligence scale in Paris, and World War I effected a partial merger of these two important streams in the United States. That the merger was only partial was made clear by the different emphases, in the 1920s, of educators such as John Brewer (1932), with his stress on exploratory experiences in guidance, and of psychologists such as Clark Hull (1928), with his hopes for psychological tests as the basis of vocational counseling.

The economic depression of the 1930s added a new current to the stream of history. Large-scale unemployment highlighted vocational guidance as a job-placement activity as well as an educational function. The Minnesota Employment Stabilization Research Institute experimented with psychological tests, occupational information, and retraining as methods of getting adult workers back into the active labor force. Then many private and public vocational counseling centers, together with the United States Employment Service, quickly took over the research and counseling methods developed in this pioneer project. The union of education, of social work, and of psychometrics in the vocational guidance of youth and adults was now somewhat more complete, as shown by the strength of the National Vocational Guidance Association and the activities of the National Occupational Conference. NVGA's membership came from the fields of education, psychology, community service, business, and government. Psychology as an organized field at this time showed some interest in guidance only through a small group of applied psychologists who, in 1937, organized the American Association for Applied Psychology, but it is significant that, while this organization included sections concerned with clinical, consulting, educational, and industrial psychology, none was concerned particularly with vocational guidance.

During the 1930s another movement gathered force, this one under the auspices of clinical psychology, namely, an interest in psychotherapy. One of the products of this new focus of psychological research and practice was Carl Rogers' book on *Counseling and Psychotherapy* (Rogers, 1942). The years following its publication in 1942 saw a growth of interest in psychotherapeutic procedures which soon became even greater than interest in psychometrics. This movement, and the numerous research and theoretical contributions that have accompanied it, has had its impact on vocational guidance (Super, 1951). It has made vocational counselors, whether psychologists or otherwise, more aware of the unity of personality, of the fact that one counsels *people* rather than *problems,* of the fact that problems of adjustment in one aspect of living have effects on other aspects of life, and of the complexity of the processes of counseling concerning any type of individual adjustment, whether in the field of occupation, of group living, or of personal values. It has, perhaps even more importantly, provided counselors of all types with a better understanding of counseling processes and techniques. It is significant, as pointed out elsewhere (Super, 1954), that the three North American textbooks that in the 1930s purported to deal with counseling methods actually dealt only with diagnostics, that of the three which were published in the 1940s only one actually dealt with counseling, and of the ten that appeared during the 1950s, up to the time of writing, as many as seven actually dealt with counseling methods in some detail.

The merging of these several streams of development means that the movement that started as vocational guidance in the United States, first with an emphasis on vocational orientation activities and then with a parallel and eventually merging emphasis on aptitude testing—both leading to placement—recently also assimilated a psychotherapeutic approach and has emerged as the "new" field of counseling psychology. Although it includes vocational guidance, it goes beyond it to deal with the person as a person, attempting to help him with all types of life adjustments. Its underlying principle is that it is the adjusting individual who needs help, rather than merely an occupational, marital, or personal problem which needs solution. However, counseling psychology recognizes, unlike some therapeutic approaches, that the adjusting individual lives in a real world in which situational as well as attitudinal problems are encountered, and hence it uses aptitude tests, occupational information, exploratory activities, and structured situations as well as therapeutic interviews (APA, 1953).

PHILOSOPHY, SCOPE, AND METHOD

This leads us to questions of the philosophy, scope, and method of counseling psychology. Even with the clarification that has taken place so rapidly during the past few years, many American psychologists ask what difference exists between counseling psychology, on the one hand, and clinical, educational, or personnel psychology on the other. In fact, there are presently quite a few clinical psychologists who believe that counseling psychology is logically a branch of clinical psychology and that the two should officially merge. It is significant, however, that the same belief is encountered among a number of educational, school, and personnel psychologists, each field stressing its kinship to counseling psychology while denying equal kinship to the other special fields.

It is frequently stated by counseling psychologists that their field is concerned primarily with the normal person (Gustad, 1953). These psychologists state that the objective of this field is to help the normal individual, whether student, worker, parent, or other, to achieve a better integration and to find more adequate outlets than he otherwise might in our complex and confused world. Although this is true so far as it goes, many other counseling psychologists, including this writer, maintain that this is not enough. Counseling psychology is also concerned with handicapped, abnormal, or maladjusted persons, but in a way that is different from what has characterized psychology.

Clinical psychology has typically been concerned with diagnosing the nature and extent of *psychopathology,* with the abnormalities even of normal persons, with uncovering adjustment difficulties and maladaptive tendencies, and with the acceptance and understanding of these tendencies so that they may be modified (Louttit, 1939).

Counseling psychology, on the contrary, concerns itself with *hygiology,* with the normalities even of abnormal persons, with locating and developing personal and social resources and adaptive tendencies so that the individual can be assisted in making more effective use of them (Gustad, 1953).

Some clinical psychologists are beginning to say, now that counseling psychology has made clear this surprisingly novel philosophy and these nonetheless time-honored methods, that clinical psychology made a serious error in defining itself as it did, that it should have been more independent of psychiatric traditions and interests and concerned itself with hygiology as well as pathology. Perhaps in due course the two fields will merge, in a more broadly trained and oriented field.

SETTING

Another important distinction between counseling psychology and the other applied fields is that of setting. Clinical psychologists function, with rare exceptions, in medical settings (unless their functions are instructional). Educational psychologists are typically professors, and when employed in other capacities they generally work as researchers in educational settings. School psychologists, as their nomenclature indicates, work in schools, and their orientation is educational even though their work in many ways resembles that of clinical psychologists. Personnel psychologists typically work in government, industry, or business, and they are often appropriately more concerned with their administrative-productive-distributive setting than they are with individuals.

Counseling psychologists, on the other hand, work in a variety of settings. They are employed in university counseling centers, in secondary schools, in hospitals, in rehabilitation centers, in social welfare agencies, in industry, in business, in government. They work in educational, medical, social work, and administrative settings—wherever there are people who need help in mobilizing their personal resources and in using the environment in order to make better adjustments. Wherever they work, they share one common treatment philosophy, one common collection of methods, and they acquire varying situational orientations according to the nature of the setting in which they are to work with people. In this, perhaps, lies counseling psychology's unique strength and its rapidly developing future: the counseling psychologist sees beyond the setting, whether it be medical, educational, social, or other, and deals with the individual who lives and functions in a variety of settings.

STRUCTURE AND ORGANIZATION

The principal professional association for vocational guidance in the United States has been the National Vocational Guidance Association. It has been brought out, also, that leadership in organizing the field of counseling psychology was exercised by the American Psychological Association's Division of Counseling and Guidance, now officially renamed the Division of Counseling Psychology. There is, of course, some overlapping of membership in these two organizations, but there are important differences.

We have seen that NVGA is made up of persons from the fields of education, community service, psychology, and business, whereas the Division of Counseling Psychology consists solely of psychologists. This means that NVGA contains many members whose primary affiliation is elsewhere, whereas APA's Division 17 (Counseling Psychology) contains members who tend to think of it as their primary affiliation. It means that NVGA has a revolving membership, as high school counselors become principals and drop their guidance activities, as social workers move from agencies doing vocational counseling to other agencies without this function, as business men move from personnel work to some other branch of management. Division 17, on the other hand, has a stable membership of persons who tend to keep up their interest in the field regardless of transfers or promotions. NVGA members may have considerable or little professional training in guidance, whereas Division 17 members have at least two years of specialized graduate preparation plus experience in their field. All this gives the Division of Counseling Psychology, with 700 members, a homogeneity and strength which NVGA, with 4000 members, does not and perhaps cannot have.

There is another important reason why leadership in this evolving area has been exercised by psychology rather than by the heterogeneous field of guidance. This is the general recognition of the unity of the individual, the widespread emphasis on the guidance of persons and on the guidance of development, the current interest in life adjustment that includes vocation rather than merely in vocational choice and adjustment. The major advances in understandings, methods, and techniques of life adjustment have been psychological: psychology developed the tests used in diagnosis, prediction, and assessment; psychology systematized the study of occupations (except for trend studies contributed by economists); psychology (building partly on psychoanalysis) analyzed interviewing and counseling methods and applied this new understanding to life adjustment problems.

Although the National Vocational Guidance Association spent a score of years in the sporadic but animated debate of whether or not to drop the adjective *vocational* from its title and statement of purpose, psychologists interested in counseling concerning life adjustment problems found a focus for their interest in the developing divisions of the American Association for Applied Psychology and of the American Psychological Association with which it merged during World War II. Better prepared to study, understand, and assist individual development and adjustment than most educators; closer to their scientific foundations and hence more versatile than most social workers; more interested in people than most administrators in business, industry, or government—counseling psychologists had a clearer idea of what needed to be done and how to do it than had most others interested in guidance.

In 1952 the National Vocational Guidance Association merged with several other similar associations to form the American Personnel and Guidance Association, thereby giving more adequate expression to the current interest in general adjustment while preserving the necessary special interest in occupational problems in its divisional structure. The APGA is today a strong and important association. But it is still more an *interest* than a *professional* association, and the contributions made by psychology to guidance were implicitly recognized in the new association by the election of two counseling psychologists both to its first and to its second slate of three officers, and by the inclusion of five counseling psychologists in its 15-member Executive Council of 1953-54. (This is in contrast with the one psychologist who was on the 11-man Board of Trustees of NVGA 20 years earlier.) Four of APGA's five psychologist-council members have been officers of APA's Division of Counseling Psychology, including two past presidents (C. Gilbert Wrenn and the writer) and two past secretaries (Frank M. Fletcher and Clifford P. Froehlich).

We have seen that the American Psychological Association's Division of Counseling Psychology has set standards for the training of counseling psychologists, standards which are now used by the APA's Education and Training Board in accrediting doctoral training programs in the universities. In addition, the Division has been regularly represented not only on the committees of that Board but also on the American Board of Examiners in Professional Psychology (1953) that has, since 1947, issued the Diploma in Counseling and Guidance to persons with the doctorate and five subsequent years of experience in counseling psychology who pass appropriate written, oral, and practical examinations. It has also been represented on the Committee on Ethical Standards that, in 1953, published the APA's Code of Ethics (APA, 1953) that deals, among other topics, with counseling.

Further recognition of the importance of this field of applied psychology in the United States exists in the program for financing the training of counseling psychologists established in 1952 by the Veterans Administration. In this program substantial numbers of university-selected men and women are currently pursuing doctoral studies which include a paid internship in a veterans hospital (Moore, 1952). The Veterans Administration initiated this and a related inservice education program in order to fill more adequately its own unmet needs for counseling psychologists in its hospitals and regional offices. It did this after rewriting job specifications and requirements for vocational counselors to replace the latter with counseling psychologists as turnover or upgrading of incumbents and the availability of trained personnel makes it possible (this has since World War II been a shortage field, with only a handful of clearly qualified practitioners in 1940).

The role of the counseling psychologist in rehabilitation work is being studied by Veterans Administration psychologists and by other counseling psychologists interested in the work of the federal and state civilian rehabilitation programs. They are concerned with making sure that the more extensive and intensive professional training that counseling psychologists are bringing to the work of the vocational counselor finds ways of making the greatest possible contribution to the rehabilitation process. Counseling psychologists in industry and in education have been doing this for some time, but now rehabilitation also has begun to make demands on vocational counseling that are appropriate to counseling psychology and which command its attention.

As implied in the above, the development of the field of counseling psychology has been reflected also in the programs of American universities. For example, in 1951–52 the Department of Guidance of Teachers College, Columbia University, made a thorough study of its programs and reorganized some of them while renaming others. It was recognized that in the Guidance Department the 25-year-old area of specialization locally known as Vocational Guidance and Occupational Adjustment had, for some time in fact, been offering five different programs: a doctoral program for counseling psychologists, another doctoral program for personnel psychologists, and three master's programs for school counselors, vocational counselors in social agencies, and personnel technicians in business, industry, or government. This recognition led to a departmental reorganization. The doctoral programs in counseling and in personnel psychology were so named and associated more closely with those in clinical and in school psychology, all in an area called Psychological Services. The master's program for school counselors was merged with that in another, nonpsychological, area called Student Personnel Administration. In many other universities a similar but not identical reorganizing and renaming of existing programs has taken place during the past three years, with the result that a total of 18 programs in counseling psychology are now accredited by the American Psychological Association (APA, 1954).

For a field to be of age it must have not only a professional organization, professional certification, professional training programs, a professional code of ethics, and professional employment outlets, but also a professional journal. This the field now has, in the *Journal of Counseling Psychology*, founded by some 20 psychologists and first published early in 1954.

CONCLUSIONS

The field of counseling psychology is still evolving, and important developments will most certainly take place during the next few years, especially in connection with rehabilitation work. Counseling psychology, already closely affiliated with clinical psychology in some universities and agencies but closer to educational psychology or to personnel psychology in others, may move even closer to one or all of these in the years to come. Already there is some talk of a need for a second "Boulder Conference" (Raimy, 1950) and a second "Northwestern Conference" (APA, 1952a, 1952b), the Runnymedes respectively of clinical and of counseling psychology, this time as two coordinated conferences or one joint conference, at which progress in the two fields might be reviewed and the rapprochement desired by some might be effected.

Perhaps the end result will be the emergence of a field of applied individual psychology, or consulting psychology, in which psychologists will be prepared to function as consultants to people in varying situations and with varying types of adjustment problems. Perhaps, on the other hand, true differences in the several fields will emerge more clearly, and both applied psychologists and the general public will develop a new recognition of and respect for the various applied specialties. In either case, the current trends in counseling psychology in the United States impress those of us who are involved in them as full of challenge, demanding the best that scientific method, professional skill, and human understanding can bring to bear.

REFERENCES

American Board of Examiners in Professional Psychology. *The certification of advanced specialists in professional psychology.* Washington: American Psychological Association, 1953.
American Psychological Association. Division of Counseling and Guidance,

Committee on Counselor Training. The practicum training of counseling psychologists. *American Psychologist,* 1952, *7,* 182–188. (a)

American Psychological Association. Division of Counseling and Guidance, Committee on Counselor Training. Recommended standards for training counseling psychologists at the doctorate level. *American Psychologist,* 1952, *7,* 175–181. (b)

American Psychological Association. Committee on Ethical Standards for Psychology. *Ethical standards for psychologists.* Washington: American Psychological Association, 1953.

American Psychological Association. Education and Training Board. Doctoral training programs in clinical psychology and in counseling psychology. *American Psychologist,* 1954, *9,* 258.

Brewer, J. M. *Education as guidance.* N.Y.: Macmillan, 1932.

Brewer, J. M. *History of vocational guidance.* N.Y.: Harper and Brothers, 1942.

Gustad, J. W. The definition of counseling. In R. F. Berdie (Ed.), Roles and relationships in counseling. *Minnesota Studies in Student Personnel Work,* No. 3, 1953.

Hull, C. L. *Aptitude testing.* Yonkers: World Book Co., 1928.

Louttit, C. M. The nature of clinical psychology. *Psychological Bulletin,* 1939, *36,* 361–389.

Moore, B. V., & Bouthillet, Lorraine. The VA program for counseling psychologists. *American Psychologist,* 1952, *7,* 684–685.

Raimy, V. C. *Training in clinical psychology.* N.Y.: Prentice-Hall, 1950.

Rogers, C. *Counseling and psychotherapy.* Boston: Houghton Mifflin, 1942.

Super, D. E. Vocational adjustment: Implementing a self-concept. *Occupations,* 1951, *30,* 88–92.

Super, D. E. Comments on current books. *Journal of Counseling Psychology,* 1954, *1,* 123–124.

Chapter 3
History of the Division of
Counseling Psychology: 1945-1963

C. WINFIELD SCOTT

INTRODUCTION

At the time of the 1954 annual meeting of the American Psychological Association in New York City, the Executive Committee of Division 17 decided that a history of the Division should be written. Minutes of Executive Committee Meetings and a complete file of *Counseling News and Views* were the most important sources of data. Other sources were the secretary-treasurer's file of prior and current correspondence, committee reports, and applications for membership. Some present and previous officers of the Association, on request, supplied certain missing information.

ORIGIN

Out of the long-standing conflict between theoretical and applied psychologists and the demands for psychological service that accompanied World War II, both the reorganized American Psychological Association and its Division 17 emerged in the middle 40s.

Insofar as official records go, the Division sprang full bloom at the first annual business meeting of the Division, September 5, 1946 in Philadelphia, Pennsylvania. One might be more metaphoric and say that it emerged in maturity from the brows of Edmund G. Williamson and John G. Darley, who, in the minutes of this meeting, were listed as being, respectively, president and secretary-treasurer. The minutes begin with the simple statement that the meeting was called to order by the president at 11 a.m. Tersely and clearly written, this first extant official document, other than the By-Laws which were adopted by mail ballot in May, 1946, gives no hint of actions that preceded the meeting or of any recognition by the group assembled that counseling psychology history was in the making. For information about precedent activity, one must rely mainly on published reports on the

This is an edited and much shorter version of the manuscript that the author submitted to the Executive Committee of Division 17 in 1963 while he was serving as chairman of the Division's History Committee. This is the first publication of this article. All rights reserved. Permission to reprint must be obtained from the publisher.

reorganization of APA, which appeared largely in the *Psychological Bulletin* (Allport, Anderson, Boring, Doll, Bryan, & Hilgard, 1943). In 1943, the Joint Constitutional Committee of the APA and the American Association of Applied Psychology initiated a survey of psychologists, one part of which included a list of 19 possible divisions for APA, one of which was personnel psychology, and blank spaces for the suggestion of others (Recommendations of the Intersociety Constitutional Convention, 1943, p. 646).

The ballot was mailed "to all American psychologists, regardless of society affiliation early in 1944" (Hilgard, 1945a, p. 20). Usable returns from 3680 of the 6000 psychologists surveyed placed personnel psychology next to the top of the list, it being outranked only by clinical. Three hundred and sixteen respondents gave personnel psychology as their primary and only choice and 47% of the total number included it among their choices. Corresponding figures for clinical psychology were 618 and 53, respectively. Child psychology ranked third in the list. These findings caused Hilgard to conclude that "the center of gravity of interests of psychologists has shifted toward applied fields" (Hilgard, 1945a, pp. 22–23). Write-ins for guidance, vocational and educational, presumably influenced the choice of the title Division of Personnel and Guidance Psychologists as the first official name of Division 17 (Anderson, 1944).

During the formative period the Division was intended for "those whose primary interests are in selection, training, and guidance in schools, colleges, and guidance agencies" (Anderson, 1944, p. 236). No mention of counseling psychology appears in the *Psychological Bulletin* reports or in Doll's (1946) well developed discussion of divisional structure. However, the organizers of the Division began early to substitute the term *Counseling* for *Personnel* and the first by-laws adopted were for the Division of Counseling and Guidance. This title was used until September 5, 1955, when the Division, at its annual business meeting, approved the title Division of Counseling Psychology by a well-nigh unanimous vote.

By action of the Division Organization Committee of the APA in 1945, Edmund G. Williamson was named temporary chairman of the Division and Catherine C. Miles, secretary (Hilgard, 1945b, p. 295). These individuals and their counterparts in other divisions were responsible for developing nominations for the various divisional offices and for handling the affairs of their divisions until the 53rd annual meeting of the APA in September, 1945. At this meeting, the report on election of officers showed the following slate for Division 17: Edmund G. Williamson, Chairman; John G. Darley, Secretary, and Dr. Darley, Alvin C. Eurich, Harold A. Edgerton, and Carrol L. Shartle, Divisional Representatives.

No member of the five committees, including the Emergency Committee on Psychology, that planned and conducted the reorganization of the APA has ever been listed in an APA directory as a member of Division 17, and only one delegate and one alternate to the Intersociety Constitutional Convention, which developed the legal framework for the new organization, has been so listed. Experimental psychology was the most prevalent interest in the group and social psychology the second most common. Twenty-three of the 54 individuals in the combined group later became members of the Division of Experimental Psychology and 16 of the Society for the Psychological Study of Social Issues. Eleven later affiliated with the Division of Military Psychology, ten with the Division of Personality and Social Psychology and nine with Educational Psychology. Although the applied psychology viewpoint was probably more diffuse in the combined groups than was that of psychology as science, it was probably as well represented as the other.

What activity on the part of guidance and personnel psychologists lies back of the bare facts of the origin of Division 17 remains largely unknown. There may have been a number of informal and perhaps impromptu discussions in "psychology foxholes" of the war effort and also some planned informal meetings. Hugh M. Bell says that while he was in the War Department from 1944 to 1946, he "heard this matter (Organization of Division 17) discussed from time to time" and recalls "having been in on only one of the planning sessions." This meeting was held in 1945–46 in the offices of the American Council on Education (letter to the author, 9/26/56). Carrol L. Shartle recalls having had "conversations with Jack Darley and Mitchell Dreese concerning the founding of the Division" (letter to the author, 9/24/56). Two other names that seem to be definitely associated with the embryonic period are those of E. G. Williamson, already identified, and G. Frederic Kuder.

That John G. Darley wrote the first by-laws for the Division is well established by some of the contents of E. G. Williamson's personal file on the Division. He attended the business meeting of the new APA in Columbus, Ohio, December, 1945, at which divisional organization was the focus of much attention, and volunteered soon thereafter to "draft a set of by-laws" (letter to E. G. Williamson, January 7, 1946). On May 3, 1946, he sent the proposed by-laws to Dr. Williamson with a note which said he could mimeograph and mail them to the provisional membership for comment and action. Dr. Williamson's enthusiastic response by Western Union telegram May 31, 1946, was as follows: "By-Laws very satisfactory. Proceed with distribution. Greet members from me. Shall I arrange a Roman circus or give them bread?"

Dr. Williamson is the only person who has held the highest office in the Division more than one year. After his appointment as chairman in 1945, he was nominated for and elected to the position of chairman for 1945–46. In 1946, the Division implicitly continued in office for the ensuing year both the president and secretary-treasurer by failing to provide for nominations for these offices. However, the election procedure apparently became confused and the APA later announced that Williamson had been chosen president. Since this coincided to a 50% extent with the intent of the Division, announced election results were allowed to stand and the Division had no president-elect in 1946–47 (letter from John G. Darley to Dael Wolfle, 9/25/46, and response, 10/8/46).

Although he was at the helm of the new organization for almost three years, Dr. Williamson holds that his role was "somewhat of a passive one" and that actually "Jack Darley was the guiding genius or midwife" (letter to the author, 9/19/56). That Dr. Darley did play an important part in the origin of the Division is evident from facts already cited and from an expression of appreciation that president Frederic G. Kuder included in a message to members dated January 9, 1948. After reporting Dr. Darley's resignation as secretary-treasurer because of "the pressure of other duties," the message stated that his responsibilities in the Division had been "particularly heavy because of the large amount of correspondence and planning involved in getting the Division started" and thanked him for his contribution.

FUNCTION

Generally speaking, the goal of Division 17 has always been and still is to promote and safeguard in a specialized area "psychology as a science, as a profession, and as a means of promoting human welfare" (Article I, APA By-Laws). This concept of the role of psychology in American society represents a long-term development from the organization of APA in 1892 to promote psychology as a science. Societal demands for the application of psychology to human problems—for example, the measurement of general intelligence—and the interests and activities of psychologists rather early produced a schism between the scientists in psychology and the "applicationists." This led to separate organizations and to an apparently increasing hiatus that might still be growing had World War II not forced psychologists to bury or subdue their differences and contribute their knowledge and skill to the effort to survive.

As has already been noted, the Subcommittee on Survey and Planning for Psychology recognized as part of its task the formulation of a pattern for the development of psychology after the war period. This report used the term "mental engineering" to denote application of psychological science to the problems of human affairs and spoke of the need for professionalization of psychology so that its applications might "keep pace with emerging human needs and demands for personal and social guidance" (Boring, Bryan, Doll, Elliott, Hilgard, Stone, & Yerkes, 1942, pp. 623-624). The position was unequivocally taken that psychology should be an instrument of social progress and that socialization of psychology as a profession was preferable to its development generally or exclusively as private practice (Boring et al., 1942, pp. 628-629).

It seems obvious that the scientific orientation of many of the members of the groups that reorganized the APA proved no deterrent to their helping to develop a unified organization with scientific and applied emphasis. One such member, Robert M. Yerkes, deserves special consideration for his interest in the application of psychology to human problems. An experimental psychologist who will long be remembered, he turned his skill to the development of intelligence testing in World War I and played the leading role in the reorganization of APA so as to have it embrace and emphasize applied psychology. Division 17, as well as all others, owes him a debt of gratitude.

As for the early formulation of the purpose of Division 17, only the statement in the proposed By-Laws exists. It runs thus:

The purpose of the organization shall be:

a.   to extend the techniques and methods of psychology to counseling and guidance activities in vocational, personal, educational, and group adjustments, including the disciplinary and behavioral problems, encountered in educational institutions;

b.   to promote high standards of practice in the psychometric, diagnostic, and therapeutic phases of counseling and guidance, as they are carried out in educational institutions, governmental agencies, private practice, and in the community, non-profit agencies that are spreading throughout the country;

c.   to encourage and support scientific and professional inquiry into all aspects of counseling and guidance;

d.   to assist in the formulation of professional standards and ethical codes for workers in the field of counseling and guidance;

e.   to assist in the promulgation of adequate scholastic and professional training requirements for workers in these fields;

f.   to collaborate with those clinical psychologists who are primarily attached to medical activities in arriving at definitions and working relationships between these related psychological specialties.

John G. Darley, who drafted the By-Laws, has summarized the reason why the Division came into being in these words: "Looking back over the stretch of the years, I am quite sure that the Division sought organizational status to protect the integrity of the field of counseling as a legitimate applied specialty within the new APA organization" (letter to the author, 9/25/56).

The latest formal statement of the purpose of the Division appears in the Revised By-Laws (1954) as follows:

The purpose of this Division is to bring together psychologists specializing in counseling psychology and to further the development of practice and research in this field. Such an organization has a unique contribution to make in the professional and technical development of counseling psychology, supplementing the promotional and organizational work of kindred associations whose membership includes professional workers in other fields. The interests of the Division are classified and described under three major headings.

a.   Scientific Investigation

1.   to encourage surveys of research in the field of counseling psychology, summarizing present knowledge and practices;

2.   to isolate problems in special need of investigation in this area; and

3.   to encourage research projects pertinent to administration and practice in this field, defined in section *b*, by members of the Division and other appropriate groups.

b. Administration and Practice

1. to extend the application of the methods and techniques of psychology to counseling and guidance in educational, vocational, and personal adjustment, whether in educational institutions, industrial or business enterprises, government agencies, social agencies or in private practice;
2. to promote high standards of practice in the use of individual and group psychometrics, diagnostic, and counseling techniques; in the use of educational, occupational, and related information; and in the development of organizational patterns and administrative procedures in the above types of organizations and practice;
3. to assist in the formulation and observance of a code of ethics for professional psychologists, and to cooperate with other professional associations in the development of a similar code for counseling and guidance workers; and
4. to formulate appropriate requirements of professional education and experience for specialists in counseling psychology and to promote their adoption, in cooperation with kindred professional associations and agencies.

c. Dissemination of Information

1. to organize and promote pertinent meetings and conferences;
2. to encourage the preparation and publication of critical reviews of research and practice in counseling psychology;
3. to encourage the preparation and publication of manuals and other aids;
4. to promote public understanding of counseling psychology.

Under its broad concept of purpose, the Division engaged in rather extensive and varied activities and compiled a record of considerable achievement.

ACHIEVEMENTS AND ISSUES

From its origin through 1963, Division 17 established itself as a strong organization ranking second or third in size among all APA divisions, with Division 12, Clinical, always larger and Division 8, Personality and Social, usually so. Its membership increased from 464 in 1948, the first year for which APA membership directory data were available, to 1211 in 1963, a percentage gain of 161.0. Annual income increased from $1064.00 in 1950, the first year for which both income and expenditure figures were located, to $4007.31 in 1962, a percentage gain of 276.6. Corresponding totals for expenditures were $625.67 and $2350.33; and the percentage gain was 275.7.

Among its varied activities were provision of a respectable and at times provocative program at each annual APA meeting, maintenance of temporary special committees to deal with specific problems, and support of federal legislation related to counseling psychology. It showed special interest in professional training, study of itself, and professional identity. Presidents were particularly influential in all activities while in office and were more involved than most members before and after this period. Their retrospective views, obtained by the author in 1962, provide an authentic and useful overview of Divisional achievements and problems.

All past presidents through 1962 were asked by letter to submit their opinions on the most important achievements of Division 17 and the "gravest issues" the Division had faced. A list of all presidents through 1962-63 follows:[1]

Edmund G. Williamson	1945–46
Edmund G. Williamson	1946–47
Frederic Kuder	1947–48
Hugh M. Bell	1948–49
John G. Darley	1949–50
C. Gilbert Wrenn	1950–51
Donald E. Super	1951–52
Mitchell Dreese	1952–53
Milton E. Hahn	1953–54
Francis P. Robinson	1954–55
Edward S. Bordin	1955–56
Harold B. Pepinsky	1956–57
Ralph F. Berdie	1957–58
E. Joseph Shoben, Jr.	1958–59
Leona E. Tyler	1959–60
Harold G. Seashore	1960–61
Robert S. Waldrop	1961–62
Albert S. Thompson	1962–63

Practically all of the past presidents responded and in ways that made possible a limited overview of Divisional achievements and a fuller summary of issues the Division has faced, some of which remain unresolved. Excerpts from the responses follow, closing with professional identity and suggestions.

Accomplishments through 1962

All of the following statements through the conclusion of the chapter are from letters to C. Winfield Scott written at his invitation:

It is difficult to name particular events or activities as *outstanding* achievements since such development is a matter of innumerable small accretions. However, the following seem particularly countable as milestones in this development. In 1951 the Northwestern Conference produced statements on doctoral training and practicum standards in counseling psychology; the first was then adopted by the Veteran's Administration in 1952 as the basis for their sponsorship of doctoral training of counseling psychologists for VA hospitals.

The division changed its name to Counseling Psychology in 1953 and the *Journal of Counseling Psychology* was started in 1954. During my tenure as president (1954–55) two committees were appointed which have also helped with this development: The Committee on Definition (H. B. Pepinsky, Chairman) and the Committee on the History of Division 17 (C. W. Scott, Chairman). Since then various other committees have reported, but among them I would particularly note the recent reports on the Scope and Standards of Preparation in Psychology for School Counselors (W. F. Johnson, Chairman) and The Current Status of Counseling Psychology (Leona Tyler, Chairman). I expect that we will have future committees searching out and describing new developments in our field [F. P. Robinson, 9/21/62].

This statement, offered by a has-been ex-president of Division 17, must necessarily be a personal one. The kinds of involvement that the presidency entails are those in which the ego is a prime participant, and one's sense of personal identity, through the experience of office, becomes charged with one's perception of the group one serves. It is with some regret, therefore, that I must confess that my own reading of counseling psychology's situation at the moment is a compound of enthusiasm and pessimism with the latter, unhappily, somewhat predominant.

I came to the presidency from three years as Secretary-Treasurer, during which I had formed the impression that counseling psychology was defining itself as a new profession within the psychological family. With new opportunities before it almost palpably in the VA and in the burgeoning field of rehabilitation, with the society at large newly awakened to the worth of "developmental" in addition to "remedial" counseling, and with widespread acceptance in training institutions of the necessity for high intellectual standards, those who represented counseling psychology seemed possessed of a vision of how the new profession could helpfully mediate between the consulting room and the actual world in which a client lived and moved and had his being. Moreover, the odds then seemed to me to favor the development of new areas of fruitful research concentration and even some stimulating and novel efforts to cross that desperate gap that seems so frequently to yawn between psychology as science, on the one hand, and on the other, those conceptions of value with which the members of any helping profession must grapple when they meet the responsibility of an actual client.

To some extent, it is true, I believe, that the vision has been somewhat clarified and made more articulate, and counseling psychology has made many gains of which it can be thoroughly proud. During my year in the divisional presidency, I was particularly pleased by three developments: (1) The response of Division 17 first in support of the passage of the National Defense Education Act and then in articulate efforts to implement those of its Titles relevant to counseling in the various programs of the states which the NDEA made possible, (2) the establishment of the Committee on the Scientific Status of Counseling Psychology, and (3) the serious interest of the Division in the preparation of school counselors, spearheaded by the work of a special committee.

At the same time, I began to be troubled. There were signs—always remembering the many and notable exceptions—that counseling psychology as a professional group seemed more inclined to claim full professional status rather than to achieve it through imaginative and sustained work. There seemed to be a bit of lethargy about seeking those new frontiers where a new helping profession could function both distinctively and in socially useful ways. There seemed to be rather more envy of such other psychological specialties as clinical psychology than pride in the establishment of new services and new lines of thought and research that would define counseling psychology as an admirable addition in its own right to the broad spectrum of applied psychology.

These impressions are certainly subjective, but they are not without documentation. There is, first, the decline in the number of doctoral training programs in counseling psychology throughout the United States. There is the corresponding decline in the number of persons making application for ABEPP diplomas in counseling psychology. There is such evidence as Granger's (*Journal of Counseling Psychology*, 1959, *6*, 183-188) that counseling psychology, in the eyes of a sample of APA members, enjoys the lowest status of all specialties in psychology requiring the doctorate. There is the remarkable degree of overlap in doctoral training between counseling psychology and clinical psychology, strongly suggestive of the notion that the distinctiveness of the former is hard to find. There is as yet no response, known to me, to an old challenge of Jack Darley's that we have no philosophy of why we should help people, no articulate criteria of how we can tell whether we have helped people, or any research-based evidence that we do help people. Indeed, such a book as Barry and Wolf's *Epitaph for Vocational Guidance* underscores rather than meets this challenge in the most traditional domain of counseling psychologists [Edward Joseph Shoben, Jr., 8/9/62]!

Issues through 1962

As for the issues, I would mention several. One of the early ones had to do with the assumed universality of counseling techniques; that is, that counseling techniques as then being developed by psychologists could be used by counselors in industry and government positions and vocational rehabilitation and community clinics, as well as in schools. I have never subscribed to this point of view because I think the educational context of counseling is quite different from that of a private consultant or a private employee in a clinic, which is not concerned strictly with education, and I am using education in the sense of developmental philosophy rather than strictly and narrowly conceived as classroom instruction only.

The second and major issue of the Division 17 contingent of the counseling field was the decision about 1954, if I remember correctly, to explicitly construct a psychological foundation for counseling as contrasted with guidance procedures. This has been a divisive issue ever since 1910, when vocational educators took over the vocational guidance movement and Kittson [sic] among others, invented the do-it-yourself analysis procedure. The vocational guidance movement bogged down into a set of information-giving procedures and ceased to be the psychological technology which Parsons had envisioned. I believe we are about to close out this issue, which should not have been a divisive one in the first place [Edmund G. Williamson, 10/9/62].

In looking back over the history of Division 17, I think one of the most critical issues that we faced was that arising out of the differences between people in the field of vocational guidance and psychologists. This conflict was often described as a feud between the Kitson group at Teachers' College and the Williamson-Darley group at the University of Minnesota.

The year that I was president the Executive Committee of Division 17 debated this issue at great length, and there was a definite cleavage in the committee. However, we agreed to support a particular action, but the next day at the regular business meeting the vocational guidance group refused to go along with the action that they had agreed to in the Executive Committee, and led a movement in the business meeting which caused a great deal of hard feeling among the psychology people. Subsequently, this difference was ironed out and has been forgotten as the years go by. Specifically, the point at issue was a report that the vocational guidance group had planned and completed, and then wanted Division 17 to endorse before it was released. The psychological group in Division 17 felt that we should have been in on the project from the beginning and not dragged in at the end to endorse it.

This single issue is an example of the tension that had built up over the years between the two groups, which, if it had not been for Division 17, might have resulted in a break between the two groups which would have had serious effects upon counseling [Hugh M. Bell, 8/24/62].

The final major problem for the divisional membership lies in the fact that they must, to do their jobs adequately, have one foot in the camp of psychology and one foot in the camp of education, at all levels. Thus the high overlap of membership with APGA; thus the problem of training standards for school systems that may not afford PhD's; thus the recurring issue of the counselor's need or lack of need for teaching experience. The very nature of the field requires it to have these dual identities [John G. Darley, 9/12/62].

I think the substantive issue in my Presidential Address which was published in 1953 is still alive in some ways. We are still in search of a better theory to guide us in our work of educational and vocational counseling, as is evidenced in John Holland's chapter for the forthcoming anniversary volume of the National Vocational Guidance Association. Holland has attempted there to review programmatic research in vocational development, and comes up with some well warranted criticisms of the still rudimentary stage in which we find ourselves. Borow has reflected these also in the *Journal of Counseling Psychology* a year or two ago, in an article in which he discussed programmatic research in career development. His report is somewhat more optimistic, I think, than Holland's, because he is impressed by the amount of work that is going on, but he also has noted the lack of general theory and the problems of developing and testing meaningful hypotheses. Despite these problems, I share Borow's optimism, and I am impressed with the fact that there is a great deal of important research going on in vocational development and in counseling methods, all of which augurs well for the substantive future and the technical future of counseling psychology [Donald E. Super, 9/12/76].

There were a number of other matters dealing with standards of preparation, but another major issue I think came up during my time was the changing of our title—the title of the division to the Division of Counseling

Psychologist [sic]. It seems to me also we were asked to participate with the deliberations of the Board of Education and Training on the request from the Veterans Administration for appraising counseling psychologist programs as had been done for clinical psychologist programs. I know that I had become a member of the Board of Education and Training, and it seems to me that was right after my term of office as president of Division 17. As you recall, all of this change about counseling psychologists came about '51 and '52 [C. Gilbert Wrenn, 8/22/62].

During my administration as president the name of the Division was changed from the Division of Counseling and Guidance to the Division of Counseling Psychology. I have always regretted that this change took place during my administration for I still feel that it was a mistake. Milt Hahn who succeeded me as president was determined that the name be changed and he won out in the matter. I believe as a result many pupils and student personnel workers of doctoral competence who do not regard themselves as counseling psychologists feel that the organization is not for them. Furthermore, as I watched the development of the Division during the past ten years, I find it difficult to differentiate between the Division of Clinical Psychology and the Division of Counseling Psychology. The fact that most clinical psychologists function in a medical setting is a thin line of demarcation. I am inclined to think that the time will come when the two Divisions in question will merge [Mitchell Dreese, 10/13/62].

It is difficult to highlight issues which have been particularly serious for our development, but the following seem to me to have caused more difficulty. First has been an over-lingering on the issue of the relationship of counseling to clinical psychology; there is obvious overlap in some aspects, but such overlap exists with other areas in psychology. Second has been some difficulty in working with the development of school counselor training programs; this I would attribute to two institutional developments: First, Arts College psychology departments and Colleges of Education have traditionally scrapped over who is to provide courses in psychology for teacher training, and so with the rapid development of school counselor training under NDEA this historical division has prevented as effective cooperation as might be. The second factor causing difficulty has been that our rapid professional development and centering on Ph.D. training have caused some educators to feel that we are not as cognizant of their needs as we should be [E. P. Robinson, 9/21/62].

I think the greatest problem and challenge facing Division 17 is that of making persons aware of the contribution that psychology can make, that it helps make psychologically healthy persons more effectively and efficiently exploit their social and personal resources, and at the same time contributes to the welfare of the community. Counseling psychologists have made some progress in withstanding the pressures that tend to concentrate their work on the ill, the disordered, and the pathological, but these pressures are inevitable, and only by demonstrating what we can do with 95% of our students and our employees and our patients will we be allowed by society to work with others than the five % whose need is most obvious and who at the same time are least capable of benefiting from our skills.

I believe the most important thing in counseling psychology is the establishment in many universities and colleges of counseling centers that provide counseling psychologists to work with the most promising people in our population. If we can continue to make psychology available to everyone as we attempt to construct a reasonable and satisfying personal life, then we have achieved almost all one could wish [Ralph F. Berdie, 8/20/62].

Professional Identity through 1962

The second point that I wish to make has to do with goals which are yet to be attained by our division. The first of these has to do with our thinking through the distinct function that counseling psychology has among the other divisions of psychology. Merely changing the name to counseling psychology is not enough. We have to think through the way in which we are alike, but particularly the way which we differ from clinical psychologists and the other specializations. In my presidential address I tried to point out some of these distinct features, but I am sure that this is incomplete. I feel that our number one emphasis should be on working with well people; that is, the nonneurotic and the nonpsychotic client. I think we should draw a rather sharp line between ourselves and the medical profession and psychiatrists, in particular. They have a specific job to do, and we have a specific job to do. I feel the clinical psychologists have gotten themselves too closely tied in with the medical profession and are in danger of being swallowed by it [Hugh M. Bell, 8/24/62].

However, I have some convictions that the division has not lived up to its potentials, and this seems to me to be the result of two historical forces: the major surge in the broad field of clinical psychology, and the inability of the divisional membership in 17 to define the roles and functions of a counselor [John G. Darley, 9/12/62].

One of the main issues in Super (1953) is that of the establishment of the identity of counseling psychology and the question of whether or not counseling psychology would become more clearly a field in its own right, or in due course merge with clinical psychology as some people were advocating. During the past two or three years this has still been an issue, but I believe that it has been resolved by the findings of the Tyler Committee and by other evidences of growing strength in our field. I suspect, as indicated in Waldrop's Presidential Report this year, that counseling psychology has indeed established its identity and that the going for our specialty will be somewhat smoother in the years immediately ahead [Donald E. Super, 9/12/62].

In short, I have been disappointed at the lack of evidence that counseling psychology is dealing straightforwardly and inventively with the problem of its professional identity. Again, it is necessary to point out the existence of some brilliant exceptions, but I remain disturbed by the tangential character of these bright stars in an otherwise dark sky. At the same time, I retain a faith, based largely on the efforts and achievements of some of the people who have been most active in Division 17, that if it is possible at all, counseling psychology will yet perceive the new horizons toward which it can distinctively and productively work, demonstrating a social awareness and responsibility, a bold willingness to deal responsibly with questions of value, and a technical competence that is at once creative and solid in both its research and its direct services to clients. Organizationally, it seems to me that the mission of Division 17 remains that of finding ways to facilitate developments of this kind, to provide vital assistance and imaginative leadership in training counseling psychologists with a new vision of the work they can do and a pride in that work that transcends any envy of any other group. In the context of social need, there is neither justification nor room for one helping profession to be envious of any other [Edward Joseph Shoben, Jr., 8/9/62].

It seems to me that the Division has worked through a sort of identity crisis during the past decade and is closer now to a clear formulation of where it is going. I probably couldn't express my views of what this formulation is any better than they were expressed by the committee in the report prepared for the E and T Board last year [Leona E. Tyler, 8/7/62].

Over my 17 years of involvement in Division 17, the persisting question has been: What is counseling psychology? This nagging query irritates many who feel there should be an answer. My belief is that we should keep asking the question forever. When we think we have framed a precise and permanent answer, the field of interest we represent will start withering. Asking the question leads us to think about substance—both scientific and applicational—for which some organizational structure is needed. As an organization Division 17 should address itself mainly to defining and redefining and then facilitating the substance. Overemphasis on organization *per se* can be treacherous; we must be willing to restructure not only the Division but the whole APA whenever structure gets in the way of psychological substance.

The common concern of the substantive field in which we till and toil and sometimes harvest a little resides in the word *normal*. The normal person with problems, more than casual but less than totally debilitating, is our psychological subject. Matters of careers—education, interpersonal competence, value systems, and self-regard, for example—are our substance over the whole range from childhood to old age. We draw on all psychology to find better ways of assisting nonsick people to cope better with life, accept themselves more easily, find their vocational and avocational niches, learn how to work and enjoy work—the list is large. How we counsel and what we need to know to counsel well are but variants of the perennial question: What is counseling psychology [Harold Seashore, 8/8/62].

Suggestions for the Division of Counseling Psychology

I think our division needs to give a lot of thought to the problem of the training needed by students who wish to become counseling psychologists. I think we need to indicate where the training should overlap with clinical psychology and industrial psychology, and also where it differs. I think our trainees should have some hospital experience in their internship and that the major emphasis should be upon an internship experience with normal individuals and experience in a broad social context [Hugh M. Bell, 8/24/62].

My suggestions to the Division are as follows:

1. that Division 17 take the leadership in bringing together for discussion, representatives from the various APA divisions the objectives of which, like those of 17, are aimed at the ADAPTATION-Distribution-adjustment and DISTRIBUTION-Adaptation-adjustment problems of the normal individual in the age-span from 15-senility.

2. that Division 17 determine whether or not to expand its own emphasis to the total life span or continue with the major attention which it is now giving to the 15–30 age group.

3. that Division 17, through its Exec. Comm., or other appropriate committee, consider the separationist tendencies of a number of us who feel that the Division no longer provided for our professional area of interest (the normal, mature, self-actualizing individual).

4. that the Division consider the problems of publication space which some of us thought were solved in large part by the establishment of the *Journal of Counseling Psychology* at the Northwestern Conference. Some of us feel that almost all of the theoretical material has come from eminent clinical psychologists—Rogers, Shoben, Tyler, Bordin, Berg, and so forth—and that only Don Super has been able to break through from the adaptation-distribution standpoint. Some, including myself, have had to turn to other journals such as *American Psychologist, Educational and Psychological Measurement, Personnel and Guidance* (for example, Williamson's article on values). As the founder of the *JCP* along with Seashore, I am not happy that I have never had an article in *JCP* with the exception of the rehabilitation panel report of 1953. Well, perhaps Gil has standards beyond my competence?

5. that the Division take a stand on a professional degree, returning the Ph.D. to its rightful owners, the research people. You will find some of the rationale in enclosure #2. Major points include:

   a. the pressure on Psychology Departments to meet the short supply of "pure" people. There is legitimate and growing opposition to the time needed for the form but not always the substance of a research thesis which some consider inappropriate for professional use.

   b. the evidence that, while professional psychologists are not less bright, or of a lower order, they do present different personality patterns. (Kreidt, 1948; Kelly & Fiske, 1948; Kreidt, 1952; Adkins, 1953; Roe, 1956; Bragante, 1962).

   c. the increased use of the Ed.D. as a professional degree in counseling, and even clinical, psychology. I have no objections to this as there are so many really excellent departments of Ed. Psych. However, the psych departments must decide whether or not the movement is one which is necessary by default or by positive action.

   d. the desire to conform to practice in two other degree areas. The M.D. is a professional degree. The holder of this degree can, and often does, seek and obtain the scholarly degree, Ph.D. The same situation holds for the Ed.D.

In my opinion, these issues will be decided on the various university campi through the appropriate departments, schools, and colleges. Such a movement could be helped if the Division studies the matter and offered a "White Paper" with the pros and cons and some recommendations. Our UCLA Departmental Committee to reappraise professional psychology begins its deliberations in October, 1962 [Milton E. Hahn, 8/8/62].

REFERENCES

Allport, G. W., Anderson, J. E., Boring, E. G., Doll, E. A., Bryan, A. I., & Hilgard, E. R. Recommendations of the Intersociety Constitutional Convention of Psychologists: II. Statement of the Continuation Committee of the Convention. *Psychological Bulletin,* 1943, *40,* 623–625.

Anderson, J. E. A note on the meeting of the Joint Constitutional Committee of the APA and AAAP, February 26 and 27, 1944. *Psychological Bulletin,* 1944, *41,* 235–236.

Boring, E. G., Bryan, A. I., Doll, E. A., Elliott, R. M., Hilgard, E. R., Stone, C. P., & Yerkes, R. M. Psychology and the war: First report of the Subcommittee on Survey and Planning for Psychology. *Psychological Bulletin,* 1942, *39,* 619–630.

By-Laws of the Division of Counseling Psychology of the American Psychological Association (revised 1954).

Doll, E. A. The divisional structure of the APA. *American Psychologist,* 1946, *1,* 336–345.

Hilgard, E. R. Psychologists' preferences for divisions under the proposed APA by-laws. *Psychological Bulletin,* 1945, *42,* 20–26. (a)

Hilgard, E. R. Temporary chairmen and secretaries for proposed APA divisions. *Psychological Bulletin,* 1945, *42,* 294–296. (b)

Recommendations of the Intersociety Constitutional Convention of Psychologists: IV. Sample blank for survey of opinion on the proposed by-laws. *Psychological Bulletin,* 1943, *40,* 646–647.

Super, D. A Theory of vocational development. *American Psychologist,* 1953, *8,* 185–190.

FOOTNOTE

[1]For the historical record, the presidents from 1963–64 through 1978–79 are as follows:

Irwin A. Berg	1963–64
Frank M. Fletcher	1964–65
David V. Tiedeman	1965–66
William C. Cottle	1966–67
Dorothy M. Clendenen	1967–68
John F. McGowan	1968–69
John L. Holland	1969–70
Arthur H. Brayfield	1970–71
Cecil H. Patterson	1971–72
John O. Crites	1972–73
Barbara A. Kirk	1973–74

John D. Krumboltz   1974–75
Thomas M. Magoon ⌐   1975–76
Roger A. Myers   ⌐
Norman I. Kagan   1976–77
Samuel H. Osipow   1977–78
Carl E. Thoresen   1978–79

Chapter 4
Birth and Early Childhood of a Journal

C. GILBERT WRENN

The Journal of Counseling Psychology was conceived in 1952 and born in February, 1954, when No. 1 of Vol. 1 appeared. Four men were its creators: Milton E. Hahn, Harold G. Seashore, Donald E. Super, and myself. If I, as the first editor of this fledgling journal, was its mother, then Milt Hahn was its father, although blood tests would be necessary to establish the dominant factor in its mixed paternity. (Perhaps I have gone further than is wise in this analogy!) Without question Hahn must be credited with the initiation of the new journal idea. He early found in Harold Seashore an enthusiastic supporter of his convictions and the two of them soon called in Donald Super and me with the thought that we would pick up the editorial responsibilities. So the four of us formed a team that worked rather intensively during the fall of 1952. As I re-read the correspondence of those early days I can sense that Hahn's constant enthusiasm and support was probably what kept us moving. Don Super was the thoughtful critic and implicit rationalist *par excellence,* Harold the organizer and hard facts man, Milt the driving enthusiast, psychological reinforcer, and idea generator.

A PERIOD OF FERMENT IN COUNSELING

This was a period during which many new perceptions in counseling were developing. I had just finished (1950–51) serving as president of Division 17 of APA, and Donald E. Super was then president (Hahn became president in 1953–54, Robinson 1954–55, and Seashore 1960–61). During my period of office the Division secured an APA subsidy to hold a two-day conference at Northwestern University for 50 carefully selected leaders in the field on the professional education of counselors at the Ph.D. level. This resulted not only in our change of name in 1953 from "Division of Counseling and Guidance" to "Division of Counseling Psychology" but also in the publication of a basic statement on preparation: "Recommended Standards for Training Counsel-

"Birth and Early Childhood of a Journal," by C. G. Wrenn, *Journal of Counseling Psychology,* 1966, *13,* 485–488. Copyright 1966 by the American Psychological Association. Reprinted by permission.

ing Psychologists at the Doctorate Level" (APA, 1952). As I recall, Francis P. Robinson was chairman of the Division 17 Committee on Professional Education during my term of office, and he and Edward S. Bordin prepared the published report. The Division 17 conference on preparation at the doctorate level had been preceded by two sessions for about 12 of us at the University of Michigan in 1949 and 1950, subsidized by the National Institute of Mental Health, on counselor preparation at the subdoctorate level. These seminar deliberations resulted in a monograph (Bordin, 1951), again with the basic writing responsibility being assumed by Bordin.

In 1952 the Veterans Administration, deliberately following the Northwestern Conference report, established a Civil Service position of "Counseling Psychologist" in the V.A. Division of Medicine and Neurology. This same year or the following year, and while I was on the APA Doctoral Education Committee (1951–53), APA, upon request from the V.A., agreed to evaluate University Ph.D. programs in Counseling Psychology so that trainees could be appointed in V.A. hospitals. In 1951 I succeeded John G. Darley for a six-year term on the American Board of Examiners in Professional Psychology, and in 1955 we changed the name of one of the Board's three fields of responsibility from "Counseling and Guidance" to "Counseling Psychology." It was a period of ferment in counseling and counseling psychology, to be sure. Only a little later, the Division of Counseling Psychology set up a committee to *define* counseling psychology ("What *is* this thing anyway?") resulting in a report on "Counseling Psychology as a Specialty" (APA, 1956).

EARLY DAYS OF INNOVATION AND ORGANIZATION

There were several basic concerns in our consideration of the establishment of a new journal. Purpose and content of journal was a paramount concern. Another was its financing. The *need* for a publication outlet in this field seemed obvious to all of us. The questions were "What?" and "How support it?" To get at the nature of the journal, I hammered out in the fall of 1952 a proposal which was re-written several times in order to incorporate the reactions and ideas of the other three.

From the outset our *Journal* team considered financing only on a self-contained basis—no seeking of foundation or organization subsidy. We were a "do it ourselves and get a few others to chip in with us" group. (Would we again be this self-sufficient or would our first thought now be a grant?) We established a list of probable stockholders who would represent various dimensions in counseling, each to be asked to buy a limited number of shares at $50 a share. None was to have over ten shares even if he was foolish enough to want to risk that much money (eight was the actual top and only one at that financial apex), for it was clearly stated that this was a risk investment! "Here is a chance to invest in your profession with no assurance of ever regaining your capital. Will you put your pocketbook behind your profession?" We really had less trouble than anticipated. Having set out to raise $6000 as our basic subsidy for the operation, we sold a little over 100 shares during 1953 and decided that this was adequate. The response was remarkable. I found an early list of 28 prospects, balanced as to type of work in counseling, and checked it against the stockholders listed in Vol. 1, No. 1. There were 19 of the 28 who had become stockholders—and I'm not even sure that we invited all on this particular list! Such a sense of professional responsibility was very heartening. Without this quality of support the *Journal* could never have gotten under way regardless of the enthusiasm and efforts of the four of us.

The opening list of stockholders read as follows:

Hugh Bell	Nathan Kohn
George Bennett	Edward Landy
Margaret Bennett	Fred McKinney
Irwin Berg	Francis Robinson
Edward Bordin	Carl Rogers
Arthur Brayfield	Harold Seashore
Dorothy Clendenen	Joseph Shoben
Mitchell Dreese	Dewey Stuit
Paul Dressel	Donald Super
Frank Fletcher	David Tiedeman
Milton Hahn	Alexander Wesman
Nicholas Hobbs	Cornelia Williams (McCune)
Donald Kitch	Gilbert Wrenn

To this list was added William Cottle by the end of 1954 and Robert Waldrop in 1955. (This group remained quite constant over the 14 years, with only three relinquishing their stock because of retirement, and so forth, and one through death—Harold Seashore.)

These stockholders deserve high praise for their confidence in the field and in the *Journal*. It is gratifying to know that their faith has been rewarded financially. The assets of the *Journal* eventually became adequate enough to provide a modest stipend for editor and managing editor. (We served for the first four years without any financial compensation and, in fact, without really anticipating one.) Still later the *Journal* paid two dividends which, together with the surrender value of the stock at the time it was incorporated into APA, repaid each stockholder all of his investment and a substantial amount over. It is pleasant to cast your bread upon the waters expecting it to be snapped up by a school of fish and find it returned to you as cake!

The stockholders in 1953 elected the first board (Berg, Hahn, Seashore, Shoben, Super, Williams, and Wrenn) with Seashore as president, Hahn as vice president, and Shoben as secretary-treasurer. I was formally appointed editor somewhere along the line, but apparently the assumption from the outset was that I was to serve as editor and Super as associate editor. It was most important that the managing editor and I be able to work together closely so I had major responsibility for locating the "right" man. My luck (and perhaps judgment!) has never been better than when Frank Fletcher turned out to be not only the board's choice but mine—and Frank accepted!

He has been the most single constant factor in the financial stability and success of the *Journal*—and a wonderfully helpful man with whom to work. Frank Fletcher, managing editor throughout the life of the *Journal*, we owe you a great deal. Harold Seashore also contributed much legal and business help in developing the *Journal* and from 1961 to his death in 1965 acted as secretary-treasurer of the board of directors. George Bennett then stepped in as secretary-treasurer and provided the expert advice essential to a smooth transfer of ownership to APA.

During 1953 the editor was a busy fellow. He had to determine journal size and format, locate manuscripts out of nowhere, find a publisher convenient to both him and the managing editor, determine Journal cost per volume so that he could suggest a subscription figure, write promotion material that would bring in qualified manuscripts as well as subscriptions (Irwin A. Berg and Seashore carried responsibility for much of the promotion activities themselves). It is gratifying that our first estimate of a $6.00 subscription rate proved adequate for our needs then and for the next nine years, even though the size of the *Journal* increased from 64 to 96 pages an issue during that period. (It is now 128 pages.)

Finding high quality manuscripts for the first volume proved a formidable task. It was here that the stockholders did an invaluable and continuous job of locating possible manuscripts. Getting together a first issue may be deceptively easy but the total first year quality counts—and even more the second year. Many journals fail after their initial supply runs low—the gold-bearing lode is likely to run out unless it has been well prospected or other lodes have been staked out. I was chairman of the Publications Committee of APGA in 1953 and was very anxious not be thought of as having a "conflict of interest" in trying to feed manuscripts to a new journal, but William D. Wilkins, then editor of *The Personnel and Guidance Journal,* was most helpful. He gave me much counsel and even offered not to "scout" for papers at annual conventions until we had had a chance at them! Later, Joseph Samler, as editor of the *P & G Journal,* and I cooperated in many ways even to the extent of systematically exchanging lists of "manuscripts accepted" so that the occasional author would not submit a very similar article to two journals. (Both Samler and I have pulled such manuscripts out of impending issues and returned them to the author with questions!) The same kind of cordial relationship existed with Laurance Shaffer, and later Edward Bordin, as editors of *The Journal of Consulting Psychology.*

The first issue finally appeared and the journal was under way. Those readers for whom 1954 was "history" may be interested in the Table of Contents of that issue:

> *A Follow-up After Three Years of Clients Counseled by Two Methods:* Edward
>   W. Forgy and John D. Black
> *An Interest Inventory as a Measure of Personality:* Manuel N. Brown
> *Career Patterns as a Basis for Vocational Counseling:* Donald E. Super
> *Analysis of Counselor Style by Discussion Units:* W. J. Dipboye

THE EDITORS AND POLICY

In the evaluation of manuscripts an editor must have help—much help and technical help. The first two associate editors, Donald E. Super (1954-65) and Paul Dressel (1954-57), and later Leona E. Tyler (1958-65), gave a second reading to all manuscripts which passed the editor's first scrutiny. They were his right hand in every matter of judgment and policy—a tower of strength to a frequently beleaguered editor who had to make the final decision. Super and Tyler are tremendous people by almost any standards and certainly they were so for me. The group of consulting editors, each selected for a particular kind of counseling or writing expertise, stayed fairly constant until a rotation policy was inaugurated in 1962. The Vol. 1 cover carries these names: Edward S. Bordin, Milton E. Hahn, Harold B. Pepinsky, Edward J. Shoben, William U. Snyder, Leona E. Tyler, Edmund G. Williamson. They gave a second or a third reading to manuscripts where their unique critical skills were needed.

We inaugurated not only a new journal but several new features: (1) Comments on leading or controversial articles (this was first suggested to me by Clarence Mahler in August, 1952); (2) grouping articles of a similar nature and listing them in the table of contents under a topical heading; (3) "Research Notes from Here and There" under Harold Pepinsky (1954-63), later entitled "Research Frontier" under Henry Borow (1961-66) and John Muthard (1964-66); (4) "Current Books and the Passing Scene," the creation of Donald Super (1954-63), later Irwin Berg (1958-66) and finally Wrenn (1964-66); (5) "Letters and Comments" was not an innovation but a feature which proved popular from the beginning; (6) "Test Reviews" has been a steady feature since 1956 under Laurence Siegel (1956-63), Gordon Anderson (1960), John Crites (1961-66), and Jack Merwin (1964-66). The publishing of "Manuscripts Received for Publication" as an aid to research workers was at one time an innovation but even more are the bibliography cards with abstracts of each article which Donald Super suggested and I investigated but which Frank Robinson as the incoming editor in 1964 put into being.

It is significant perhaps of some of the early planning to note that the "Purpose" of the *Journal* as given on the inside front cover has been unchanged from Vol. 1 to Vol. 13. The purpose statement grew out of the thinking of us all, but I would like here to quote a paragraph from a letter to me from Harold Seashore, dated April 21, 1953: "I think that our articles ought to be either out-and-out research or first rate experimental-theoretical material. I do not object to a review, but it ought to be a review in a research setting and not a review of 'practice' as such. Another way of saying this is that we want the bulk of the *Journal* to be research *content* with the remainder being primarily research planning and summarizing."

The *Journal* hasn't wandered far from this early standard under either Francis Robinson or me, although I expect that I accepted more "theory" articles than Harold would have done! Even the first three volumes showed a fair balance, however, as indicated by a topical analysis of the contents of Vols. 1, 2, and 3, published in the final issue of Vol. 3.

Topical Area	No. of Articles
Counseling and Personality Theory	22
Counseling Process	21
Research Theory and Method	21
Studies of Students	20
Vocational and Rehabilitation Counseling	28
Measurement in Counseling	25
Counselor and His Professional Growth	22

An analysis of the latest three volumes might show a different pattern of emphasis. Certainly the "younger" writers are more in the ascendancy and I can think of some topics covered in 1964–66 that weren't even *known* in 1954–56. Just for fun, I checked the 42 authors of articles in Vol. 1 against the authors appearing in Vols. 11 and 12. Only four Vol. 1 authors wrote for either the 1964 or the 1965 volume—Berdie, Pepinsky, Layton, and Tyler. Some authors *remain* young!

The present comprehensive and smoothly organized professional-research journal produced by editor Francis P. Robinson and his colleagues has come a long way from its first staggering steps. So has counseling and I like to think that the *Journal* has contributed to counseling's development. If so, then much is owed to many.

REFERENCES

American Psychological Association. Division of Counseling and Guidance, Committee on Counselor Training. Recommended standards for training counseling psychologists. *American Psychologist,* 1952, *7,* 175–181.

American Psychological Association. Division of Counseling Psychology, Committee on Definition. Counseling psychology as a specialty. *American Psychologist,* 1956, *11,* 282–285.

Bordin, E. S. (Ed.). *The training of psychological counselors.* Ann Arbor: University of Michigan Press, 1951.

Chapter 5
The Journal of Counseling Psychology as a Matter of Policies

HAROLD B. PEPINSKY
KAY HILL-FREDERICK
DOUGLAS L. EPPERSON

Twenty-five years ago, leaders in the fledgling APA Division of Counseling Psychology initiated the *Journal of Counseling Psychology*. What has evolved as journal policy, we note, reflects early developments in the history of the division. A steady growth in the proportion of empirical as against nonempirical articles and a dramatic rise in the proportion of process-outcome studies in the journal symbolize the division's continuing need for unity of thought; *The Counseling Psychologist*, by contrast, is an outlet in which divisional members may express their need for individuality of action.

The three of us who have written this anniversary tribute represent contrasting generations in the life of the psychological specialty from which the *Journal of Counseling Psychology* derives its name: Two of us are advanced graduate students in an APA-approved program of studies in

Editor's Note. An event such as the Silver Anniversary of a professional periodical should be commemorated; who other than someone active in counseling psychology history and the *Journal of Counseling Psychology's* creation and development—someone who helped make it happen—could do better at such a task. Thus, in order to commemorate the 25th anniversary of the publication of the *Journal of Counseling Psychology*, I invited Harold B. Pepinsky to write an article reviewing the historical events leading up to the creation of the journal along with his observations of the course the journal has followed since that time. Pepinsky went one step further and invited two younger colleagues to join him in the task, thus broadening the article's perspective and educating younger colleagues at the same time about counseling psychology's history. Pepinsky and his coauthors have labored hard to review, to reflect, to synthesize, and to interpret our professional history. I hope you will find their work as interesting as I did (Samuel H. Osipow).

"The *Journal of Counseling Psychology* As a Matter of Policies," by H. B. Pepinsky, K. Hill-Frederick, and D. L. Epperson, *Journal of Counseling Psychology*, 1978, *25*, 483–498. Copyright 1978 by the American Psychological Association. Reprinted by permission.

The first author acknowledges the influence of Gilbert Wrenn, Harold Lasswell, and Ohio State University's Mershon Center upon his ideas about counseling and social policy. We all thank Don Dell and Pauline Pepinsky for comments on an earlier draft of this article.

Requests for reprints should be sent to Harold B. Pepinsky, Ohio State University, Department of Psychology, 1945 North High Street, Columbus, Ohio 43210.

47

counseling psychology; the third is a charter member of the American Psychological Association's Division of Counseling Psychology—itself a charter division of the APA—and one of those privileged to serve under the editorship of Gilbert Wrenn as a contributor and reader of manuscripts for the journal. In this article, we have sought to identify constituent features of the journal, thereby illuminating references to social and political circumstances of its development over the past quarter century. Published accounts are embellished by those of the first author, who, as eyewitness to much that has happened to shape the specialty and its namesake, has been invited also to reminisce about these things. For all three of us, preparation of the article has melded what we knew and didn't know into fresh perspective.

SOCIAL AND POLITICAL CONDITIONS

Introduction

The early 1950s was a landmark period both for the Division of Counseling Psychology (Wrenn, 1977) and for the journal that bears its name (Wrenn, 1966). As stated in a published report of the division's Committee on Definition (APA, 1956), the labels *counseling psychology* and *counseling psychologist* were recommended by persons attending an invitational conference held at Northwestern University prior to the APA's annual convention and under divisional sponsorship in 1951. During the annual convention, the division itself adopted these terms. In 1952, the phrase *counseling psychologist* was used in a published report by the division's Committee on Counselor Training (APA, 1952), and at the APA's annual convention for that year, the division formally changed its designation from "Counseling and Guidance" to "Counseling Psychology."

To accord with the new terminology, the Veterans Administration (VA) obligingly reclassified as "Counseling Psychologist (VR & E)" one of the positions in its Division of Vocational Rehabilitation and Education and created under medical auspices the new position of "Counseling Psychologist (Vocational)" (cf. Moore & Bouthilet, 1952). Initial publication of the *Journal of Counseling Psychology* occurred under the editorship of Gilbert Wrenn in 1954. In 1955, the American Board of Examiners in Professional Psychology (now the American Board of Professional Psychology) obligingly changed the title of a diploma, which it confers as a badge of professional competence, from "Counseling and Guidance" to "Counseling Psychology."

Our discussion of the early years highlights two sets of events that have not been emphasized in previous histories. One occurred in 1946, shortly before the baptismal years; the other as an accompaniment (1951–1956) and aftermath (1958–1965) of the landmark years. Both accounts feature relations between the Division of Counseling Psychology and its parent organization, the American Psychological Association.

The Year Was 1946 . . .

In September 1946, the American Psychological Association had its first annual convention after a suspension of such meetings during the war years. The convention was held in Philadelphia on the campus of the University of Pennsylvania. It was a curious affair, with many in attendance still in uniform and the occasion, as a whole, dominated by the experimentalists. Yet there were foreshadowings of what was to become a major transformation of APA policies and practices. Applied psychology, which had come into national prominence as a result of the massive psychological testing of U. S. Army inductees during World War I, received added visibility with the more pervasive and sophisticated programs of classification for the U. S. armed forces of World War II. Such programs also included group testing for the purpose of screening out persons to be rejected as intellectually or personally unfit for military services. For the most part, these tests were administered by enlisted persons, themselves job classified to perform this and other clerical services. Initial judgments about "personal" fitness, however, were often based on interviews conducted by commissioned officers—either MDs, many of whom had been suddenly transposed into psychiatrists, or non-MDs labeled as clinical psychologists. Among the latter, only a few had been formally educated as psychologists; even fewer had been trained in the specialty. In hospital units of one kind or another, programs of clinical diagnosis and treatment for military personnel were conducted under medical supervision, but often by persons identified as clinical psychologists. Special units with elite members also included persons whose duties were esoterically psychological; for example, the mysterious, quasi-military, and glamorous Office of Strategic Services—forerunner of the Central Intelligence Agency. Other select units of civilian and military personnel, attached to particular branches of the services, developed psychometric tests and/or conducted assessments of selection, classification, and training programs, more rarely of missions in the field.

Here was an unprecedented demand for psychological services, a publicly mandated response to the exigency of creating abruptly a massive yet efficient military machine, whose human components had been drafted largely from the ranks of young male adult civilians. This was followed at the end of the war by a huge demand for psychological services, equally unprecedented but now prompted by the need for getting veterans of military service back into civilian life. As a matter of public policy, psychological treatment was to occur under the auspices of the Veterans Administration, with mandates for two major programs of rehabilitation: (a) educational and occupational and (b) emotional.

By the time of the APA convention in 1946, provision had been made for dealing with problems of the second kind. In the VA Division of Medicine and Neurology, a new category of Civil Service position had been created, that of "Clinical Psychologist." To cope with problems of the first kind, there were—

within the VA Division of Vocational Rehabilitation and Education—
"counselors" to guide clients into appropriate education or training.
Significantly, however, the VA had also contracted with a number of colleges
and universities to provide this type of vocational-educational "advisement."
With this financial inducement, many agencies were established on campuses
to perform services that were variously identified—for example, as
advisement, counseling, guidance, and testing.

If the services were to be performed—so went the reasoning among
psychologists who were politically active at the time—there also must be
persons trained to offer them. Older, established programs of graduate
training, as at the University of Minnesota, The Ohio State University, and
Teachers College, Columbia University, were reconstituted, expanded, and
formalized.

By September of 1946, moreover, many new training programs had
been instituted at other colleges and universities; others were soon to follow.
There was no clear-cut pattern of training among these, nor were there clearly
identifiable objectives that could enable prospective students to know what
they might be trained for. Even the locus of training was uncertain; prominent
departments of psychology and educational psychology were discovered to be
housed in schools and colleges of teacher education. Out of an earlier
tradition, there were hybrid departments of philosophy and psychology.

If 1946 was a time of accelerated change for institutionalized
psychology, it was also marked by organizational change within the American
Psychological Association. No longer was the association to be dominated by
persons who prided themselves on being "pure" psychologists and for whom
"professional practice" was an object of contempt. At that historic convention
in Philadelphia, a merger having been effected between the APA and the
American Association for Applied Psychology, the APA itself was
reorganized into a conglomerate of divisions. Nearly half of these had distinct
implications for professional practice—for example, the Divisions of Clinical
Psychology (12), Consulting Psychology (13), Industrial Psychology (14),
Educational Psychology (15), School Psychology (16), Counseling and
Guidance (17), Psychologists in Public Service (18), and Military Psychology
(19). To mark the occasion further, Carl Rogers—an avowedly applied
psychologist—was introduced at that annual convention as president-elect of
the APA.

As noted here and earlier, Division 17 came into being as a charter
division of the APA under the title of "Counseling and Guidance." That was
in recognition of common ground among founding parents—for example,
Hugh Bell, Edward Bordin, John G. Darley, Mitchell Dreese, Frank Fletcher,
William Gilbert, Milton Hahn, Francis Robinson, Winfield Scott, Dewey
Stuit, Donald Super, Edmund Williamson, and Gilbert Wrenn, who were
university teachers and administrators or, like George Bennett and Harold
Seashore, were in the business of producing and selling psychological tests.
Almost all of these persons had overlapping memberships in two non-APA
organizations: the American College Personnel Association (ACPA)—

centered on student personnel work in colleges and universities—and the National Vocational Guidance Association (NVGA)—largely concerned with vocational guidance activities at the junior and senior high school levels. Although several of that group also were members of the APA's Division of Clinical Psychology, relatively few were visibly identified with clinical as well as counseling psychology.

Interregnum, 1951-1956

Five years later, the NVGA and the ACPA, along with several other organizations informally related as a Council of Guidance and Personnel Associations, incorporated to become the American Personnel and Guidance Association (APGA). Frank Fletcher (Note 1) tells the story of how he and Robert Shaffer, president of the reconstituted APGA, hunted all over Washington, D. C., to find housing for the fledgling Association. Eventually, thanks to Fletcher's acquaintance with Dael Wolfle, then executive secretary of the American Psychological Association, APGA was able to rent from the APA an old carriage house behind its own central office building. In those years, Gilbert Wrenn and Donald Super served almost concurrently as presidents of the APGA and of the APA's Division of Counseling Psychology. Fletcher, who was APGA president in 1957-1958, later became president of the division. Edmund Williamson and Ralph Berdie, early presidents of the division, later became APGA presidents. These close and cordial relationships extended to the *Personnel and Guidance Journal,* an official publication of the APGA, and the *Journal of Counseling Psychology* (Wrenn, 1966).

Ironically, these and many other persons active in both organizations during 1951-1955 were also instigating changes in name for the division and its members. As noted above, the new titles were "Counseling Psychology" and "Counseling Psychologist." The prospect, soon realized, of funding for trainees and consultants within the Veterans Administration was accompanied by that of enhanced prestige for counseling psychologists (Robinson, 1964). Like clinical psychologists, they, too, could now work in hospitals, even if somewhat ambivalently under medical auspices. Job opportunities for counseling psychologists were enhanced in number and in variety of settings for employment. Ten years later, however, Robinson (1964) recalled that some of those early leaders, like himself, had been made uneasy by the modified titles. As things turned out, their concern—presumably over what the change from "Counseling *and Guidance"* (italics added) implied—was not unjustified.

Response to Sputnik I, 1958-1965

Although divisional leaders had been politically successful in upgrading the levels of training for counseling psychologists in the Veterans Administration, counseling *psychologists* as such had much less impact upon the training of rehabilitation counselors. In part that was because other professions, such as social work, were able to resist pressure to require doctoral training for these positions. In part, however, the federal Vocational Rehabilitation Act of 1954 created a demand for many more counseling positions than could be staffed by psychologists. The American Personnel and Guidance Association thus could be assisted by psychologists who were members of the APA to seek and obtain newly available funds for the training of rehabilitation counselors at the master's level.

The training of counselors under other than psychological auspices was given an even greater boost by the National Defense Education Act (NDEA) of 1958, part of the United States' agitated response to the launching of Sputnik I. Again encouraged by APA members, the APGA lobbied effectively for funds with which to train counselors for work in elementary and secondary schools. The NDEA Guidance Institutes, under the aegis of schools of education, were a major consequence of this effort. These provided an alternative to existing programs of graduate education, briefer in length and not culminating in a traditional graduate degree.

Neither the Division of Counseling Psychology nor the APA saw fit to establish formal liaison with the APGA to aid in developing guidelines for the new programs. Instead, the APA formed a major committee to negotiate with representatives of the American Psychiatric Association on territorial disputes between the two organizations. Concurrently, an invitational conference on graduate education in psychology (there were no professional schools of psychology in those days) recommended emphasis upon the doctorate as a minimally essential level of training for psychologists. Because resources were limited, so ran the prevailing argument, there could be only token sponsorship of subdoctoral training programs (cf. Roe, Gustad, Moore, Ross, & Skodak, 1959).

The Division of Counseling Psychology's inaction vis-à-vis the APGA at this time is also understandable. Earlier, it had endorsed the idea of the doctorate as a requisite level of training for counseling psychologists (APA, 1952). More recently, as noted above, divisional ties with rehabilitation and school counseling were allowed to erode while counseling psychologists in large numbers were receiving doctoral training and subsequent employment in VA hospitals. The VA had ample funds for trainees, staff, and consultants. Counseling psychology thus was able to compete successfully with clinical psychology for its share of a lucrative market for psychological services. These events contributed toward a blurring of distinctions between the two psychological specialties.

By 1959, in view of counseling psychology's apparent drift, the APA's Education and Training Board was moved to ask whether the area should continue to be recognized as an independent specialty. The matter was not permitted to become a subject of debate within the APA generally,[1] but the

---

[1]That part of counseling psychology's history, hitherto suppressed, will be aired by invitation of John Whiteley in a forthcoming publication on the specialty, which he is editing.

division was moved to renewed self-searching and to consequent publicizing through reports emanating from a special committee of inquiry in 1961 (later published in Thompson & Super, 1964, pp. 151–161) and from a second invitational conference, held at the Greyston Center in 1964 (Thompson & Super, 1964). Counseling psychologists were affirmed to have common cause, for example, in helping individuals to develop their strengths, yet out of highly diverse interests and means of helping to provide such assistance.

Appropriately, the conference at Greyston was reported to identify counseling psychologists as having "unity in diversity" (Thompson & Super, 1964, pp. 25–26). Still, there were invited speakers who called attention to the special heritage of counseling psychologists in such activities as vocational appraisal and counseling. And there was evidence of unease over the direction things had taken. For example, Francis Robinson (1964, p. 36) recalled that there were many persons to whom the earlier change in title from "Counseling and Guidance" to "Counseling Psychology" had sounded inappropriate. Later in his talk, however, he glossed over the connection between divisional decisions of this sort and a "storm of aggressive misinterpretation" with which school counselors and their trainers in schools of education were said to have greeted the published report of a Divisional Committee on Training in Psychology for School Counselors (Robinson, 1964, pp. 40–41).

Finally, the division's marginal status within its parent organization at the time of the conference at Greyston is attested to by the fact that prior efforts to obtain financial support of the conference from the APA were not successful (Thompson & Super, 1964, p. vi). In contrast, the second major invitational conference of the Division of Clinical Psychology, held a year later in Chicago, was not only sponsored but amply funded through the APA (Hoch, Ross, & Winder, 1966).

Later Events

These will be touched upon only briefly here, since they are more familiar to readers of the *Journal of Counseling Psychology.* The APA's decision to acquire the journal as one of its major publications in 1967, of course, brought the journal into line with the association's general rules for its publications. As we shall see in our discussion of the journal, which follows immediately, publication of *The Counseling Psychologist* (begun in 1969) and of *The Journal of Vocational Behavior* (in 1971) has had little direct impact on policies of the *Journal of Counseling Psychology;* rather, it has supported them. Though recent events have had a major effect upon American society, their effect upon the journal is less immediately evident. The war in Vietnam, social and political movements on behalf of ethnic minority groups and women, and concurrent social, political, and economic upheavals (for example, the energy crisis, inflation, unemployment, global restiveness) are reflected more in the subject matter of manuscripts published than in either the manner of collecting and interpreting information or the forms in which they are presented. While the latter are governed with increasing explicitness by rules contained in the APA's *Publication Manual* (APA, 1974), the *Journal of Counseling Psychology*'s own rules of procedure appear to have been determined more by earlier rather than later circumstances in its history. Even the Vail conference on training in professional psychology, held in 1973, seems to have had little impact on how information is presented in the journal, despite the fact that counseling psychologists had strong reactions to that conference (Fretz, 1974); a similar pattern was found for the APA's 1976 and 1977 conferences on credentialing (Fretz, 1977; Wellner, 1976, 1977).

Implications for the Journal of Counseling Psychology

In the midst of all the *Sturm und Drang* in its environment, the journal has charted and maintained a steady course. In our view, this has been influenced by early (1946–1956) developments in the history of the division. First, its current emphasis on counseling as a kind of process (Osipow, 1976) is consistent with the Charter Division of Counseling and Guidance (in 1946), which encompassed two related *activities,* and is to be distinguished from the later Division of Counseling Psychology, in which *counseling* has become a modifier to define a specialty that encompasses diverse activities and interests (Osipow, 1977; Thompson & Super, 1964). Second, in its upward mobility within the APA (from 1951 to 1956), the division's early recommendations emphasized the need for training in research at the doctoral level (APA, 1952). We shall now document this claim by reference to the contents of the *Journal of Counseling Psychology.*

The Journal of Counseling Psychology *and Its Policies*

In this 25th year of the journal, thanks to the aforementioned societal upheaval, there is a good deal of talk about *policy.* In trying to understand why this is so and what is meant by the term, we are impelled to believe that questions of policy arise when things are in an unsettled state and need to be resolved. Policy, thus, has the objective of reducing discrepancy between what is perceived to be an actual and a desired state of affairs (cf. Pepinsky & Patton, 1971). For example, when funds for basic research began to dry up and there was money instead to support projects that seemed to have immediate practical applications, we heard a good deal about *science policy.* More recently, following the actions of OPEC, we are confronted with *energy policy* still to be decided upon. These events may be restated in the form of an "If . . . , then . . ." proposition, where the "If . . . ," portion describes a contingency (like the oil crisis) that must be dealt with, and the "then . . . ." part expresses a basic idea of what is being or ought to be done about it.

In their classic study of the international negotiations of the American business community and its relation to United States foreign policy, Bauer, Pool, and Dexter (1963) introduced a second important attribute, which helps us to understand how policy is formulated. Instead of being guided by U. S. governmental policy, businesses were seen to be acting in their own self-interest; policy was thus to be identified *after the fact* of business transactions. In general, Bauer (1968) asserted later, policy is as much to be inferred from actions that take place as the actions themselves are apt to be determined by preformulated policy. Hence, we may also conceive *policy* to be a *premise in the form of general rules that either presuppose—or are presupposed by—a category of social actions* (Pepinsky, 1974).

Consider the *Journal of Counseling Psychology* as a category of social actions that enters into its production and its policies as ground rules that have guided its production during the past 25 years. We may now examine the journal's policies both as described by its editors and as rules to be inferred from analysis of their productions.

Editorial Statements

A word about the journal's editors is in order. To date, there have been four of them: Gilbert Wrenn (1954–1963), Francis Robinson (1964–1969), Ralph Berdie (1970–1974), and Samuel Osipow (1975–1981). Stanley Strong and David Weiss helpfully served as acting co-editors (August–December 1974) following Berdie's death in 1974. As Osipow (1976) describes the editorships of his predecessors, Wrenn's was the period in which the journal was established; Robinson's, an era of transition from independent ownership to management by the APA; and Berdie's, a time of substantive consolidation. Under Osipow's direction, as implied in his initial statement of editorial policy (Osipow, 1976), there has been further consolidation and delimiting of the journal's contents. Wrenn, Robinson, and Berdie all had served as presidents of the Division of Counseling Psychology; Osipow, also the youngest of the four during his editorship, became president of the division early in his term as editor.

The first author has had the privilege of knowing well all of the editors. He may be excused for taking this occasion to pay special tribute to Gilbert Wrenn—doctoral adviser, teacher, friend, and later colleague—an important, constructive influence on his personal and professional development. Those qualities of warmth, generosity, and wisdom that Wrenn showed toward his students, he also manifested abundantly during the times of his many national offices and in his service on behalf of the journal. His perspective on the journal (Wrenn, 1966) and, most recently, on the division (Wrenn, 1977) continues to evince a rare openness to new ideas and experiences, an ability to draw sustenance from the past and to be challenged by the present.

Qualities such as these made Gilbert Wrenn an inspirational leader, a fitting person to launch the journal as a center of dialogue for the Division of Counseling Psychology as a fledgling organization. The guiding policy of his editorship was clearly displayed in his initial editorial (Wrenn, 1954) and subsequent reviews of the journal's early years under his editorship (Wrenn,

1956, 1966). The last of these (Wrenn, 1966) is particularly important, not alone for the view it gives of an early and necessarily flexible set of guidelines but also for the description by an expert witness of the journal in its first decade.

There is a clue toward what would become an increasingly firm policy of the journal in Wrenn's (1954, 1956, 1966) statements about a greater than anticipated volume of nonresearch articles. He makes clear his dilemma in wanting to attract more data-based articles as against the need to attract publishable articles in sufficient volume. Even in the first two years of Robinson's editorship, Wrenn (1966) noted and lauded a shift in journal emphasis toward one of "professional research." Both Wrenn (1954) and Robinson (1964) encouraged manuscripts from a "newer generation," including articles based on dissertation research. Again, the policy was one of encouraging—later, of accepting—an increasingly large volume of *research* as against *nonresearch* articles. This was possible because the rejection rate was becoming higher: In 1964, less than one third of submitted articles were being accepted for publication (Robinson, 1964). As Robinson (1970) pointed out at the time of his retirement, the transfer of ownership to the APA called forth many additional manuscripts for review.

Under Robinson's regime, as he tells us (Robinson, 1970), the necessity of rejecting manuscripts because of space limitations was itself the enactment of implicit policy. Manuscripts had to become briefer; even so, there was increased risk of eliminating otherwise acceptable manuscripts. At the same time, it became possible for the editor and his two reviewers for each manuscript to enforce what they construed to be higher standards in the quality of writing and in the sophistication of the research itself. Incidentally, his retirement article (Robinson, 1970) contains an excellent set of guidelines for conducting and reporting one's research. By this time, it is evident that research-based articles were preferred.

Survey research, which Robinson (1970) described as a source of "sociological information," was also encouraged. He cited a number of these (Bohn, 1966; Foreman, 1966; Goldstein, 1963; Myers & DeLevie, 1966; Walsh, Feeney, & Resnick, 1969) published during his term of office.

During his time of consolidation, Berdie (1973) lamented the numerous manuscripts submitted that reflected current fads. His comment emphasizes, by implication, the extent to which an editor and his or her referees can determine what is or is not acceptable for publication. The kind of research Berdie would like to have seen is discussed by him in the journal and elsewhere (Berdie, 1973; Williamson, 1974).

It remained for Osipow (1976), however, to be the most explicit about what kinds of substantive content would be more and less acceptable for inclusion in the journal. "The *Journal*'s focus on counseling itself should increase because of new policies," he wrote in beginning his editorship. Emphasis would be given, he said, to papers on the counseling process and counselor behaviors; evaluation and outcome studies; the differential effects of various counseling interventions on different populations . . . ; descriptions and evaluations of innovations in counseling programs and procedures; counseling theory; training and selection of counselors; and methodology as it is directly concerned with the counseling activity [Osipow, 1976, p. 1].

Research other than counseling research would tend to be unacceptable for inclusion.

The Rating Game

"To Garfinkel," according to Harré (1970, pp. ix–x), is to make trouble for people in order to find out how they avoid it. We shall resist the temptation to do just that as we examine briefly the assigning of reputations to people on the basis of their association with the *Journal of Counseling Psychology*. In line with the journal's addiction to empirical research, the process of assignment rests on the premise that what exists does so in some amount and may be counted. The process assumes further that those whose names appear most frequently are to be accorded the highest prestige. One may count either the frequency with which people contribute articles or are cited in them.

Myers and DeLevie (1966) made the only study we know of in which a count was made of the number of times a given person was cited in any or all of four journals, including the *Journal of Counseling Psychology*. These were considered likely outlets for publications of special relevance to counseling psychologists. Myers and DeLevie (1966) searched through volumes of these journals for the years 1960–1964. The top three—by implication, the most eminent—persons mentioned were Allen Edwards, Carl Rogers, and Donald Super. For the *Journal of Counseling Psychology* alone, Super and Rogers were far and away the most frequently cited. Myers and DeLevie (1966) commendably hedge their bets after employing a method "honeycombed with weaknesses . . . anticipated but tolerated" (p. 246). The authors' humorous caveat against the laboriousness of their research procedure may have dissuaded others from using it since in research on the *Journal of Counseling Psychology*.

Far more information is available on the relative frequency with which organizations were represented by members' contributions to the journal. Goodstein (1963), who began it all with an analysis of Volumes 1–8 (1954–1961), reported the vast and sprawling network of VA installations to be the largest single contributor. The largest single geographic units represented were midwestern universities in the United States. As he pointed out, however, the percentages for individual organizations were small, the VA conglomerate alone accounting for but 8% of the total.

Bohn (1966) made a similar analysis of the institutional sources of contributions for Volumes 9–12 (1962–65) and found a decline in the proportion emanating from the VA. Though contributions from individual organizations remained small, the largest number consisted of universities from the Midwest. Katz and Brophy (1975) extended the analysis to include Volumes 9–20 (1962–1973). The VA's contributions continued to decline, and though midwestern universities continued to be the largest contributors, eastern universities were making inroads on that lead. Most recently, Cox and Catt (1977) analyzed graduate departments of psychology as sources of publications appearing in all 13 APA journals for 1970–1971, 1971–1972, and 1972–1973. For the *Journal of Counseling Psychology* alone, the University of Maryland contributed the most publications, showing a relatively marked increase for the last two years, whereas that from the University of Minnesota had dropped markedly. In the total for all three years, the aggregate contributions from midwestern universities was still greatest. Again, the frequencies for individual universities are small, particularly for those made year by year.

What effect these institutional sources have on policies of the journal is not wholly clear. As Walsh et al. (1969) showed in analyzing articles published during the journal's initial 14 years (1954–1967), the leading institutional sources of these articles also were educating a disproportionately large share of graduate students who ultimately would be contributing articles to the journal. All four editors of the journal, at the time of their service, have been employed by midwestern universities. We did not attempt to analyze sociometrically the network of relations between editors and their editorial boards and ad hoc reviewers of manuscripts. For one so minded, that might provide an interesting story in itself.

We can but surmise that an editor is more likely than not to appoint as colleagues persons whom the editor presumes to be, in some critical dimension, like-minded. Also, we may assume that editorial consultants, more often than not, are likely to have been prior contributors to the journal. All of this, too, in the manner of organizational elites, may have something to do with the transmission of a culture through successive generations of editors. In that sense, continuity in journal policy becomes a self-fulfilling prophecy. Berdie's (1973) editorial on what was being submitted to the journal and what he would prefer to have submitted reminded us that editors and their referees are likely to be important determiners of what eventually gets published. Do they make policy in this respect, or do they but implement existing rules of procedure? Perhaps someone will wish to answer such questions. We ourselves cannot now do so but turn instead to the journal to find out what its policies are.

Journal Policy as Reflected in Its Contents

The most explicit indication of the *Journal of Counseling Psychology*'s policies over the years is provided in an analysis of its contents. As we have seen, special features of the journal were eliminated in 1967 when the APA became its publisher. That left only editorial comments and articles submitted and accepted for publication as the essential scholarly features of the journal. Limiting himself to the published articles, Munley (1974) undertook this Herculean task for the years 1954–1972 (Volumes 1–19). In Table 1, we have extended Munley's analysis to include the next five volumes for the years 1973–1977. Munley did not report on the reliability of his observations, and though our own categorizing had to depend on the descriptions he provided, two of us were able to check on each other's work. The results are interesting.

Type of content. Robinson (1970, p. 386) reported an increase in the number of pages in each volume of the journal since it became a publication of the APA in 1967. That result is accompanied by an increase in the yearly total of articles published, which also seems to have leveled off over the past few years (see Table 1, last column). Over the years, too, the contents of the journal have changed (see Table 1). One of the most obvious is the change in the ratio of empirical to nonempirical articles. By the latter, we infer that Munley (1974) had reference to discursive, rhetorical, or conceptual articles; by the former, to articles reporting on data collected, quantified, analyzed, and interpreted for one or more specified purposes. In 1954, only one of every two articles was empirical in content. Since then, there has been an almost steady rise in the proportion until, in 1977, more than nine out of every ten articles were data based. Foreman (1966) earlier reported this trend in the *Journal of Counseling Psychology* and related journals, associating it with the increased external funding of published empirical research.

   Another dramatic change is revealed in the areas of outcome, process, and process-outcome research (Table 1, columns 7, 8, 9). Note that within the past eight years, the percentage of empirical research represented by outcome studies dropped from 22% to 2%, whereas that for process research rose from 9% to 25%, and that for process-outcome research rose from 2% to 25%. The last increase may have been influenced by the repeated admonition to relate the outcome of counseling to its process (for example, Berdie, 1973; Carkhuff, 1966; Paul, 1967). A spate of experiments on social influence in counseling, driblets of which were being published in the mid-sixties, appear to have been further stimulated by this phenomenon, we believe. Strong's (1968) article on the subject helps to account for the swollen percentage of articles dealing with the counseling process. Osipow's (1976) statement of editorial policy will surely encourage these trends.

   Other trends are apparent but less marked. For example, although the proportion of published research on vocational behavior may have declined slightly since 1969 (see column 10 of Table 1), the marked decrease which might have accompanied the appearance of the *Journal of Vocational Behavior* in 1971 has not materialized.

Sampling. As shown in Table 2, some changes in sampling procedures have occurred within the past five years. An ever greater proportion of college students have served as subjects in published research. From 1954 through

Table 1. Content analysis of the *Journal of Counseling Psychology*

Year	1	2	3	4	5	6	7	8	9	10	11	12	13	14	Total empirical articles[a]	15	16	17	Total nonempirical articles[b]	Total articles[c]
1954–55	2(4)	6(11)	4(7)	7(13)	0(0)	10(19)	5(9)	5(9)	0(0)	6(11)	2(4)	1(2)	0(0)	0(0)	54(51)	5	2	44	51(49)	105
1956–57	2(3)	1(2)	5(9)	2(3)	2(3)	20(36)	3(5)	3(5)	1(2)	7(13)	1(2)	1(2)	2(3)	2(3)	56(57)	8	1	33	42(43)	98
1958–59	4(8)	4(8)	2(4)	3(6)	2(3)	10(20)	6(12)	2(4)	0(0)	14(28)	0(0)	2(4)	3(6)	3(6)	50(51)	7	1	30	38(49)	98[c]
1960–61	2(3)	1(1)	1(1)	6(8)	3(4)	13(18)	1(1)	3(4)	3(4)	17(24)	3(4)	0(0)	4(6)	4(6)	72(62)	9	1	35	45(38)	117
1962–63	3(4)	2(2)	2(2)	11(13)	2(2)	12(15)	9(11)	3(4)	0(0)	19(23)	2(2)	1(1)	5(6)	5(6)	82(64)	9	2	35	46(36)	128
1964–65	9(9)	2(2)	6(6)	10(10)	3(3)	22(22)	17(17)	1(1)	1(1)	12(12)	1(1)	2(2)	5(5)	5(5)	103(75)	10	1	24	35(25)	138
1966–67	10(7)	7(5)	11(8)	15(10)	15(10)	20(14)	17(12)	12(12)	12(12)	15(10)	4(2)	0(0)	7(4)	7(4)	143(80)	13	0	22	35(20)	178
1968–69	18(9)	10(5)	11(8)	12(8)	12(8)	17(12)	15(10)	2(1)	1(1)	37(19)	4(2)	2(1)	5(3)	8(4)	193(91)	2	0	16	18(9)	211
1970–71	10(5)	8(4)	11(6)	7(4)	5(3)	15(8)	15(8)	4(2)	1(1)	37(19)	4(2)	0(0)	10(5)	9(5)	195(89)	3	1	20	24(11)	219
1972–73	14(7)	3(2)	4(2)	24(12)	8(4)	23(12)	22(11)	19(10)	4(2)	25(13)	4(2)	3(2)	12(6)	9(4)	196(90)	6	2	14	22(10)	218
1974–75	12(6)	3(2)	8(4)	13(6)	9(4)	19(10)	18(9)	30(15)	12(6)	12(6)	1(1)	1(1)	19(10)	9(4)	200(93)	4	0	11	15(7)	215
1976–77	8(4)	0(0)	3(2)	3(2)	8(4)	22(11)	3(2)	48(25)	27(14)	27(14)	2(1)	0(0)	20(10)	2(1)	194(94)	4	0	9	13(6)	207
Totals	96(6)	58(4)	72(5)	121(8)	59(4)	230(15)	172(11)	108(7)	62(4)	233(15)	29(2)	15(1)	92(6)	59(4)	1,538(80)	79	11	304	394(20)	1,932

Note: The data from 1954 to 1972 and all categories are taken from Munley (1974). The first number in each cell is the absolute frequency for the specified years. For categories 1–14, a second number is presented in parentheses, which represents the relative frequency (percentage) of studies for the specified years as compared to all empirical research. Categories: 1 = personality and adjustment research; 2 = research on college student characteristics; 3 = academic achievement research; 4 = research on counselor and client characteristics; 5 = research on attitudes and beliefs about counselors, counseling services, and mental health issues; 6 = research on development and evaluation of tests and measurements; 7 = counseling outcome research; 8 = counseling process research; 9 = counseling outcome and process research; 10 = research on vocational behavior; 11 = research methods and statistics; 12 = use of tests in counseling; 13 = counselor training and education; 14 = miscellaneous empirical research; 15 = research reviews and status reports on research projects; 16 = case studies; 17 = theoretical articles and essays.

[a] The number in parentheses is the percentage of empirical articles published in the years specified.

[b] The number in parentheses is the percentage of nonempirical articles published in the years specified.

[c] The total reported by Munley (1974) does not equal the sum of empirical and nonempirical articles for these years.

Table 2. Composition of samples

Composition category	% of empirical studies in specified categories		
	1954-1972[a]	1973-1977	1954-1977
Population of samples			
Preschool children	0	0	0
Elementary school children	3	0.5	2
High school students	11	6	9.5
College students (nonclients)	44	54	47
Counseling center clients	16	5	12.5
Graduate students	3	1	2.5
Adults (nonclients)	12	5	10
Adult psychiatric patients	5	1	4
Adult medical patients	2	1	1.5
Adult vocational-rehabilitation clients	2	1	1.5
Adult clients (private or agency)	0.5	0.5	0.5
Juvenile delinquents and prisoners	0.5	1	0.5
Families	1	0.5	1
Child vocational-rehabilitation clients	0	0.5	0.1
Practicing therapists or counselors	0	4	1.5
Counselors in training	0	8	2.5
Agencies	0	1	0.5
Mixed	0	9	3
Unspecified	0	0.2	0.1
Sex composition of samples			
Males only	26	12	21.5
Females only	7	12	8.5
Males and females	40	60	46
Unspecified	27	17	24
Size of Samples			
1–5	2	0.5	1.5
5–10	1	1	1
10–25	6	10	7
25–50	12	23	15.5
50–100	23	25	24
100–250	29	22	27
250–500	13	9	11.5
500–1000	8	4	7
1000–2500	4	3	3.5
2500–5000	1	1	1
Over 5000	1	1	1
Unspecified	0	0.5	0.1

[a]Data in column 1 are taken from Munley (1974).

1972, these constituted 44% of the total number of persons who thus served. Within the past five years, that figure has increased to 54%. Though there are good reasons for studying other populations (see, for example, Berdie, 1973; Munley, 1974; Schmidt & Pepinsky, 1965), college students remain the captive group most immediately accessible to graduate students and their professors in the conduct of research. Equally important is the fact that groups of subjects are simply less accessible to us. Earlier warnings that research on human subjects was being conducted in such a manner as to evoke strong resentment and resistance (cf. Pepinsky & Patton, 1971) went largely unheeded. Now, as a matter of public policy, there are strictures on research (Mitchell, Kaul, & Pepinsky, 1977). In response to heightened awareness of the need to minimize discriminative practices in research, we may note that the percentage of male *and* female samples investigated has increased from 40% to 60%, whereas the proportion of males-only samples has decreased from 26% to 12%. Curiously, although there are strictures against specifying the sex of a subject unless it is assumed or hypothesized to make a difference in the outcome of research, the percentage of subjects whose sex remains unspecified has dropped from 27% to 17%. The size of sample employed seems to have dropped slightly, though Berdie's (Williamson, 1974) recommendation that more attention be paid to intrasubject variation or Goldman's (1976) recommendation, that more emphasis be given to the individual as a "unit of study," seems to have gone largely unheeded.

Process and its outcomes. The analysis of process-outcome research also reveals that changes have occurred within the past five years (see Table 3). A comparison of our data with those of Munley (1974) reveals a continuing, predominant use of "graduate students and counselors in training" in research on the attributes of counselors; the employment of counselors in practice and other professional helpers has decreased. In the face of evidence gathered over more than 25 years, which suggests that counseling outcomes are related to the counselor's background of training and experience (Luborsky, Chandler, Auerbach, Cohen, & Bachrach, 1971), we may share Munley's (1974) concern about the educational level of counselors studied.

In the past four years, the use of undergraduates to portray counselors has increased, and there has been a marked rise in the "others" category. The latter reflects a large number of articles in which such attributes as level of experience and expertise are either simulated by reference to written descriptions or thus role played in "analogue" research. Here again, we infer the influence of public policy and accompanying legal strictures against the invasion of privacy, which delimit the conditions under which counseling research is to be conducted. Although the percentage of studies in which the counselor's educational level remains unspecified has decreased, nearly one third of all articles still failed to do so. That figure, we think, remains too high.

With respect to the manner in which counseling is said to occur (see Table 3), there has been a dramatic reduction in the frequency of reference to assumed type—for example, analytic, Adlerian, and so on (from 38% down to 15%). A comparable decrease has occurred in the "unspecified" category

Table 3. Characteristics of process and outcome research

Category	% of process and outcome studies in specified category		
	1954-1972[a]	1973-1977	1954-1977
Educational level of counselors			
Undergraduate students	3	6	4.5
Graduate students and counselors in training	29	27	28.5
Masters level counselors	5	2	4
Doctoral level counselors	13	8	8.5
Medical doctors	3	0	2
Social workers (MSW)	2	0	1.5
Others	1	28	13
Unspecified	44	29	38
Types of counseling studied			
Analytic	1.5	0	1
Adlerian	1	0.5	1
Behavioral	18	11	15
Client-centered	10	2	6.5
Eclectic	2	0.5	1.5
Gestalt	1	0.5	1
Rational–emotive therapy	1.5	0.5	1
Sensitivity and human relations training	3	9	6
Description or checklist (unable to classify)	20	56	36
Mixed	0	10	4.5
Unspecified	40	10	26.5
Focus of counseling			
Personal–emotional	32	20	26.5
Vocational–educational	21	9	16
Study skills	14	0	8
Sensitivity and human relations	3	9	5.5
Specific behavioral problem	18	44	29.5
Mixed	0	1	0.5
Unspecified	12	17	14
Method of counseling			
Individual	65	59	62
Group	29	32	30
Both	6	6	6
Unspecified	0	3	2

[a]Data in column 1 are taken from Munley (1974).

(from 40% to 10%). In the same time period, there was an equally dramatic rise in the frequency of recourse to a description or checked list of specific behaviors, a recent trend earlier reported and applauded but not documented by Munley (1974). To us, that is a welcome step toward an accurate recounting of what took place and is consistent with, if not influenced by, Paul's (1967) recommended strategy for the conduct of outcome research. A modest, apparent rise in the use of "sensitivity and human relations" training methods is consistent with Kagan's (1977) current identification of counseling as a means of helping clients to develop interpersonal skills.

Again, in considering the stated focus of counseling in published articles, we find a sharp rise in the specification of behavioral problems to be remedied (from 18% to 44% in Table 3) and a modest increase in counseling for heightened sensitivity and improved human relations. A slightly greater proportion of reports failed to identify any such focus (from 12% to 17%), a puzzling omission that we encountered even in accounts of videotaped analogue research. As in the earlier period covered by Munley (1974), individual counseling continues to predominate, though the recent trend toward group interventions—which he notes but does not document—is maintained.

Our impression is that counseling psychologists are more actively involved in group treatment programs than is reflected in published articles (32% over the past four years). Perhaps research on this currently popular mode of psychological treatment is simply more difficult to conduct in a fashion that meets standards acceptable to editors of the *Journal of Counseling Psychology;* maybe research on the treatment of groups has many other outlets for publication. Our own data do not provide warrant for choice among such inference.

Implications. If present trends continue, then the journal's articles are more than ever likely to be empirical in content, with increasing emphasis on the analysis of counseling process and its related outcomes. The sex of persons who serve as research subjects is more likely to be specified, with a larger proportion of both males and females thus employed in any one study, and most of these are apt to be college students. The counselor studied is most apt to be someone who is in training for the role, even when it is play acted through recourse to methods of simulation. The analysis of counseling process shows signs of becoming more pragmatic and less dependent on preconceptions of how counseling is supposed to be done, with an accompanying pragmatism in specifying behavior to be modified. Individual programs of treatment are likely to be reported upon more frequently than those involving groups. Whatever view one takes of these trends, they provide a clear indication of editorial *policies* affecting what appears in the *Journal of Counseling Psychology* beyond the more general rules governing publications of the APA.

DISCUSSION

There is a parable for us in a comment that Myrtle Wright (1974) makes about the Norwegians she lived and worked among during the German occupation of that country in World War II. "Much of the fate of Norway," she writes, "was determined by a unity of outlook coupled with individuality of action which is characteristic of the people" (Wright, 1974, p. iv). The history of the Division of Counseling Psychology is one of an organization that began in 1946 with what appeared to be considerable unanimity of outlook among its members, a state that seemed to persist through its first decade and for at least two years beyond the launching of its new journal. By the time of the division's second invitational conference in 1964, we were told, there was considerable diversity of interest among divisional members yet "unity in diversity." By last year, we infer, that diversity of belief and practice had become even greater.

Yet the emphasis on doctoral education within the division and the APA has even been heightened in response to legal strictures imposed by state licensing laws and to the carrot held out to many of us in the opportunity to participate in "comprehensive health care programs" and receive "third party" payments. Once again, as 25 years ago, it has become politically and economically attractive for members of the division—or even persons trained in counseling and guidance, who are not—to identify themselves as, first and foremost, psychologists.

After surveying APA-approved departments vis-à-vis other established programs of counselor training, Fretz (1975) was distressed by the lack of a common core of psychology courses for trainees and wondered whether counseling psychologists had a professional identity. Soon thereafter, the APA's conferences on credentialing (Wellner, 1976, 1977) helpfully recommended core areas in psychology that conferees could regard as minimally essential. And Krauskopf, Thoreson, and McAleer (1973) were helpful in pointing at differences between the graduates of APA-approved doctoral programs in counseling psychology and those in counseling training not under APA auspices and in different departments. Counselor educators looked more like teachers and administrators, whereas the graduates of psychology programs were more oriented toward scientific and professional concerns.

It seems to us that the two journals most evidently relevant to the division provide necessary and complementary outlets for counseling psychologists: *The Counseling Psychologist* provides a forum for rhetoric, speculation, and debate, as well as catering to highly diverse interests and practices among the division's members. The *Journal of Counseling Psychology* provides in narrowing focus a symbol of what may well be counseling psychologists' distinctive competence, namely, the activity of counseling. This focus is not narrow or doctrinaire enough to satisfy some (cf. Patterson, 1969) nor broad enough to satisfy others (cf. Oetting, 1967). Kagan (1977), in his presidential address to the division, implicitly supported our assumption in calling attention to the counseling psychologist's roles in providing "primary care" and in helping others to develop interpersonal skills.

During his own presidency, Osipow (1977) deplored the tendency among counseling psychologists to treat *counseling* as if it were a verb while elevating *clinical* to the status of a noun. Whatever the *clinician* does is thus sanctioned as a professional act; *counseling*, in contrast, is downgraded to the status of a generic activity, which requires no special investiture. As an antidote, Osipow (1977) urged counseling psychologists to concentrate on "the facilitation of normal development, with a focus on career development" (p. 93). By implication, that kind of professional objective demands professional knowledge and skills, prominent among which—as a distinctive competence for the counseling psychologist, we infer—is the professional practice of counseling.

However debatable the idea of counseling as a distinctive psychological competence may be on other grounds, the presumption is given weight by renewed pressures toward the delineation of practices, which the APA can identify and advertise as psychological in nature. Here, the declared objective is to standardize further the accreditation of programs and the licensing of individuals for professional practice (Wellner, 1976, 1977). In this context, there is warrant for Osipow's (1976) stated policy for the *Journal of Counseling Psychology* of emphasizing research on the practice of counseling. Both the *Journal of Counseling Psychology* and *The Counseling Psychologist*, it should be noted, thus are centered upon practices, as opposed to theoretical issues.[2] In this respect, too, both journals are representative of a scientific and professional psychology that is authentically American.

We think there is an even more attractive reason for Osipow's (1976) editorial policy and note that the trend toward it was manifest prior to his editorship. In the basic training of counseling psychologists, we believe, training in counseling provides a critical kind of craftsmanship—artisanship, if you will—in working with clients. There is an analogy here to becoming a professional musician or an artist. Picasso, for example, had become highly proficient at drafting before he began his extravagant departures from a representational art. Among professional musicians, it is not at all uncommon to learn one instrument as a basis for becoming skilled in the use of another.

The late Donald Paterson, mentor to one of us, claimed that one could learn a great deal of job-related activity on the job. Our position today is that one can adapt better to diverse job-related activities if one has first been thoroughly disciplined in a mode of working with other people. Counseling provides such a mode, one that also takes us back in our division's history to a time when counseling was considered a minimally essential, respectable kind of work. It is in that sense, we believe, that the journal's current policy is more closely linked to the division's earlier history than to its present, more diffuse state. Editor Sam Osipow unquestionably acknowledges our common focus on counseling as a core activity. Such an assumption enables us to believe that we have unity of thought yet allows us at the same time the comfortable license of individuality of action in our daily routines.

[2]Sam Osipow says he'd welcome more good theoretical papers; too few are submitted for review (Osipow, Note 2).

REFERENCE NOTES

1. Fletcher, F. M. Personal communication, June 1978. (This and other reminiscences are to appear in a forthcoming publication of memoirs by former presidents of the APGA and its divisions, edited by V. Sheeley.)
2. Osipow, S. H. Personal communication, July 18, 1978.

REFERENCES

American Psychological Association. *Publication manual of the American Psychological Association* (2nd ed.). Washington, D. C.: American Psychological Association, 1974.
American Psychological Association, Division of Counseling and Guidance, Committee on Counselor Training. Recommended standards for training counseling psychologists at the doctorate level. *American Psychologist,* 1952, *7,* 175–181.
American Psychological Association, Division of Counseling Psychology. Counseling psychology as a specialty. *American Psychologist,* 1956, *11,* 282–285.
Bauer, R. A. The study of policy formation: An introduction. In R. A. Bauer & K. J. Gergen (Eds.), *The study of policy formation.* N. Y.: Free Press, 1968.
Bauer, R. A., Pool, I. de S., & Dexter, L. A. *American business and public policy.* N. Y.: Atherton, 1963.
Berdie, R. F. Editorial. *Journal of Counseling Psychology,* 1973, *20*(5) [front matter in unbound issue].
Bohn, M. J., Jr. Institutional sources of articles in this *Journal of Counseling Psychology*—four years later. *Journal of Counseling Psychology,* 1966, *13,* 489–490.
Carkhuff, R. R. Counseling research, theory and practice—1965. *Journal of Counseling Psychology,* 1966, *13,* 467–480.
Cox, W. M., & Catt, V. Productivity ratings of graduate departments of psychology based on publication in the journals of the American Psychological Association. *American Psychologist,* 1977, *32,* 793–813.
Foreman, M. E. Publication trends in counseling journals. *Journal of Counseling Psychology,* 1966, *13,* 481–485.
Fretz, B. R. Counseling psychology and the Vail Conference. *The Counseling Psychologist,* 1974, *4*(3), 64–66.
Fretz, B. R. Psychology in counseling psychology: Whither or wither? *Journal of Counseling Psychology,* 1975, *22,* 238–242.
Fretz, B. R. (Guest Ed.). Professional identity. *The Counseling Psychologist,* 1977, *7*(2), 8–94.
Goldman, L. A revolution in counseling research. *Journal of Counseling Psychology,* 1976, *23,* 543–552.
Goodstein, L. D. The institutional sources of articles in the *Journal of Counseling Psychology. Journal of Counseling Psychology,* 1963, *10,* 94–95.
Harré, R. Foreword. In S. M. Lyman & M. B. Scott (Eds.), *A sociology of the absurd.* N. Y.: Meredith Corporation, 1970.
Hoch, E. L., Ross, A. O., & Winder, C. L. (Eds.). *Professional preparation of clinical psychologists.* Washington, D. C.: American Psychological Association, 1966.

Kagan, N. Presidential address, Division 17. *The Counseling Psychologist,* 1977, 7(2), 4–7.

Katz, G. M., & Brophy, A. L. Institutional sources of articles in the *Journal of Counseling Psychology,* 1962–1973. *Journal of Counseling Psychology,* 1975, 22, 160–163.

Krauskopf, C. J., Thoreson, R. W., & McAleer, C. A. Counseling psychology: The who, what, and where of our profession. *Journal of Counseling Psychology,* 1973, 20, 370–374.

Luborsky, L., Chandler, M., Auerbach, A. H., Cohen, J., & Bachrach, H. M. Factors influencing the outcome of psychotherapy: A review of the quantitative research. *Psychological Bulletin,* 1971, 75, 145–185.

Mitchell, E. V., Kaul, T. J., & Pepinsky, H. B. The limited role of psychology in the roleplaying controversy. *Personality and Social Psychology Bulletin,* 1977, 3, 514–518.

Moore, B. V., & Bouthilet, L. The Veterans Administration program for counseling psychologists. *American Psychologist,* 1952, 7, 684–685.

Munley, P. H. A content analysis of the *Journal of Counseling Psychology. Journal of Counseling Psychology,* 1974, 21, 305–310.

Myers, R. A., & DeLevie, A. S. Frequency of citation as a criterion of eminence. *Journal of Counseling Psychology,* 1966, 13, 245–246.

Oetting, E. R. Developmental definition of counseling psychology. *Journal of Counseling Psychology,* 1967, 14, 382–385.

Osipow, S. H. New directions: Editorial. *Journal of Counseling Psychology,* 1976, 23, 1–2.

Osipow, S. H. Will the real counseling psychologist please stand up? *The Counseling Psychologist,* 1977, 7(2), 93–94.

Patterson, C. H. What is counseling psychology? *Journal of Counseling Psychology,* 1969, 16, 23–29.

Paul, G. L. Strategy of outcome research in psychotherapy. *Journal of Consulting Psychology,* 1967, 31, 109–118.

Pepinsky, H. B. A metalanguage for systematic research on human communication via natural language. *Journal of the American Society for Information Science,* 1974, 25(1), 59–69.

Pepinsky, H. B. A metalanguage of text. In H. Fisher & R. Diaz-Guerrero (Eds.), *Language and logic in personality and society.* N. Y.: Academic Press, in press. (Copies of the chapter may be obtained from H. B. Pepinsky, Ohio State University, Department of Psychology, 1945 N. High St., Columbus, Ohio 43210.)

Pepinsky, H. B., & Patton, M. J. (Eds.). *The psychological experiment, a practical accomplishment.* Elmsford, N. J.: Pergamon, 1971.

Robinson, F. P. Transition and continuation. *Journal of Counseling Psychology,* 1964, 11, 2.

Robinson, F. P. The growth of counseling psychology. *Journal of Counseling Psychology,* 1970, 17, 385–387.

Roe, A., Gustad, J. W., Moore, B. V., Ross, S., & Skodak, M. (Eds.). *Graduate education in psychology* (Report of the Conference on Graduate Education in Psychology at Miami Beach, Florida). Washington, D. C.: American Psychological Association, 1959.

Schmidt, L. D., & Pepinsky, H. B. Counseling research in 1963. *Journal of Counseling Psychology,* 1965, 12, 418–427.

Strong, S. R. Counseling: An interpersonal influence process. *Journal of Counseling Psychology,* 1968, *15,* 215–224.

Thompson, A. S., & Super, D. E. (Eds.). *The professional preparation of counseling psychologists, report of the 1964 Greyston Conference.* N. Y.: Columbia University, Teachers College, Bureau of Publications, 1964.

Walsh, W. B., Feeney, D., & Resnick, H. Graduate school origins of *Journal of Counseling Psychology* authors. *Journal of Counseling Psychology,* 1969, *16,* 375–376.

Wellner, A. M. *Education and credentialing in psychology. Preliminary report of a meeting.* Washington, D. C.: Office of Professional Affairs, American Psychological Association, 1976.

Wellner, A. M. *Education and credentialing in psychology. II. Report of a meeting.* Washington, D. C.: Office of Professional Affairs, American Psychological Association, 1977.

Williamson, E. G. Ralph Berdie: Editor, *Journal of Counseling Psychology* (1970–1974). *Journal of Counseling Psychology,* 1974, *21,* 461–462.

Wrenn, C. G. Editorial comment. *Journal of Counseling Psychology,* 1954, *1.*

Wrenn, C. G. Topical analysis of 169 research and theory articles in counseling. *Journal of Counseling Psychology,* 1956, *3,* 312–317.

Wrenn, C. G. Birth and early childhood of a journal. *Journal of Counseling Psychology,* 1966, *13,* 485–488.

Wrenn, C. G. Landmarks and the growing edge. *The Counseling Psychologist,* 1977, *7*(2), 10–13.

Wright, M. *Norwegian Diary, 1940-1945.* London, England: Friends Peace International Committee, 1974.

INAUGURAL DEFINITIONS OF A PROFESSION: 1952-1956 3

Chapter 6
Recommended Standards for Training Counseling Psychologists at the Doctorate Level

COMMITTEE ON COUNSELOR TRAINING
Division of Counseling and Guidance
American Psychological Association

In the light of the increasing demand for professional psychological services, there is need for a clear statement of the training that should be given to various types of psychological practitioners. This report will provide an explicit statement of the standards for training counseling psychologists.

Because of the growing concern with the problem of the mental health of our nation, and with the effective use of the nation's human resources, counseling psychologists have been spurred to re-examine their functions as they relate to society. This means a concern for the training programs which contribute to the fullest development of these functions. Following two previous conferences (Bordin, 1951; *Counselor Preparation,* 1949), the Counselor Training Committee of the Division of Counseling and Guidance, through the effective work of a subcommittee in PhD training, and with the concurrence of the Division's 1950–51 Executive Committee, presented a formal statement on doctoral-level training to an invited group of the Division's membership in Chicago, August 29–30, 1951. The accompanying proposal of training standards is the outgrowth of the work of this conference and of the Division's Committee. It has been reviewed and approved by the 1951–52 Executive Committee of the Division and, by action of the membership at the 1951 annual business meeting, thus becomes an official statement of the Division.[1]

This statement should be of interest not only to counseling psychologists but to psychologists generally since it clarifies training standards in one field of psychology. It should serve as an aid to university departments engaged in training counseling psychologists. This report should enable foundations, governmental agencies, and other relevant social institutions that support training for this type of psychological practice to become more discriminating in their support. Society at large should, through this statement, become more aware of the attempts being made to develop needed psychological services at adequate levels of competence.

ROLE AND FUNCTIONS OF COUNSELING PSYCHOLOGISTS

The professional goal of the counseling psychologist is to foster the psychological development of the individual. This includes all people on the adjustment continuum from those who function at tolerable levels of adequacy to those suffering from more severe psychological disturbances. Counseling psychologists will spend the bulk of their time with individuals within the normal range, but their training should qualify them to work in some degree with individuals at any level of psychological adjustment. Counseling stresses the positive and preventative. It focuses upon the stimulation of personal development in order to maximize personal and social effectiveness and to forestall psychologically crippling disabilities. This facilitation of personal growth takes place through utilizing the interrelated techniques of psychological assessment and effective intercommunication between client and counselor. It means also the utilization of the interpersonal relationships involved in group situations as well as in individual counseling.

With the stress on facilitating optimal personal development, it is understandable that educational institutions provide a central setting in which counseling is carried on. Considering the relative plasticity of children and adolescents and the social responsibility of schools and colleges for this age group, it is both historically and socially fitting that educational facilities remain the most important institutional home for psychological counseling functions. Other settings in which counseling psychologists function are business and industry, hospitals, and community agencies such as churches,

---

[1]The memberships of the two-day Conference and of the Executive and Counselor Training Committees of the Division are given at the close of this report.

"Recommended Standards for Training Counseling Psychologists at the Doctorate Level," American Psychological Association, Division of Counseling and Guidance, Committee on Counselor Training, *American Psychologist*, 1952, *7*, 175–181. Copyright 1952 by the American Psychological Association. Reprinted by permission.

youth organizations, marital clinics, parenthood foundations, vocational guidance centers, and rehabilitation agencies. The training program should qualify the counseling psychologist to work effectively in such varied settings.

Closely related to this matter of setting is the fact that doctorally trained counseling psychologists often carry administrative, supervisory, training, research, and public relations responsibilities. Thus, counseling psychologists must be able to supervise the testing and counseling activities of the less intensively trained staff, to make diagnostic decisions regarding cases requiring collaboration with other specialists, and to interpret counseling functions to higher levels of administration, to other professional workers, and to the public at large. They need to be skillful in working out effective organizational relationships and a favorable work climate within the total institutional setting. They must provide the leadership that encourages high productivity and morale among staff members. The counseling psychologist must also provide training for others both through supervision and formal teaching. There is a marked current need for counseling psychologists with sufficient breadth and experience to assume training roles in colleges and universities.

The activities of counseling psychologists and the types of clients and problems with which they deal place an emphasis on collaboration with people in many professional settings. These include teachers and educational administrators, physicians and psychiatrists, social case workers, group workers, other psychologists, community officials and administrators of social agencies, executives, and other personnel in commerce and industry.

Finally, it must be emphasized that on counseling psychologists falls the chief responsibility for conducting the research upon which depends the possibility of more effective counseling. Any applied field needs roots in the basic scientific discipline that lend substance to its work. It is therefore imperative that psychological counseling remain firmly established within the orbit of basic psychological science and the related disciplines, and that counseling psychologists acquire the research skills which make possible the enlargement of knowledge. We feel strongly that research must continue as a basic job of the counseling psychologist and that he must be trained accordingly.

SELECTION OF STUDENTS

In selection, we can state our goals with clarity and, at the same time, recognize the crudity of the selection methods now at our disposal. Our goal is the selection of students who are intellectually able, professionally motivated, emotionally and socially mature, and curious about the unknowns in the field of psychology. Limited training time and resources, as well as the welfare of prospective students, make it highly desirable to utilize effective selection procedures.

We are aware that, despite the importance of intellectual ability, professional motivation, maturity, and interest in extending psychological knowledge, the characteristics are insufficient predictors of performance in counseling psychology. They do not completely describe the dimensions of effective counseling psychologists and do not differentiate between counseling psychologists and other specialists within psychology. In the light of the importance to the prospective student, to the training institution, and to society of adequate selection procedures, it is important that research be done on the distinguishing attributes of those persons who complete their training programs and work effectively as counseling psychologists. This is necessary not only to enable universities to admit appropriate students but also to permit students to evaluate themselves against the demands of the profession and to choose their careers with a greater degree of knowledge and security.

The selection methods to which we can give the greatest weight involve the use of such familiar approaches as the academic records of the applicant, tests of intellectual status and attainment, personality tests, interviews, and evaluation of work experience. In this last connection attention should be given to evidence of successful work with people in job situations as well as in volunteer capacities. Without more research evidence concerning what is meant by both "effective" and "counseling," in trying to select those who will become effective counselors, we must admit extensive margins of error with these or any other methods.

Selection is in many ways a continuous process. Students meet critical evaluation points not only at the time of their entrance into the department but also at the point of course and matriculation examinations, practicum evaluation, and indeed in their daily work. This calls for a system of selection and evaluation that will periodically require the assessment of a student's status so that progressive advancement or elimination can take place without waste of time and resources. Because self-understanding is requisite to intelligent motivation and performance, selection should be a reciprocal process between student and staff. The student as well as the institution has a voice in the selection process. It is clear that this process has definite counseling implications.

The prospective counselor's undergraduate program should represent a balance among the physical, biological, and social sciences, mathematics, and the humanities. Too often prospective counselors are permitted to elect specialized technique courses in the undergraduate phases of their training. Students should have an adequate background in the field of psychology, but these introductory courses should be of a broad nature. They should introduce them to the theoretical and factual foundation of psychological thought, and they should give them an overview of, but not training in, psychological practice.

GRADUATE TRAINING

The counseling psychologist should be given opportunity to acquire a core of basic concepts, tools, and techniques that should be common to all psychologists. The title of the sponsoring department is not as vital as the training and experience of the faculty members who offer the training. Too often faculties sponsoring counselor training programs consist of persons whose own training is not primarily psychological and whose experience in counseling is limited. Such a staff cannot provide adequate facilities for training counselors at the doctoral level. Training in counseling psychology will be greatly facilitated by interdepartmental cooperation and collaboration and by giving primary attention to the content and quality of instruction without regard for departmental labels.

Breadth of Training versus Specialization

The counseling psychologist assists clients who have many types of problems—for example, emotional, vocational, marital, language, and study methods. Counseling agencies differ in the manner in which they handle this wide range of problems: some have general counselors who handle all types of problems, others refer clients to counselors specializing in particular areas. The counseling psychologist should have had some experience in all of these areas, in order to handle such problems or in order to work effectively with other counselors. It is recognized, on the other hand, that individuals in training and even training institutions may wish to give particular emphasis to certain of these problem areas in their training programs. The opportunity for training institutions to try out new areas and emphases is one important means of furthering the most effective evolution of the counseling process. Although the training program should insure a broad knowledge of both psychology generally and of the various counseling specialties, it should not be too rigidly prescribed. Opportunity needs to be given for individual specialization and institutional experimentation.

An effective doctoral training program can be postulated only if one assumes that training is a process continuing throughout the counselor's professional career and that the predoctoral program provides a base for the more specialized training that must follow. Counselors begin training in specialized areas of counseling, in line with their interests and aptitudes, during their graduate study, but in the main their graduate work in counseling is of a general rather than a specialized nature. At the completion of the doctorate a counselor's training is far from complete and thus the expansion of postdoctoral training becomes increasingly important.

This inevitable incompleteness of the doctoral training program has other implications. One is that the training program that attempts to turn out individuals capable of being all things to all people is doomed to failure. The emphasis on breadth, although important, must be kept within limits consonant with the student's ability to gain competence in various areas of counseling practice. Beyond this it seems likely that the persons most likely to function usefully will be those who best know their professional and personal strengths and weaknesses. It will be these who are motivated to capitalize on further training opportunities. Each department should therefore give explicit attention to the student's personal development throughout his or her training period. This should not only help him or her to live with himself or herself in full knowledge of his or her limitations and with a genuine and reasonable desire to overcome them, but it should also facilitate optimal learning during the doctoral training period.

The doctoral program itself should include, in addition to the common core mentioned in the first sentence of this section, the areas described below. Instructions in each of these areas may be given in courses, seminars, and practice.

1. *Personality organization and development.* This is an area of central importance to the counseling psychologist. Included in this area would be opportunities for review of academic theories of personality as well as those implicit in current concepts and practices of counseling and psychotherapy. It should also include opportunities for analysis of developmental patterns of behavior from a longitudinal as well as a cross-sectional point of view. Emphasis should be placed on the variability of developmental patterns rather than on the frequency of discrete items of behavior. This area should also include analysis of the psychological characteristics of deviant individuals including abnormal personalities, intellectual deviates, and social deviates. Special attention should also be given to the social and cultural determinants of personality as well as to social learning and communication as factors in the development of personality.

2. *Knowledge of social environment.* In addition to knowing how individuals learn to interact within social groups, it is assumed that counseling psychologists must have a knowledge of a great many aspects of our social structure. They should be familiar with the broad problems of social structure and organization, with cultural conditions, and with the heterogeneity of subgroup patterns within our culture. On a more specific level they should be acquainted with community resources for meeting educational, employment, health, social, and marital needs, and with socioeconomic and occupational trends.

3. *Appraisal of the individual.* The student should acquire extensive knowledge of and skill in using various types of psychological tests. This includes basic training in test theory, in the use and interpretation of both objective and projective techniques, and in the use of such informal methods of group and individual appraisal as interviews, autobiographies, questionnaires, and rating scales. The counseling psychologist's diagnostic competence should be sufficient to enable him or her to make diagnoses in his or her own field and to recognize the need for diagnostic referrals to other specialists.

4. *Counseling.* The program should involve a comprehensive review of the major theories of counseling and psychotherapy. Students should gain

extensive familiarity with basic ideas and techniques involved in individual counseling and therapeutic work. They should also be introduced to such procedures as bibliotherapy, group therapy, group discussion techniques with a variety of kinds of groups, and utilization of student activity programs and mental hygiene lectures. An awareness should be developed of the advantages and limitations of these various individual and group methods.

One way by which the student may gain an enlarged basis for understanding the counseling process is by having been on the receiving end of a counseling experience. Despite this value for training, such an experience has greatest value when it comes about as a result of the student's own motivation. This report does not therefore suggest that a didactic counseling experience be required. Many students may themselves need counseling, however, in order to achieve and maintain adequate personal maturity. It is the responsibility of the training department to do everything feasible to understand and meet such a need.

5. *Professional orientation.* An important aspect of the training of the counseling psychologist is the development of sensitivity to the counselor's responsibilities in social and interprofessional relationships. In addition, there are the many ethical considerations involved in practice, as well as the problems posed by the necessity for maintaining a balance between loyalties to clients, to the institution, and to society. Still another desideratum is the development of awareness of the various administrative patterns characteristic of the several types of social agencies within which the counseling process takes place; for example, a counseling psychologist working on a college campus needs to understand the administrative structure of higher education.

How this goal is to be implemented is deliberately left an open question in this report. Training agencies will and should differ in the ways that they will find most appropriate to meet this vital part of counselor preparation. Some will prefer to cultivate the relevant attitudes and knowledges through courses offered late in the doctoral sequence. Others will choose to do the job through seminars and informal discussions during the internship period. Still others may find it most feasible to handle professional orientation through the supervisory or student-adviser relationships. It is important for all training experiences to be permeated with proper regard for problems of a professional nature. But this casual and indirect approach to the required knowledges and attitudes does not seem sufficient. Specific attention must be given to the adequate orientation of the student to the profession of psychological counseling in its various contexts.

6. *Practicum.* The objective of the practicum is to provide counseling psychologists with a sense of the realities of the counselor/client relationship and of various staff relationships. It provides them with opportunities to apply their academic knowledge to practical problems of personal adjustment and to integrate the various skills required for understanding and helping a person. Competence in counseling is its goal.

The type and amount of practicum experience needed by a given student depend on the types and amounts of experience that the student has already had. In most cases, the counseling psychologist will need to develop practical competence by means of a planned sequence of supervised laboratory courses, field work, and an internship. In cases where the department and the student decide that certain competencies have already been acquired by the student, the practicum phase of training can be shortened accordingly.

The proposed sequence of practicum work consists of prepracticum or laboratory work related to academic courses, followed by field work for one or two days per week for a semester or a year, followed (in the third or fourth year) by a half-time internship for two years or a full-time internship for one academic year. Patterns of practice will vary according to students' attained competence, their objectives, and the available resources. Most of the didactic background specific to that part of the counseling process should be acquired before entering a given stage of the practicum. It is important that adequate supervision be provided by both the university and the practicum agency so that the experience may be truly progressive and instructional.

The nature of this supervision, provided either by the university or the practicum agency, is a critical factor in the training program. In addition to safeguarding the interests of clients, adequate supervision is necessary to provide a truly progressive instructional experience. Sensitive, permissive supervisors, who are themselves mature counselors, can be one of the most important influences on students' ability to understand and evaluate their motivation to counsel and to adjust their motivation to the best interests of their clients. There is great need, however, for research on the supervisory process itself. We know too little about how to provide supervision so that students gain measurably both in counseling skills and in the supervisory techniques that they will use later in their own careers.

The counseling psychologist should be exposed to as wide a range of counseling situations as possible, but the major emphasis should be upon work with normal individuals and upon the attainment of competence in basic skills. The practicum should provide some experience with emotionally maladjusted and with physically and socially handicapped clients. This latter experience should be in collaboration with other specialists such as physicians, psychiatrists, social case workers, and teachers.

Elaboration of these points will be found in the separate report of the Subcommittee on Practicum Training (APA Committee on Counselor Training, 1952).

7. *Research.* Training for research should include provision for actual research experiences. Most training institutions have arranged for students to carry out minor research studies in addition to the major research project represented by the doctoral thesis. Although training in research is considered essential for all counseling psychologists, allowance must be made for the range of research abilities that will be found among students, no matter how carefully selected. It can be expected that counseling psychologists will range

from those who will make minimal research contributions to those whose major professional contribution will fall in this sphere.

At a minimum, such training should aim to develop the ability to review and to make use of the results of research. Psychological counseling is and should be founded upon basic psychological science and related disciplines. Counseling psychologists can make unique contributions to psychological knowledge because their counseling experience provides an especially fruitful opportunity to formulate hypotheses. It is therefore essential to maximize their research training. How to achieve a balance between practice and research during the training period is an unsolved problem. A flexible program of training in research that takes into account the range of research potentialities of its students will go a long way, however, toward solving this problem.

TENTATIVE TIME ALLOTMENTS
TO AREAS OF TRAINING

The recommendations that follow are intended to provide a basis for the more uniform interpretation of the foregoing proposals. They are meant as guides for individual variations in programs, not as rigid specifications. The suggested ranges of time allotments provide for the proposed four-year program including one year of internship. Percentages represent proportions of a year of full-time study. It should be noted that these are not estimates of credit hours, but rather relative weights recommended for the various areas of training.

Proportions of One Year's Study in the Various Areas
of Training (Total of 4 years = 400)

Core	65–70	Diversification	30–50
Personality	20–30	Professional orientation	10–20
Social environment	15–20	Practica: Field work	120–135
Appraisal	35–45	and internship	
Counseling	20–30	Research	45–50

Although only 70% of a year's work has been allotted to training in basic psychological science, the actual allotment exceeds the equivalent of one year because the personality and appraisal areas ordinarily include basic courses such as personality theory, theory of measurement, and social psychology.

The relatively small allotment of time to the counseling area concerns only didactic work. It should be kept in mind that much of the practicum will be devoted to counseling experiences.

The recommendation for professional orientation deserves special mention. This aspect of training should permeate the entire program—course offerings, practicum experiences, and the relationship between the student and staff, in addition to what amounts to a relatively small amount of specific course and seminar offerings.

The area of diversification represents a pool of time that may be used to broaden the training experience. This may be done by enlarging the emphasis given to any of the described areas, by including outside didactic or practicum experiences, or by preparing for related teaching or administrative responsibilities. This permits institutions to modify emphases in their programs in the light of their particular conceptions and to meet individual student needs.

FURTHER STEPS

Following a quarter of a century of training counseling psychologists, this report represents an initial step in formulating standards in the light of new and greatly increased demands for psychological services. Obligations to society and responsibility to the profession require the extension of the work begun here. One primary need in this connection is for training institutions to experiment with their programs. This should be done with an eye toward developing an explicit empirical base for the revision of standards and for the progressive improvement of the training experiences. Further study should also be made of such matters as post-doctoral training and relationships to other specialties (APA Committee on Intraprofessional Relationships in Psychology, 1951).

In this latter connection the training program for counseling psychologists overlaps with training for other psychological fields. The delineation of similarities and differences in either practice or training is not, however, an appropriate problem for unilateral action by representatives of one area. This collaborative effort lies in the future.

Report prepared by:

Edward S. Bordin, Chairman, Subcommittee on PhD Training Programs
Ralph F. Berdie
Earl F. Carnes
Edward J. Shoben, Jr.
Julius Seeman
Francis P. Robinson, Chairman, Committee on Counselor Training
C. Gilbert Wrenn, President, Division of Counseling and Guidance, 1950–1951
Donald E. Super, President, Division of Counseling and Guidance, 1951–1952
and the following members of the Conference on the Training of Counseling Psychologists, Northwestern University, August 29–30, 1951:

Seth Arsenian	Frank H. Finch
Kenneth B. Ashcraft	Frank M. Fletcher, Jr.
Ralph Bedell	William M. Gilbert
Delton C. Beier	Milton E. Hahn
Irwin A. Berg	Arthur A. Hitchcock
Douglas D. Blocksma	Nathan Kohn, Jr.
Joseph M. Bobbitt	Louis Long
Collins W. Burnett	H. B. McDaniel

John M. Butler	Robert H. Mathewson
Dorothy M. Clendenen	Harold B. Pepinsky
William Coleman	Herman J. Peters
L. E. Drake	Edward C. Roeber
Paul L. Dressel	Joseph Samler
Willis E. Dugan	Winifred S. Scott
Royal B. Embree, Jr.	Marie Skodak
Catherine Evans	A. C. Van Dusen
Norman Feingold	Philip Zlatchin

REFERENCES

American Psychological Association. Committee on Intraprofessional Relationships in Psychology. Fields of psychology and their implications for practice and training. *American Psychologist,* 1951, *6,* 90–93.

American Psychological Association. Division of Counseling and Guidance, Committee on Counselor Training. The practicum training of counseling psychologists. *American Psychologist,* 1952, *7,* 182–188.

Bordin, E. S. (Ed.). *Training of psychological counselors.* Ann Arbor: University of Michigan Press, 1951.

Counselor preparation. Washington: National Vocational Guidance Association, 1949.

Chapter 7
The Practicum Training of
Counseling Psychologists

COMMITTEE ON COUNSELOR TRAINING
Division of Counseling and Guidance
American Psychological Association

NEEDS FOR AND OBJECTIVES OF
PRACTICUM TRAINING IN COUNSELING[1]

Need for Practicum Training in Counseling

The practicum is in some respects the most important phase of the whole process of training in counseling. Without this, students may be unable to apply their academic knowledge or to integrate required skills to understand and help their clients. The discipline of the supervised practicum in counseling safeguards the public by preparing the neophyte for professional practice. Agencies employing counseling psychologists therefore have an obligation to society and to the profession to participate actively in practicum training programs. Such an obligation should sit lightly, however, since such participation is probably the best way to insure a supply of adequately trained personnel.

The meaning of the practicum experience for student counselors may vary according to their interpretation of their own needs. Students will commonly find in the practicum an opportunity to synthesize the more or less fragmented phases of their previous academic work and to bring these learnings to a focus upon the actual problems of individual clients. Thus, potential professional knowledge and skill will be centered, not on purely academic ends, but upon the adjustment, orientation, and development of clients themselves.

One of a series of reports by the Committee on Counselor Training of the Division of Counseling and Guidance of the American Psychological Association.

"The Practicum Training of Counseling Psychologists," American Psychological Association, Division of Counseling and Guidance, Committee on Counselor Training, *American Psychologist*, 1952, 7, 182–188. Copyright 1952 by the American Psychological Association. Reprinted by permission.

[1]In preparing this statement, use was made of that prepared by the APA Committee on Training in Clinical Psychology for that field (*American Psychologist*, 1950, 5, 594–609).

Objectives of the Practicum Training

The essence of the practicum must be the acquisition by the trainee of a sense of the realities of the counselor/client relationship. The trainee's attitude toward this relationship will be of the utmost importance. Thus a highly significant aim of practicum training will be to bring trainees into that psychological state where they clearly perceive for themselves that their client's personal adjustment and development is their first consideration and loyalty. Of foremost significance also will be mastery of counseling technique by the student-counselor. The preparation of guidance workers has often been too academic in nature. There is no economical way to acquire professional competence except through well-organized and supervised practica. The *practicum program* therefore emerges as one of the keystones of any program for the education of counseling psychologists.

Among other desirable outcomes of the practicum will be the seasoning of the student-counselor in the realities of everyday institutional experience; an acquaintance with working conditions and organizational processes; and an introduction to the problems of maintaining a regular counseling schedule, of building a favorable personal and professional relationship with associates and administrative heads, and of retaining personal mental health under the impact of sustained counseling responsibility.

It is well to recognize that the inevitable restrictions of time and facility impose on most institutions definite limits as to what can actually be accomplished during the practicum period. This means that the practicum training proposed in the literature and announced by training institutions should be realistically in accord with what can be provided. For the rest, responsibility must fall upon the professional personnel supervising the postpracticum experience of counselors in the early period of their professional practice.

Ethical Considerations

Too frequently, inadequately planned and supervised practica degenerate into clerkships, recordkeeping, busywork, or other forms of lower-grade experience inadequate to the essential professional development of the student-counselor. Such experiences may sometimes be rationalized as providing necessary seasoning under realistic job conditions, but these should never be recognized as valid forms of practicum training. Responsibility for the activities of the trainee must necessarily be held jointly by the training institution and by the field agency providing the training opportunity. This is true because only the field agency can be on hand for a substantial portion of the time. Nevertheless, the training institution cannot completely relinquish responsibility for its student, but must share the burden with the operating agency at least to the extent of cooperatively planning and evaluating the student's practicum experience. This creates the necessity for a clear initial understanding between institution and agency as to the type of worker required, personal and professional qualifications needed, types of activity to be conducted, extent and methods of supervision to be exercised by both, and other stipulations.

The paramount allegiance of counselors being to their clients, problems sometimes arise among student-counselors as to how they are to act when institutional considerations or administrative restrictions seem to be in conflict with the welfare of the client. Also, student-counselors may observe practices that they have been taught to regard as wrong or obsolete, and they are in a quandary as to what to do about them. Mature practicing counselors may also encôunter such problems, but they have the option of attempting to modify what they regard as faulty practices or of resigning their jobs. Student-counselors, however, are not yet in a position to pass mature judgment on the professional actions of others or on the policies of institutions, nor are they in a position to withdraw from an uncomfortable situation. Such situations, however, constitute one of the realities of professional living, and it is the responsibility of the training staff of both the university and the practicum agency to provide opportunities for trainees to discuss problems of this sort and to enlarge their understanding of them.

Likewise, student-counselors may be helped to realize, through adequate handling of situations of this sort, that practice rarely attains the level of theory. They learn that practical situations always impose limitations and that, at the best, a balance is attained in which negative factors are outweighed by the positive.

LEVELS OF PREPRACTICUM AND PRACTICUM TRAINING

Background preparation such as that recommended in the report, "Standards for Training Counseling Psychologists" (APA, 1952), should provide a basic psychological understanding of (a) prospective clients, especially in terms of their social and cultural relationships, (b) the tools and skills of counseling, and (c) community agencies and their evolving function in the broader social context.

The training center should provide:

a. *Laboratory experiences,* to help the student-counselor master basic tools and basic skills. These normally are provided in the first and second years of study, as a part of academic courses, for which the student pays tuition and laboratory fees.

b. *Field-work experiences,* to help student-counselors relate their tools and skills to one another, use their tools and skills to understand and meet the needs of clients in the functional setting of an agency, and to learn to see clients as persons. These are usually provided in the second semester of the first year and during the second year of training, the agency providing the experiences as a service to the profession and the students undergoing them as part of their training, without pay.

c. *Internship in an agency* is the terminal phase of their practicum training, in which student-counselors integrate their skills with a crystallizing philosophy of service to clients, to the agency, and to the community served by the agency (usually in the third or fourth year of study), for pay appropriate to learners.

The progressive development of the student-counselor from content mastery through the prepracticum and various practicum levels of training can be seen more clearly if briefly outlined in terms of several criteria.

Time in Practica

Time spent in practica will vary with the level. The *prepracticum* or laboratory experience may be viewed as course-related activity that continues for one or two semesters, depending upon the length of the course. It normally requires from three or four hours per week in the prepracticum, course-related, mastery of skills (learning to administer and score group and individual tests, conducting simple registration or information-getting interviews, and so forth). The *field-work* experience usually continues for a semester or a year, depending upon the experience of the student and the number of hours devoted by the student each week; the period should involve a minimum of 100 to 200 hours. Part of the field work may be done in the second semester of the MA program, part subsequently to that. Field work usually requires from one to two days each week. The *internship* calls for half time (20 hours per week) for two years or full time (35 to 45 hours per week) for one academic year devoted to agency activity and related community service.

Levels of Skill

In the *laboratory* or prepracticum level student-counselors are learning the fundamental tools and skills (testing, interviewing, recording) and may employ the laboratory experience to improve their techniques, learn the limitations of each of their instruments, and to develop beginning understanding of how to assess and influence client behavior, although it is not likely at this stage that they will work with actual clients.

The *field-work* experience affords student-counselors an opportunity to work more intensively with their tools and skills within an actual agency setting, in carefully graded ways and under close supervision, with selected clients. At first their activity will be limited to assisting, observing, and applying their skills to parts of the total problem presented by a client. As their technical skills develop and their understanding of the agency's function deepens, they may be permitted to carry increasingly greater responsibilities for working with clients. By the close of their field-work experience students should have mastered basic techniques and be ready to serve actual agency clients reporting relatively simple kinds of problems.

The *internship* takes for granted mastery of the basic skills of counseling psychology and provides the student-counselor with opportunity to carry a variety of cases under supervision, the closeness of the supervision varying with the intern's competence and with the type of case.

PREREQUISITE EDUCATION

Since the practicum experience is seen as a continuing program, education prerequisite to it is seen not as just the academic background preceding the initial field work, but as the development of a series of skills, understandings, and knowledges coordinated with and directed toward increased responsibilities and ever widening experience with actual clients.

1. Education prerequisite to initial field work:

a. The basic core recommended by the APA (*American Psychologist,* 1947, 2, 539–558) as background for graduate study in clinical psychology is in general considered desirable background for counseling psychologists. It has been discussed with particular reference to this field in a companion report (APA, 1952).

b. Additional classroom instruction essential to understanding counseling tools, processes, and functions, and to understanding the counselee as a person, is reserved for graduate study. As specified in the statement on doctoral programs the following *areas* (not necessarily specific courses) are important to the field-work experience:

> Personality organization and development.
> Knowledge of social environment: cultural and social factors affecting behavior, sources of information, educational resources, financial aid, health services, employment services.
> Appraisal of the individual: principles and techniques of measurement; evaluation of normative data; test analysis and review.
> Attendance at case seminars, toward helping the student see aspects of his currently acquired information in the setting of full case material.
> Laboratory work in test administration, scoring and reporting of results, and interviewing.

c. The experience of being a counselee is desirable for the student if it can be a bona fide one.

2. Education prerequisite to an interview relationship with a client. The difference between this and the next section is in terms of the degree of responsibility to the client that is assumed by the student. Use of actual case material, preferably from students' field work, helps to keep the client and his problems from being lost to view in the focus of attention on techniques. Directly related to field work is didactic instruction in the following areas:

> Counseling theory: philosophy and principles of counseling.
> Appraisal of the individual: techniques for studying the individual

(including interview, questionnaires, observation, and tests and inventories); observation and discussion of interviews; synthesis of data from various sources.

Professional orientation: interprofessional relations, ethical practices, loyalties, professional and agency organization.

3. Education prerequisite to carrying, under supervision, major responsibility for a client. Much of the preparation for increased responsibility will be achieved through field work, continuous seminars, case conferences, critical analysis of case records and of recorded or observed interviews, and following the progress of clients with whom students have had contact during their field work. In addition, material in the following area is important to the student-counselor's effectiveness: Counseling theory—procedures and techniques (including initiation, maintenance, and termination of the counseling relationship, referral, follow-up, and evaluation).

THE NATURE OF THE PRACTICUM EXPERIENCE

The nature of the practicum experience necessarily varies with the amount of training possessed by students, the functions of the organization in which they work, and the amount of time given by the students to practicum activities. The field worker normally brings less training and devotes less time to his practicum work than does the intern.

Variety of counseling problems. Each community guidance center, school or college counseling service, rehabilitation service, or other agency in which practicum experience may be obtained, necessarily works with a limited variety of clients. They may be adolescents in school or college, young adults about to enter or who have recently entered the world of work, tubercular patients of all ages, older adults, or some other rather specialized groups. The problem raised by these clients may center largely on education, vocational choice or entry, progress in a field of work, value conflicts, family relations, use of leisure time, some phase of personal-social adjustment, or some other area.

It is desirable for counseling psychologists to have a combination of breadth and depth in their practicum training within the limitations imposed by the availability and nature of suitable practicum training facilities. They should see a variety of students and clients and should have a first-hand familiarity with problems of educational choice and adjustment, vocational choice and planning, and personal-social adjustment and development. They should develop competence in diagnosis, counseling, referral, use of resources, and interprofessional relations, and in dealing with problems of ethics. At the same time, the student-counselor should work intensively enough in one or more areas to be able to carry on work of that type with little or no supervision.

Breadth of practicum experience can probably best be attained by a combination of field work placements that enable the student to (a) observe, interview, and test a variety of cases handled by more experienced counselors, and (b) participate in case conferences in which varied problems are considered and different procedures and resources are reported and discussed.

Depth can best be gotten by working intensively as an intern with a limited variety of problems in order to develop a deeper understanding of, and more skill in, diagnosing and counseling problems of that type.

Types of institutional settings. What has been said about the variety of counseling material encountered in practicum training has implications for the types of institutional settings in which practice may be provided. No one setting is likely to provide a great variety of experience, but it can provide some variety and considerable depth.

For example, a college student counseling service can normally provide intensive experience with problems of curricular and vocational choice, aspiration and achievement levels, vocational planning, adjustment to family and group living, and value conflicts; it may provide experience in diagnosing and counseling cases of personal adjustment problems of a more deep-seated type, in psychotherapy with the mild neuroses, in working with handicapped persons, in helping with problems of marital adjustment, and in referral for specialized services. Although it is not likely to provide the intensive experience in helping persons who are floundering vocationally during their first years of work that another type of community guidance center might provide, and although it is not likely to supply either the experience in the coordination of community resources for the training and placement of various kinds of handicapped persons that a social agency can supply, or much experience in the diagnosis of the psychoses, it can do something in those directions.

Student-counselors' internships are usually best served in institutional settings comparable to that in which they plan to work, so that they may acquire special familiarity with the peculiar problems of that type of setting. Thus, if they are likely to work in a college, an internship in a student counseling center would normally be most appropriate. For students with other objectives, internships in public schools, community guidance centers, rehabilitation services, child welfare agencies, family service agencies, or industrial consulting organizations may be more appropriate. Although attaining competence in a specialty is desirable, the university, the practicum agency, and the student should never lose sight of the need for versatility. The Committee feels strongly that counseling psychologists, especially those trained to the doctorate, should have command of a wide variety of skills and knowledges, permitting them to adapt to a number of different professional situations.

Knowledge, approaches, appreciations, and skills learned. Field-work students generally need opportunities to use skills and apply knowledge learned on the campus to real clients in life situations, so that they may be able to perform specific services under supervision. What is normally needed at the point of entering *internship* is (a) skill in establishing effective professional relationships, (b) diagnostic, prognostic, and treatment skills (that is, skill in reaching an understanding of causative factors as contrasted with mere skill in testing or interviewing), (c) self-understanding and self-discipline, (d) understanding of and ability to fit into an actual institutional or agency setting, to work effectively with a variety of professional colleagues, and to deal appropriately with ethical problems, and (e) understanding of the community and societal functions of guidance and of the institution or agencies in which guidance is provided. The internship experience is uniquely suited for the development of these understandings and skills, and should be so planned as to contribute to their development to the highest possible degree. By the time they finish the internship, interns should be functioning as regular junior members of the agency staff.

Methods, types, and quality of supervision. As the practicum student's role in the practicum agency is comparable to that of a closely supervised regular employee of that agency, the supervisory function is primarily that of the practicum agency. Although the university in which the field worker or intern is a student may provide some supervision, the training center's contribution is most effectively made via the agency staff member who is responsible for on-the-job supervision and in periodic contacts such as those provided by joint seminars and consultations.

The supervision provided by the practicum agency consists of (a) planning the students' practicum work in consultation with the university, in terms of their readiness to assume various types of responsibility or to function in various capacities, and in terms of their needs, (b) keeping students occupied with a meaningful succession of practicum work, (c) observing and evaluating their functioning, and (d) sharing these evaluations with students so that they may learn from their experiences and with the university so that it too may maximally contribute to the students' growth.

A competent practicum supervisor is a counseling psychologist who has had substantial graduate training in psychology, followed by a number of years of successful counseling experience. Possession of the Diploma in Counseling and Guidance awarded by the American Board of Examiners in Professional Psychology is a desirable type of evidence of competence, but training and experience alone are not enough; supervisors should be interested in providing practical training for others, effective in sharing their insights with professional students, and free to devote time and thought to providing and evaluating these experiences. In other words, they must also be teachers and frequently counselors to the counselor-in-training.

The lack of a tradition of paid internships and of field agency supervision of practicum work (such as exists in the field of social work) may well make difficult the early achievement of standards such as these. During the transition stage it may sometimes be desirable for the universities to play a more active part in the immediate supervision of practicum students. Joint appointments and shared or dual supervision, especially at the field-work level, may be temporary solutions.

Allocation of time in the practicum. Students' time in practicum training should be so planned as to give them the types of experience they most need, in amounts sufficient to enable them to learn from the experience. It is probably easier to put *field workers* in the testing department of a guidance center and have them administer and score tests for the duration of their field work (with the possible justification that even in that time they will not acquire complete competence in testing) than it is to rotate them through other departments and give them a little experience in their work. But field workers' concurrent and subsequent studies are made far more meaningful for them if their practicum experience is broad enough to give them some understanding of the various aspects of their field as seen in practical situations.

Interns may spend the bulk of their time in counseling, with special types of cases, in order that they may develop the basic skills and understandings of work with individuals. But counseling also includes report writing, case conferences, and consultations. The flow of their work should be so planned that they may spend some time with cases of types other than those in which they have specialized, and some time in reading the cases of other counselors, observing the work of other staff members and other agencies, conducting research, and reading on special problems.

Duration of practicum training. Since *field workers* are primarily students, giving most of their time to academic work on the university campus and spending one or at most two days each week in the field, it is necessary that the field work experience extend over a sufficiently long period of time for the students to acquire a modicum of proficiency in the use of some techniques and to develop some understanding of the problems encountered by the agency and its clients. Field work should therefore probably be planned on a semester (or quarter) basis and might well continue for a whole year, the second semester being planned to provide experience of a different type or in a different setting. An alternate plan is for the field worker to spend a month or more between terms in an agency on a full-time basis, thus becoming a more integral part of the institution although not remaining there long enough for it to serve the purposes of an internship.

Although *interns* spend all or possibly half of their time in the practicum agency and are primarily related to that agency rather than to the university in that phase of their training, the principal reason for making the internship virtually a full-time activity is to provide intensity or depth of experience for the intern. Whereas field work may be of only a semester's duration, the internship should normally be planned for at least one academic year. This is necessary if interns are to have the experience of carrying a regular work load toward the end of their practicum, if they are to work intensively with a large enough variety of clients, and if they are to have an opportunity to function for a time virtually as regular staff members in an operating situation.

Evaluation of field workers and interns. Practicum supervisors have unique opportunities to observe and evaluate the student at work with clients and with professional colleagues; they also have unique opportunities for guiding the student in the light of these observations. The student's principal supervisor in the practicum agency should synthesize the observations of all supervisors having contact with him or her, communicate these evaluations to the student in a way that will contribute to his or her professional growth or to his or her leaving the field of guidance in a constructive way, and share them with the training center, so that it too may use the information in counseling and evaluating the student. Such evaluations should be made at least at the end of each field-work experience and at least twice each semester during the internship.

Through a systematic and continuing evaluation of student-counselors, combined with cooperative research programs, it should become possible to: (a) modify and improve criteria for selection of subsequent candidates for the internship, (b) develop more effective means of improving learning in the field, (c) improve academic course offerings and prepracticum experiences as needs become apparent, and (d) help field agencies improve their practica.

ESTABLISHING AND OPERATING A PRACTICUM TRAINING PROGRAM

Agreement between practicum agency and university. It is important that parties representing both the agency and the university meet informally and discuss the various phases of the practicum training program (purpose of the program, obligations to be assumed by each party, length and level of the program, stipend, hours, methods and types of supervision, and so forth). After an agreement has been reached, a written statement should be drawn up for use by both parties. This statement will be helpful in the indoctrination of students assigned by the university to the agency. A complete understanding on the part of the student of the relationship between the agency and the university will help to avoid misunderstandings that might otherwise arise. Furthermore, for each practicum student the university and the practicum agency must work out an appropriate planned sequence of experiences.

Administrative records. An adequate log of their training experience should be kept by the students so that the quality and extent of their agency work can be evaluated in terms of the general plan and the students' individual plans. Such logs should include the number of clients seen, type of clients (problems presented and treatment called for), and type of techniques (tests, interviews, and so forth) used. The students' own evaluations of their experience should also be recorded. The keeping of these records is not to be confused, of course, with the keeping of case records.

The agency should keep such records as may be needed in preparing for the university a detailed evaluation of the work done by the student.

Selection of field workers and interns. The final decision as to whether or not a student will be accepted must, of course, be left to the agency. The university, however, has a responsibility for the initial selection, and it can help in the final selection of students by working with the agency in setting up standards and by studying the effectiveness of the selection procedure used by the agency.

An effective system of communication between the agency and the university must be set up. One way in which this can sometimes be accomplished is to have reciprocal appointments. Other techniques, including preplacement conferences of supervisors to plan field experiences, attendance at staff conferences and seminars, and research by doctoral candidates in the field agencies, need exploration and development.

Report prepared by:

Subcommittee on Practicum Training:
Donald E. Super, Chairman
Louis Long
Robert H. Mathewson
Winifred S. Scott
Edward J. Shoben, Jr.
Philip Zlatchin

Committee on Counselor Training:
Francis P. Robinson, Chairman

Division of Counseling and Guidance, APA:
C. Gilbert Wrenn, President, 1950–51
Donald E. Super, President, 1951–52

REFERENCE

American Psychological Association. Division of Counseling and Guidance, Committee on Counselor Training. Recommended standards for the training of counseling psychologists at the doctorate level. *American Psychologist,* 1952, 7, 175–181.

Chapter 8
Counseling Psychology
as a Specialty

COMMITTEE ON DEFINITION
Division of Counseling Psychology[1]

In 1952 the Division of Counseling Psychology published two reports on recommended standards of professional education for counseling psychologists at the doctoral level (APA, 1952b) and, as part of this program, on practicum training (APA, 1952a). These followed logically the report of the Michigan conference on the preparation of psychological counselors (Bordin, 1951). A carefully stated definition of the specialty of counseling psychology was needed at that time, but none was available. Since the two statements on professional training proved to be sufficient tasks, the earlier committee contented itself with a brief description of the specialty and postponed to a later period the task of more elaborate definition. This document is the present committee's attempt to supply a more complete statement of what is counseling psychology.

The term *counseling psychology* has only recently come into official and extensive use, but in the past few years the adoption of the term and the recognition of the specialty have become widespread (Bordin, 1955; Hahn, 1955; Hahn & MacLean, 1955; Pepinsky & Pepinsky, 1954; Super, 1955; Wrenn, 1951, 1952, 1954; Wrenn & Darley, 1942).[2] The term was adopted by the Division in 1951 and was given currency in 1952, with the publication of the two reports on professional education. In 1952, also, the Division changed its official designation from that of Counseling and Guidance to Counseling Psychology. Almost simultaneously, the Veterans Administration announced the establishment of two major psychological positions, bearing the titles "Counseling Psychologist (Vocational)" and "Counseling Psychologist (VR & E)." In 1954, a new professional publication, the *Journal of Counseling*

"Counseling Psychology As a Specialty," American Psychological Association, Division of Counseling Psychology, Committee on Definition. *American Psychologist,* 1956, *11,* 282–285. Copyright 1956 by the American Psychological Association. Reprinted by permission.

[1]Edward S. Bordin, Milton E. Hahn, Donald E. Super, C. Gilbert Wrenn, and Harold B. Pepinsky (Chairman). This report has been accepted and its publication authorized by the Executive Committee of the Division.

[2]An interesting picture of developments in counseling psychology from 1950 to 1956 is provided in the chapters on "counseling" in the *Annual Review of Psychology* (see articles by Berdie, Bordin, Stuit, Pepinsky, Gilbert, Williamson, Wrenn, Hobbs and Seeman, and Shoben).

Psychology, made its appearance. In 1955, the American Board of Examiners in Professional Psychology adapted to these developments by changing the title of one of the specialty fields in which it issues a diploma from "Counseling and Guidance" to "Counseling Psychology." These events have made expedient the present attempt to provide a more explicit definition of counseling psychology than has been available heretofore. More urgently, the existence within the Veterans Administration of related operations in counseling psychology and clinical psychology and their antecedents in university programs that prepare students for these kinds of work, make highly desirable the spelling out of similarities and differences in these two psychological specialties. Such a delineation of specialty areas within the field of psychology becomes even more timely since the conference on the overlapping field of school psychology has just made its report (Cutts, 1955). Of course, it is appropriately the function of the American Psychological Association to make official pronouncements regarding its specialty fields, but its Divisions have been expected to exercise initiative in the preparation of these statements. Any formulation such as that presented here should be viewed as part of an ongoing activity within psychology and its professional association, tentative in nature, and subject to modification as warranted by changes in the science of psychology and its various applications.

HISTORICAL DEVELOPMENT

Counseling psychology has its origins in three distinct movements. Two of these, the vocational guidance and the psychological measurement movements, began simultaneously early in this century and merged some 20 years ago. The third, the emphasis upon the motivational and affective aspects of behavior, began to merge with the first two a decade later. It was this union of emphases on vocational orientation, psychometrics, and personality development that led to the emergence of counseling psychology as a specialty.

In 1909, Frank Parsons wrote of vocational guidance as a process of vocational orientation, individual analysis, and counseling (Parsons, 1909). Lack of testing and interviewing theories and techniques led to the neglect of the last two aspects of vocational guidance and to the emphasis on exploratory activities which characterized the work and writing of leaders such as Brewer (1932).

At the same time, the psychometric movement and the study of individual differences got under way, bearing fruit in the 1930s in programs such as the occupational ability pattern research of the Minnesota Employment Stabilization Research Institute (Paterson & Darley, 1936). Psychometric research workers joined forces with proponents of vocational orientation, and the revitalized vocational guidance movement proclaimed that "vocational guidance is now possible" (McConn, 1935). Individual differences in aptitudes and interests could now be studied in relation to occupations, and students and clients could be given adequate information about occupational opportunities and requirements.

But this enthusiasm now seems premature. In the 1940s, the influence of the psychoanalytic concepts of repression and anxiety and their significances for the understanding of behavior began to be felt. As those who worked with problems of personality and emotional development communicated with those who worked with problems of educational and vocational planning and adjustment, the unity of the task became apparent. As personality and learning theory became clarified and as their role in counseling was more widely recognized, it became apparent that earlier concepts of counseling as restricted to the matching of individual abilities and interests with occupational requirements needed to be modified. At the same time, psychotherapeutic methods were being modified and described in terms that made them usable in everyday counseling situations.

Whereas psychometrics focused attention on individual differences, adaptations of psychotherapy brought out their meaning to the individual in the form of attitudes and motivation, and clarified the procedures for helping the individual to understand, accept, and utilize his assets.

An important outcome of the merger of the vocational orientation, psychometric, and personality development movements has been a changed concept of the functions and training of the people who do the counseling. They were first either teachers who helped people explore the world of work or psychologists who gave and interpreted tests. Then they, who might or might not have been psychologists, were users of community resources, of occupational information, and of psychological tests. They have now emerged as psychologists. They are, however, psychologists who use varying combinations of exploratory experiences, psychometric techniques, and psychotherapeutic interviewing to assist people to grow and to develop. This is the counseling psychologist.

CURRENT STATUS

At the present time, the specialty of counseling psychology is approaching a state of balance among emphases upon contributions to (a) the development of an individual's inner life through concern with his or her motivations and emotions, (b) the individual's achievement of harmony with his or her environment through helping him or her to develop the resources that he or she must bring to this task (for example, by assisting him or her to make effective use of appropriate community resources), and (c) the influencing of society to recognize individual differences and to encourage the fullest development of all persons within it.

In connection with its attempt to help the individual develop a more mature inner life, counseling psychology draws upon contemporary personality and learning theories. In so doing, it employs concepts and tools that are also used by clinical, experimental, social, and school psychologists, among other specialty groups. Because it aims to contribute to the personal development of a great variety of people, counseling psychology does not concern itself only with the more extreme problems presented by individuals who are in need of emergency treatment. In other words, counseling psychology does not place special emphasis upon the development of tools and techniques necessary for intensive psychotherapy with individuals whose emotional growth has been severely distorted or stunted. Counseling psychology, then, leaves to other psychologists the major responsibility for the emergency treatment of psychological disasters.

The counseling psychologist wants to help individuals toward overcoming obstacles to their personal growth, wherever these may be encountered, and toward achieving optimum development of their personal resources. Therefore, this psychological specialist is found to be working in the full range of social settings—for example, school, hospital, business or industry, or community agency. The counseling psychologist may help individuals in their personal development while they are progressing through school, suffering the effects of illness or physical disability, changing jobs, or attempting to cope with marital situations or problems of parent/child relationships.

As a psychologist, the counselor has certain unique resources to offer individuals for use in achieving a harmonious relationship to their environments. Tests and other methods of psychological evaluation enable counseling psychologists to offer their clients forecasts about the probable outcomes of the alternative courses of action open to them (Paterson & Darley, 1936; Paterson, Schneidler, & Williamson, 1938; Super, 1949). Analytic techniques developed by psychologists provide the counselor with the means of assessing the psychological demands of roles an individual may play in various environmental situations (for example, Shartle, 1946). Although counseling psychologists interest themselves in many other kinds of information and skills that related disciplines have to offer the client (for example, education, sociology, or religion), they do not claim special competencies in these areas.

Although no distinct cleavage exists, we do see evidences of differences between clinical and counseling psychologists. One such difference is in the amount of emphasis given to the above-described function of increasing individuals' resources for coping with their environments. Counseling psychologists, like personnel psychologists, spend more time in attaining a comprehensive knowledge of the validities of psychological tests for predicting the outcomes of activities engaged in by clients during the normal courses of their lives (for example, educational achievement, occupational success, marital happiness, and so forth). This is balanced by less preoccupation with the use of psychological tests for the analysis of the individual's inner life and for predicting problems of hospital management and psychotherapeutic treatment.[3]

[3]Contrast a typical text on psychodiagnosis with a typical text on educational or vocational appraisal.

Counseling psychologists do not view their contribution to individuals' personal development as restricted to direct contact with them through psychological counseling. Where necessary, they are willing to follow the client out of the office and to work with other persons and groups with whom the client has to deal. In this way, the counseling psychologist shares with the social psychologist a concern for the degree to which social organization adapts itself to the meeting of individual needs. For example, in the educational sphere, counseling psychologists play a role in shaping admissions procedures, curriculum development, and extracurricular activities, and consults with teaching faculty and other educational personnel. In industry, they collaborate in training programs for supervisors, influence selection and placement procedures, and consult on personnel policies. In hospitals, they stimulate the development of hospital employment opportunities for treatment purposes, collaborate with other workers (for example, physicians, nurses, social workers, and occupational, physical, and educational therapists) in the development of a total rehabilitation program, and work with other hospital and nonhospital personnel in the development of outside employment opportunities. In all of this, the goal of counseling psychologists is to further the fullest possible self-realization of those who constitute a particular social group, not just their clients or those deviant individuals who are making less than a minimal adjustment in that social setting.

THE FUTURE

For counseling psychology, it is safe to assert that many changes are likely to occur over the next decade. Because dramatic changes are taking place now, we cannot predict what the future will hold for the specialty. It may be, for example, that counseling psychologists will work mostly with sick people; a new kind of industrial psychology may emerge out of the fusion of clinical, counseling, personnel, and applied experimental psychology in the industrial setting, or, it is possible that counseling and school psychology may merge in the educational setting. Whatever the developments, they will depend on where the functions performed by counseling psychologists find their most useful outlets.

It is our conviction that counseling psychology is still evolving as a specialty area. Although there are discernible trends toward commonality among the present psychological specialties, it is important to underline the remaining differences among them. Regardless of ultimate trends, the present accentuation of differences should permit new functions to develop. By attempts to define these specialty areas, we can help to ensure that the unique contributions of different kinds of functions will be recognized. The present organization and structure of the specialties, however, should not be regarded as permanent.

The primary concern among all practicing psychological specialists ought to be the building of a more effective applied psychology. In counseling psychology, we must not lose the present opportunity to make our unique contribution to psychological science and practice because of spurious pressures to merge with other groups. Neither should we fight genuine assimilative trends, such as counseling psychology's trend toward increased attention to personality development and that of clinical psychology toward increasing concern with extra-personal, environmental influences upon individual and group development. We think it wise to make explicit our unique functions as counseling psychologists without resisting their fulfillment by other specialty groups.

The problem of convergence may be resolved by a simplification of the existing specialty structure. A broad group of functions may come to be performed under a new and single banner, but it is important to ensure that this does not take place in such a way that important, presently performed functions are slighted or ignored. It is quite possible, therefore, that what seem to be convergence trends among the present specialty areas will lead to the parallel development of functions rather than to complete overlap.

SUMMARY

At the present time, counseling psychology is a specialty within the area broadly designated as applied psychology. It utilizes concepts and tools and techniques that are used also by several other specialty groups, notably social, personnel, and clinical psychology. Although the specialty has been practiced for many years, its designation as counseling psychology has been adopted and generally accepted only recently. Historically, it has drawn upon three distinct movements: (a) vocational guidance, (b) psychological measurement, and (c) personality development. Currently, the specialty of counseling psychology is approaching a balance among emphases upon contributions to (a) the development of an individual's inner life, (b) the individual's achievement of harmony with his environment, and (c) the influencing of society to recognize individual differences and to encourage the fullest development of all persons within it. Although counseling psychology leaves to other psychologists the major responsibility for treating psychological disasters, counseling psychologists may be found working in the full range of social settings. They have unique resources—for example, tests and other methods of psychological evaluation—for helping individuals to achieve harmonious relationships with their environments. They are willing to work directly with other persons and groups with whom their clients must deal outside of the counseling office. Their goals are to further the fullest possible self-realization of those who live in a particular social setting.

REFERENCES

American Psychological Association. Division of Counseling and Guidance, Committee on Counselor Training. The practicum training of counseling psychologists. *American Psychologist,* 1952, *7,* 182–188. (a)

American Psychological Association. Division of Counseling and Guidance, Committee on Counselor Training. Recommended standards for training counseling psychologists at the doctorate level. *American Psychologist*, 1952, *7*, 175-181. (b)

Bordin, E. S. (Ed.). *The training of psychological counselors*. Ann Arbor: University of Michigan, 1951.

Bordin, E. S. *Psychological counseling*. N. Y.: Appleton-Century-Crofts, 1955.

Brewer, J. M. *Education as guidance*. N. Y.: Macmillan, 1932.

Cutts, N. E. *School psychologists at mid-century*. Washington, D. C.: American Psychological Association, 1955.

Hahn, M. E. Counseling psychology. *American Psychologist*, 1955, *7*, 279-282.

Hahn, M. E., & MacLean, M. S. *Counseling psychology*. N. Y.: McGraw-Hill, 1955.

McConn, M. Educational guidance is now possible. *Educational Records*, 1935, *16*, 375-411.

Parsons, F. *Choosing a vocation*. Boston: Houghton Mifflin, 1909.

Paterson, D. G., & Darley, J. G. *Men, women, and jobs*. Minneapolis: University of Minnesota Press, 1936.

Paterson, D. G., Schneidler, G., & Williamson, E. G. *Student guidance techniques*. N. Y.: McGraw-Hill, 1938.

Pepinsky, H. B., & Pepinsky, P. N. *Counseling: theory and practice*. N. Y.: Ronald, 1954.

Shartle, C. L. *Occupational information*. N. Y.: Prentice-Hall, 1946.

Super, D. E. *Appraising vocational fitness*. N. Y.: Harper, 1949.

Super, D. E. Transition: from vocational guidance to counseling psychology. *Journal of Counseling Psychology*, 1955, *2*, 3-9.

Wrenn, C. G. Training of vocational guidance workers. *Occupations*, 1951, *29*, 414-419.

Wrenn, C. G. The ethics of counseling. *Educational and Psychological Measurement*, 1952, *12*, 161-177.

Wrenn, C. G. Editorial comment. *Journal of Counseling Psychologist*, 1954, *1*, 124.

Wrenn, C. G., & Darley, J. G. Counseling. *Review of Educational Research*, 1942, *12*, 45-65.

THE DIFFERING VIEWS ON A DEVELOPING PROFESSION: 1954–1962

4

Chapter 9
Counseling
Psychology: 1954

MILTON E. HAHN

For some time this country has been faced with a rapid rise in the demand for related, nonmedical professional services. Established areas such as social case work, psychiatry, and psychology are developing subspecialties and, in one instance, a new interdisciplinary subdoctoral group, rehabilitation counselors, recently has emerged. With such a condition of growth, we find each of these vigorous professional groups staking out zones of influence in unclaimed territory and occasionally laying claim to functions traditionally considered as "belonging" to other disciplines.

Although many of these conflicts are still at the level of friendly bewilderment, we are faced with the need to clarify and justify our legitimate areas and methods of practice. In particular, psychiatry, social work, clinical psychology, and counseling psychology are competing for status, legal sanction, and advantage.

In developing the concepts in this paper, there is neither the intention to forget, or to play down, the basic unity of psychology as a field of knowledge

Address of the retiring president of the Division on Counseling Psychology of the American Psychological Association, New York City, September 4, 1954.

Editorial assistance from Drs. Dorothy Clendenen, Frank Fletcher, Morse Manson, Max Houtchens, Robert Waldrop, and Gilbert Wrenn is gratefully acknowledged.

and practice nor to imply that our in-field differences are as great as those between and among other discrete disciplines. Attention is called, however, to similar problems confronting other expanding professional service disciplines—for example, medicine and social welfare. In medicine we have the differences between general practice and psychiatry, surgery, and pediatrics. In social work we have the psychiatric social worker and the general practitioner, among other specialties. Psychologists should be psychologists first and psychological specialists second, but the specialties do exist and are important to the development of psychology as a whole.

This paper is a proposal to establish counseling psychology as a functionally unique pattern of practice. Patterns of vocational activity are seldom unique in their parts and not always unique in their totality, but, using a phrase coined by Paterson, may be "relatively unique." It is difficult to demonstrate a single function or practice that, with the exception of some specialties of medicine, is completely unique to any of the professional groups we are considering. Nevertheless, it does seem possible to show a *patterning* of methods, objectives, and situations that is peculiar to any one of these groups. The basis of such patterns lies in the professional training required, the type of client, the objectives of practice, and the work situation.

All of us in these related disciplines use the same general tool kit of methodology. However, use tends to differ—for example, between the psychiatrist and the social case worker in quantity, complexity, and purpose of tool use. We all use tests, but projective devices and measures of academic achievement have quite different purposes and interpretations. We all make use of the interview, but relationship and situation, in addition to our differing objectives and the kind of client or patient, are not identical. All of the groups with which we are concerned make use of learning theory to a greater or lesser extent as a basis for helping clients to achieve better adjustment, but our structuring of the learning situations will vary.

In developing the differences that identify our patterns of practice, one is aware of the need to avoid invidious comparisons. It would be most satisfying if a positive statement could be made of what counseling psychology does and is concerned with, without reference to other disciplines. Such an attempt could become relatively ineffective because of the overlapping of methods, objectives, and types of client. There is the further problem that such a noncomparative statement will preempt functions that other groups will consider theirs. To consider the problem with any approach to completeness demands both (a) a comparison with other professional groups, and (b) a statement of relatively unique patterns of practice. Following the order of emphasis, we first consider the broad problems of interdisciplinary relationships with particular emphasis on the two fields of clinical and counseling psychology.

Among the specialties related closely to counseling psychology, superficially the one most difficult to differentiate from it clearly is clinical psychology. When one looks first at the original selection of individuals for these two services, it is quickly apparent that data on selection for these two specialties are meager. To be sure, the publications of Adkins (1954), Kelly and Fiske (1951), and Kriedt (1949) are helpful. From these researches on the kinds of people in psychology and from much general reading and observation, some generalizations can be drawn as working hypotheses. It is granted that these hypotheses are controversial and generally lacking in experimental verification.

One hypothesis is that, contrary to the thinking of many, *counseling psychologists resemble industrial psychologists to a greater extent than they do psychotherapists.* Support for this point of view is lent by the proposed reorganization of APA in which industrial and counseling psychologists would be grouped, with clinical psychologists in another division. Mobility between these two fields appears to be an easier path than the ones between either of them and clinical psychology. There appears, however, to be a greater attempt at exchange between counseling and clinical psychology with some clinical and counseling psychologists assuming that counseling and psychotherapy are synonymous in training and practice. Personal experience does not bear out this clinical-counseling mobility in practice.

A second hypothesis is that *clinical psychologists have a greater personality dimension of interests in "persons and personalities" as opposed to "processes and things" than do counseling psychologists.* The value systems appear to vary significantly in terms of the weights assigned to the good of the individual versus the good of society or a group. The counseling psychologist appears to some of us as more "hard-boiled." Along the same line, many counseling psychologists appear to embrace a normative approach to personality traits and structure, as compared to many clinical psychologists who lean more to the phenomenological viewpoint.

A third hypothesis is that *counseling psychologists tend to have greater managerial, administrative interests.* Certainly observation of practitioners over a period of years gives some support to this idea. In my experience, counseling psychologists have a strong tendency to pick up early in professional life such titles as manager, director, or, Heaven save us, even dean!

My last hypothesis is that *counseling psychology trainees take more readily to statistics and statistical research.* Landfield (1954) lends some support to this hypothesis. While Landfield addresses himself to clinical trainees, few of us appear to have found this difficulty to any great degree with counselor trainees.

In closing this section on hypotheses, I again emphasize that the hunches (or hopes) expressed are in large part an indication of areas that call for research. So little has been done in obtaining a valid descriptive basis for our practices that we have not been in a position to deal sensibly with the selection of our trainees. Until we are agreed as to what our patterns of practice are, and should be, research is indeed difficult to accomplish.

It is not the purpose here to propose a method of selecting counseling versus clinical psychology trainees. It is obvious that research is needed along new lines with emphasis on dimensions of personality since there is no evidence that the mental alertness or power of the individual is different in the two groups. However, it is my contention that we do have individuals who differ in their value judgments, their attitudes, and their interests and that, however trained, eventual professional practice will tend to follow personality dimensions rather than the specific pattern of training.

Opinions regarding possible differences in training between the two psychological specialties vary from those who believe that "only a course in occupational information divides them" to those who see little communality. There is agreement that both, including a minimal one-year internship, are at least four-year graduate training programs.

Inspection of various curricula in several institutions gives the impression that approximately two years of the academic work for both groups is devoted to the training of sound general psychologists with an orientation in experimental, physiological, social, and general psychology. Basic measurement and statistics are covered also during this period. By the end of the third year both clinical and counseling psychologists are completing groundwork in personality and learning theory. Three of the four years of academic work are much alike or even duplicates. However, learning theory has somewhat different implications and applications. The clinical psychologist is more concerned with the deviate whose anxiety level is disabling and disintegrative. The counseling psychologist tends to work with those whose anxieties are interfering and disruptive but not disabling. When therapy is based on learning theory, the counselor usually concentrates more on cognitive, intellectual levels and less on phenomenological constructs.

Differences appear too in the applications and implications of personality development and structure theory. Here, counseling psychologists concentrate on the problems of interfering value systems and judgments and the changing of attitudes. The clinical psychologist appears to work more in the medically related areas of reorganizing basic personality structure. Although the course work is often done in the same class, what is taken from the course in terms of future practice may be quite different. Counseling has greater concern with a positive approach to trait strengths and less concern with medically diagnosed personality deviations that demand remediation through psychotherapy.

Counseling psychologists frequently are marked in their training, among other emphases, by an emphasis on trait and factor theory. For them it is often material basic to practice. Their most unique skill is the psychological assessment of trait strengths and weaknesses and their implications for social living. Occupational information is of great use to the counseling psychologist in educational-vocational settings, although this use is shared by others such as those in industrial psychology. Clinical psychologists make much less use of this body of knowledge.

Differences appear too in the use-patterning of tools and techniques for clinical and counseling psychologists. For example, both use psychometric devices, but projective instruments and those used for the assessment of aptitudes, abilities, and interests are usually quite different in purpose and in the application of results. Clinical psychologists are not always at home with the many group tests whose reliability and validity vary widely as do even more, perhaps, the individual tests they more frequently use.

In contradistinction to the frequent use of "counseling" and "psychotherapy" as synonyms, there is a need for an advisory aspect in counseling that is not usually considered in order with deeply disturbed patients. Inasmuch as advising presumes that the advisor has special knowledge of high reliability and validity, and thus is a sound guide to the client, there is a content in counseling that deals with specific conditions in educational institutions, business and industry, and social living. This advisory content tends to separate training and practices of the psychotherapist and the counseling psychologist. Training in counseling psychology is based in part on these special knowledges useful, for example, in the advising of clients about such mundane affairs as jobs and how to get them, study skills, educational opportunities, and normative information for comparisons of the individual with specific social and economic groups.

Differences persist in the internship. Many university and college counseling centers provide paid internships not always open to the clinical psychologist, just as the reverse is true in some medical settings. Community agencies also make use of the counselor in nonmedical situations. Even in the hospital internships provided by the Veterans Administration, medical people make legitimate complaints when the reports of clinical and counseling psychologists do not differ noticeably in approach, language, and intent. It is of interest to note that the Chief of Counseling Psychology in many hospitals reports directly to the Chief of Professional Services and not through a psychiatrist.

In summary, there is little proof that we are training clinical and counseling psychologists to do the same things in the same ways with the same hoped-for outcomes, and this, even though three-fourths of their academic experience may be in common; nor does the evidence indicate that we are selecting and training interchangeable human units. It may well be that those who are happiest with what a clinical psychologist does will practice as psychotherapists even though they come through the training program for the counseling psychologist. The reverse claim has equal strength. To combine the training into one curriculum could well result in adding a year of graduate work. The graduates would, in my opinion, not be ambivalent in practice. In terms of personal interests, they would practice primarily in one or the other area with no appreciable gain to society or to the individual practitioner so trained from an added year of work. One practitioner concerns himself or herself primarily with *patients,* the other with *clients.* The differences are far greater in training than a course in occupational information.

The original task remains of summarizing a relatively unique pattern of function for the counseling psychologist. This pattern, it is hoped, will show clearly that we are a legitimate and discrete group of practitioners. The pattern does not appear to be duplicated in large part by our colleagues in related fields.

First, the major concern of the counseling psychologist is with *clients,* not *patients,* from the mass of people who can support themselves and live with reasonable adjustment in our society.

Second, our employment is in situations that do not place us professionally under the direction or supervision of related disciplines either as a matter of policy, law, or political or economic conditions.

Third, our tools and techniques of practice are based in general more on normative approaches than are those of related disciplines.

Fourth, we tend to emphasize learning theory at the cognitive, intellectual, and rational levels although not omitting orientation to the content of psychodynamics. We help *clients* to change attitudes and value systems, but we rarely attempt the major restructuring or rebuilding of a personality.

Fifth, we deal usually with anxiety states at the frustrating, interfering levels, not when disability or disintegration is indicated.

Sixth, and our most nearly unique single function, we are the most skilled professional workers in the assessment and appraisal of human traits for educational-vocational-social living: the casting of a psychological balance sheet to aid our *clients* to contribute to, and to take most from, living in our society.

Seventh, we are obligated to follow our *clients* beyond the office door. Until there is *client*-accepted planning for such future action as formal education or training, vocational exploration, and social direction, the counseling process is not complete.

Eighth, and last, we stress positive psychological strengths and their personal and social use as opposed to a process of diagnosing and remedying psychopathies.

I know of no professional group which duplicates this pattern of practice or approaches it closely.

REFERENCES

Adkins, D. C. The simple structure of the American Psychological Association. *American Psychologist,* 1954, *9,* 175–180.

Kelly, E. L., & Fiske, D. W. *The prediction of performance in clinical psychology.* Ann Arbor: University of Michigan Press, 1951.

Kriedt, P. H. Vocational interests of psychologists. *Journal of Applied Psychology,* 1949, *33,* 482–488.

Landfield, A. W. Research avoidance in clinical students. *American Psychologist,* 1954, *9,* 240–242.

Chapter 10
The Status of Counseling
Psychology: 1960

IRWIN BERG
HAROLD B. PEPINSKY
EDWARD J. SHOBEN

In 1959, the APA Education and Training Board appointed an *ad hoc* committee[1] to examine, review, and prepare a general report concerning the status of counseling psychology as a professional specialty. The reason for the Board's action was a general feeling among its members that all was not well with counseling psychology. Although counseling as an activity in fields other than psychology appeared to be flourishing, as witness the provision for counseling in the National Defense Education Act, *counseling psychology* appeared, in the opinion of some members of the Board, to have lagged behind other specialty areas of psychology. Two or three decades ago, counseling psychology was immensely prestigeful as a specialty, but now it appears to be in some ways on the wane. The present report is in no sense an exhaustive study of the current position of counseling psychology in the United States. Rather, it is offered as a statement of the findings obtained by committee members with rather limited time and facilities for the task at hand but who have had broad experience in the counseling psychology field. Some conclusions and recommendations are presented, but they are tendered modestly and, it must be emphasized, are subject to radical revision.

THE DECLINE OF COUNSELING PSYCHOLOGY

There is clear evidence that counseling psychology is declining. Because there is a large number of psychologists who currently bear the counseling label, the indications of a vanishing specialty are not at once apparent. But to

This is the first publication of this article. All rights reserved. Permission to reprint must be obtained from the publisher.

[1]The committee members were Harold B. Pepinsky, Edward Joseph Shoben, Jr., and Irwin A. Berg, Chairman. Because *ad hominem* issue may possibly be taken with this report, it seems desirable to qualify the committee to the E&T Board. Collectively, the committee members have held APA Counseling Psychology Division elective offices of president, secretary-treasurer, APA council representative, and executive committee member. They have also held appointive membership on most divisional committees. All the members have published a variety of research in the counseling psychology field, and all of them have earned the ABEPP diploma by examination—two members in counseling psychology and one in clinical psychology.

maintain and augment the current body of counseling psychologists, new persons must enter this field in appropriate numbers. Such has not been the trend in recent years. Some administrators of APA-approved university programs in counseling psychology have lamented that both the quantity and quality of their graduate students have fallen off during the past five years. Nothing specific can be said concerning graduate student quality in counseling psychology, but the sheer number of recent Ph.D.'s seems quite inadequate to maintain meaningfully the counseling label. In 1957-58, for example, 268 Ph.D.'s were awarded in clinical psychology, but only 41 in counseling, according to a 1959 report (Berdie & Lofquist, 1959) to the Committee on Divisional Functions of the APA Division of Counseling Psychology. At a time when clinical psychology is expanding, adding new APA-approved programs at the Universities of Alabama, Houston, and Oklahoma, counseling psychology has been shrinking, with Oregon and Stanford voluntarily eliminating their counseling programs. Some universities, like Duke, have approved programs but no students. Other universities, like Kansas State, have a few students nominally in their counseling psychology programs, but none actually completing doctorates. A common complaint of administrators of doctoral programs in counseling psychology is that many of their graduate students entered counseling only because they were rejected for training in clinical psychology.

There are several programs in counseling psychology that seem to be exceptions to the trends outlined here. These are the long-established, prestigeful programs in large universities such as Columbia, Minnesota, or Ohio State; and they are administratively located in colleges of education with affiliation of varying degrees of closeness to a department of psychology. Other well-established counseling psychology programs, such as that at the University of Illinois, appear to have no problems with respect to quality or quantity of students; but, in such places, the counseling and clinical psychology programs are virtually identical. Graduate students in both specialties take the same courses and have an internship in both clinical and counseling psychology. Like students in most programs, they have the same professors whether they are in the counseling or clinical psychology course sequence. Upon graduation, they may presumably elect either the counseling or the clinical label since they are qualified for either. Thus, where counseling psychology has apparently maintained its position, it is either identified with a college of education or is a clinical psychology program that has broadened to qualify its students for counseling psychology as well.

As for internships, there are dozens of APA-approved agencies in clinical psychology. By contrast, the APA Committee on Evaluation at the time this report was written had never received a single request for evaluation of a counseling psychology internship program. It is true that counseling internships are often organized in a "captive" training center within the academic setting. However, the APA Division of Counseling Psychology has prepared several statements on recommended standards for academic and practicum training in counseling psychology. One might assume that, were counseling psychology in robust health, at least a few internship centers would have sought APA approval of their counseling programs as a demonstration that Division 17's standards had been met. Although this point may be moot, a relevant portent of undoubted significance is the persistent and consistent avoidance of the ABEPP diploma in counseling. In 1959, 114 psychologists made application for the ABEPP written examinations in clinical psychology, but only seven applied in counseling. In 1950, it was 23 for clinical and seven again for counseling.

These are symptoms of malaise, but not the only ones. A 1959 report (Goodstein, Buchheimer, Crites, & Muthard, 1959) by the APA Division 17 *ad hoc* Committee on the Scientific Status of Counseling Psychology flatly asserted that the scientific state of counseling psychology was far from satisfactory. The report noted that there was a dearth of systematized and integrated empirical research and that the *Zeitgeist* of counseling psychology appeared to be ascientific. It may be noted in this connection that many of the highly visible counseling psychologists, those who published extensively in the counseling specialty during the past decade or so, are now largely engaged in other pursuits. A surprising number of them are college deans, department heads, or foundation and business executives who, although they periodically sally forth to call public attention to the need for counselors, are no longer contributing to the body of counseling psychology knowledge. Those who achieved professional stature through their research in counseling have in some instances switched to another research area. To some extent, of course, this may be said of the visible members of any psychological specialty; but in counseling psychology the trend seems to be considerably more pronounced than in other fields.

Apart from the activities of the visible members of the counseling specialty is the question of the status of counseling psychology itself. According to a study by Granger (1959), counseling psychology was rated by a sample of APA members as being lowest in status of all specialties in psychology requiring the Ph.D. Perhaps the apparent decline of counseling psychology as a special field is related to a decline in the status it once enjoyed.

Be that as it may, counseling psychology certainly has not had the burgeoning development that clinical psychology has had. The membership of the APA Division of Counseling Psychology has increased each year but not with the leaps and bounds of the Division of Clinical Psychology. Also, it must be kept in mind that about 50% of the members of the counseling division of APA hold membership in the clinical division as well. Perhaps the explanation for the differential growth rates of the two specialties lies partly in the semantic characteristics of the two labels. Counseling is something that everybody does—at least, they say they do. Lawyers, clergymen, teachers, scoutmasters, bankers, parents, *ad infinitum,* all do counseling and use the word *counseling* to designate certain of their behaviors. By contrast, clinical activities are definitely associated with professional training and professional settings. In the thinking of the professional and lay public, counseling conceivably could occur anywhere—in the rose garden, on the street, or in the parlor—and be carried on by anyone with a bit of wisdom and a little special knowledge. Clinical responsibilities, on the other hand, seem to be associated with hospitals, consultation rooms, and professional education. Thus, a semantic value may be involved and may account for some of the differential status of the two fields.

Certainly, differences in training do not supply an answer. It has already been noted that many approved counseling and clinical training programs are identical. Similarly, when Paterson and Lofquist surveyed the 24 departments that had approved programs in both counseling and clinical psychology, only three of the 21 departments replying stated that the course work and doctoral preliminary examinations for the two fields were definitely different. These investigators concluded that there obviously was little difference between the two specialties insofar as training was concerned. This is borne out in the Veterans Administration's registry of qualified applicants for jobs in psychology, where it is common to find psychologists who have qualified for both clinical and counseling psychology positions. When actually on the job, clinicians sometimes work in counseling positions and counselors as clinicians in the VA services.

SOME ALTERNATE SOLUTIONS

It seems probable that there is no single solution to the complex of problems outlined here. Rather, there are several alternatives that may serve to bring productive order into this odd professional chaos. It is understood that some of these alternatives may be quite disturbing to those psychologists who are reluctant to relinquish the specific label of "counseling psychology." It must be emphasized, however, that all of the possibilities offered here are intended to preserve, strengthen, and enhance the important functions and orientation of counseling psychology as it has developed in the past. Unless one of these alternatives or some variant of them is adopted, there is a real probability that this set of important contributions may be lost as the trends described in this report continue.

Fusion of Clinical and Counseling Training

One alternative is the fusion of counseling and clinical psychology at the level of doctoral training. This notion does *not* mean the absorption of counseling by the clinical specialty. It implies instead the fulfillment of Super's (1955) prediction that ". . . the two fields will merge (into) a more broadly trained and oriented" kind of profession. To be fruitful, such a merger must entail an enlarging of the scope of clinical practice and internships, the provision through both course work and field experience of wider familiarity with normal people and their problems, and a somewhat greater emphasis on developmental and facilitative (as against psychopathological and remedial) points of view.

Given such modifications, it seems probable that clinical psychology would acquire greater scope and greater usefulness both as a form of service and as a contributor to psychological science. To some degree, the direction of its development would be diverted from the traditional psychiatric model and toward a more intrinsic concept of psychological help to a very wide range of people. On the research and theoretical side, it would be infused with concern for the conceptualization and assessment of personality assets, the identification of psychological issues associated with the world of work and the development of careers, and the dimensions of interpersonal relations in such nearly universal human situations as marriage, family life, work relationships, community processes, and so on.

Counseling psychology, on the other hand, would retain its label to signify its status as an identifiable and highly contributive emphasis *within* the more developed clinical specialty. APA's Division of Counseling Psychology would be maintained, as would appropriate job titles in the Civil Service and other agencies. The ABEPP Diploma in Clinical Psychology would suffice to cover the newly created field, provided proper allowances were made in the examinations for specialty sections. There would be no diminution in the degree of autonomy of visible identity that counseling psychology currently enjoys; but the confusion resulting from its lack of precise distinctiveness would be greatly reduced, and better capital would be made in psychology generally of its valuable stress on the recurrent problems of normal persons and on the strengths and assets of human personality in its encounters with developmental crises and the potential frustrations of the social world.

The Clinical Core

As almost an extension of the fusion concept, it is easy to imagine the basic doctoral curriculum in clinical psychology as a core from which various specialties in psychology's helping disciplines would develop. With a central training pattern, occupying approximately half of a four-year program, specialization along several lines could take place through differentiated internships and the equivalent of about one year of course experience. This kind of specialization might include work with school children and school personnel from a mental health standpoint; work devoted primarily to decision-making with respect to such matters as career objectives, personal relationships, and life planning among ostensibly normal persons; developmental services to business and industrial personnel, or the preparation of people to use new housing opportunities in constructive ways, or to integrate themselves with integrity and interpersonal efficiency into communities of a kind foreign to their previous experiences.

Again, the aim here is that of enriching and increasing the usefulness of clinical psychology both professionally and theoretically while preserving the contributions and the identity of the fields of specialization, particularly counseling psychology, that have grown up around it. In a kind of negative sense, the move envisioned here would reduce the factionalism and tendencies toward fission that threaten psychological science as well as the psychological profession. Increasing the degree of commonality in training and the opportunities for sharing orientations and service points of view would seem helpful on this score. At the same time, the provision for explicit and broad areas of specialization within a single major field would insure the chances for novelty and diversity to find fertile soil in training experiences and in both the forms of service and the types of research and theory that psychology can provide. As in the first alternative, a single ABEPP diploma should suffice with due allowance for specialty interests within clinical psychology to be represented in the examinations. Also similarly, no change would seem to be required in the APA divisional structure, the use of various job titles by employing agencies, and so forth.

The Development of Genuinely Distinctive Programs

Another alternative, of course, is the development of training programs that are genuinely distinctive and patterns of service that are fully discriminable from those of other specialties within psychology. In this connection, Danskin (1959) has suggested that training programs might aim at producing counselors first and psychologists second. There are at least four possibilities here that, singly or in some combination, could conceivably provide the separate identity that some counseling psychologists seek. A primary question is that of whether the orientation and type of function for which counseling psychology has stood might not better be ramified throughout the psychological services areas rather than cabined within the restrictions that any one of these possible lines of specialization suggest.

For example, it would be perfectly conceivable for counseling psychology to return essentially to the directional emphases given by Frank D. Parsons and Harry D. Kitson and to take vocational choice and career development as its distinctive domain of study and service. Such a tendency would seem to entail a reversing of history and a flying in the face of the widespread experience that these regions of concern cannot be effectively served without a broader background than was required by the traditional vocational guidance emphasis. Nevertheless, assuming the willingness of those primarily identified with counseling psychology, it would be feasible to accept such a limitation on subject matter, transformed by more recently acquired knowledge and the interest in personality factors associated with the world of work that have recently proved their relevance.

Second, counseling psychology could take over some of the psychological functions associated with community development and preventive mental health, thus evolving a relatively new domain of thought, research, and service for itself. Little relevant attention, for example, has so far been given to the problem of delinquency and the conditions out of which it develops. This kind of crucial social question could well come within the purview of counseling psychology's developmental emphasis and its traditional interest in adolescents. Even the conventional concern with occupational assessment and increased familiarity with the occupational world might be useful here. Conceivably, a sophisticated and early appraisal of a youngster's vocational fitness, coupled with some well planned work experiences, might do much to prevent his turning toward delinquent behavior patterns, especially if this kind of service were effectively colored by the understandings that have been derived from counseling psychology's more recent accommodation of psychotherapeutic techniques, a broader gamut of personality theory, and understanding drawn from studies of social factors in individual development. Similarly, the whole problem of the aged could be conceived as an appropriate domain for investigation and service by counseling psychology. Preparation for retirement, the working through of problems associated with declining energies, and the revision of life patterns to take into account the physical and psychological processes associated with growing older are all, until shown otherwise, presumably amenable to the counseling process and constitute a most important part of the difficulties of normal people to which counseling psychology has been fruitfully committed.

Along somewhat different lines, the problem of population control is probably the central one confronting the human race in modern times. Again, the psychological factors associated with such things as the planned limitation of family size, the effectiveness of different forms of communication in educating people about the problem of population growth, and the dissemination of contraceptive information have been little studied, and virtually no one has attempted to devise a form of psychological service that would assist in meeting the awesome threat of overpopulation. This challenge presents a creative opportunity to psychology generally, and counseling psychology may be in a uniquely favorable position to respond to it.

Finally, there is the whole matter of urban planning, the development of new housing enterprises, and so on. It has been noted that people from foreign, underprivileged backgrounds are frequently unable to use these new resources in effective ways. The productive coupling of counseling techniques with an awareness of the social forces that influence people's attitudes may represent one useful answer to this kind of problem. Once again, counseling psychology seems in a position, if its leadership is so inclined, to capitalize in socially and intellectually worthwhile ways on this opportunity.

A third class of possible distinctive programs may be found in the problems of physical and psychiatric rehabilitation. This field is rapidly expanding as is witnessed by the recent establishment of a separate division, representing the concerns of rehabilitation workers, in APA. Although many different specialties in psychology may be properly concerned with the rehabilitation process, counseling psychology seems to have a particular stake in this enterprise because of the inherent emphases on assessing and utilizing assets and on reintroducing an individual into the community. The fact that most training programs for rehabilitation counselors are now administered primarily under the wing of counseling psychology increases the opportunity to dignify those committed to the rehabilitation venture by stressing the psychological side of these interdisciplinary responsibilities and educating rehabilitation workers to the doctoral level.

Fourth, counseling psychology could take over a central role in special education, concentrating on mental retardates and the gifted. This move would require a genuine form of specialization, not a mere relabeling of the concerns that have been central in the discipline for some time, giving particular weight to the problems of individual development posed by one's being at the extreme ends of the continuum of intellective ability. Some counseling psychologists have shown an interest in this field, and it may well be worthy of the serious consideration of many others.

Educational Personnel Work

Still another class of possibilities involves the concentration of counseling psychology on the educational process with a special concern for pupil personnel services, particularly at the college level. In many ways, such a move would simply formalize a trend that is already much in evidence. In many instances, counseling psychology is operating within a school or department of education rather than a department of psychology, and a good deal of the time of counseling psychologists is being devoted to the training of student personnel workers. In one sense, this form of distinctive concentration would be analogous to the way in which psychologists have brought their influence in helpful ways into medical schools or other professional training facilities outside psychology. Both the traditional concern of psychology with the general process of education and the special preoccupation of counseling psychology with the college as a setting for its own enterprise make this potentiality an attractive one. Certainly, education needs all the help that it can get from psychology, and meeting this obligation and opportunity is a welcome task for most within the psychological profession. Perhaps, the counseling psychologists are those by training and by tradition who are most fully equipped to provide this kind of service as a central and distinctive part of their professional functioning.

Technician Level of Functioning

Another alternative is that of conceiving the distinctive functions of counseling psychologists as appropriate to the M.A. or technician level of operation as recently sanctioned by the Miami Beach Report. There is a sense in which the training of relatively large numbers of vocational appraisers, counselors, guidance and personnel workers, and so forth on the basis of M.A. programs is legitimately defensible on the ground of immediate social need; and it also represents one way in which the distinctive element in the notion of the counseling psychologist as "an M.A. vocational counselor with a clinical doctorate" can be preserved. Such an arrangement would, however, encounter two serious questions: (1) Would the abrogation of the doctorate not only eliminate counseling psychology as a specialty level in psychology but also minimize the beneficial effects that its orientation and functions have seemed to have over the last decade? (2) Would such a move tend to create a group of technicians who would be regarded as second-class citizens in the psychological republic?

There may well be other alternatives that have not been listed here. In all cases, however, the possibilities briefly discussed in this report represent either ways of increasing the identity and distinctiveness of counseling psychology as a separate specialty or of making its contributions and helpful characteristics more available to other specialties. In the latter instance, the alternatives presented here constitute responses to the pattern that seems so definitely to have evolved in professional psychology: In spite of its vigor and growth, counseling psychology seems to have developed more in the way of affinities with other areas of specialization, especially clinical psychology, than a distinctive identity of service functions or training patterns. In consequence, it is not easily recognizable by the granters of supportive funds, the persons standing in need of special services, or students interested in specialized careers in psychology. It seems urgent that this kind of problem be met with both wisdom and decisiveness.

REFERENCES

Berdie, R. F., & Lofquist, L. Report to Committee on Divisional Functions, Division 17, APA. Mimeographed, 1959, APA Division 17.

Danskin, D. G. Pavlov, Poe, and Division 17. *Counseling News and Views,* 1959, *12,* 4–6.

Goodstein, L. D., Buchheimer, A., Crites, J. O., & Muthard, J. H. Report of the *ad hoc* Committee on the Scientific Status of Counseling Psychology. Mimeographed, 1959, APA Division 17.

Granger, S. G. Psychologists' prestige rankings of 20 psychological occupations. *Journal of Counseling Psychology,* 1959, *6,* 183–188.

Super, D. E. Transition: From vocational guidance to counseling psychology. *Journal of Counseling Psychology,* 1955, *2*(1), 3–9.

Chapter 11
The Current Status of Counseling Psychology: 1961

LEONA TYLER
DAVID TIEDEMAN
C. GILBERT WRENN
A Report of a Special Committee
Of the Division of Counseling Psychology, 1961

ORIGIN OF THIS STUDY

In September 1960, the Executive Committee of the Division of Counseling Psychology asked three members of the Division to draft a statement on the current status of counseling psychology as a field of study and work. Such a review of the field also had been requested by the Education and Training Board of the American Psychological Association.

The Board in 1959 had commissioned Drs. Irwin Berg, Harold Pepinsky, and Joseph Shoben to prepare an analysis of counseling psychology. The Executive Committee of Division 17 decided in 1960 that the opinions expressed in that report did not reflect the variety of interests of the members of the Division. Furthermore, the Executive Committee felt that the report (which has not yet been officially released for general circulation) did not adequately marshal the factual evidence concerning the current status of counseling psychology which should be relevant in the deliberations of the Education and Training Board. However, the Executive Committee instructed its special committee not to write a rejoinder to the aforementioned report but rather to write a positive statement deducing conclusions from documented evidence. The following considerations have guided the writing of the present report.

Counseling psychology, particularly in its important components of vocational psychology and vocational counseling, is in need of careful reexamination and clarification at this time. The scientific and professional interests of the members of Division 17 are multiple and complex. Some pulling

This report has been approved by the 1960-61 and the 1961-62 Executive Committees of the Division of Counseling Psychology.

together of some of the main threads in the more recent development of the Division is desirable.

The relatively new label, *Counseling Psychology,* has caused this well established field of work to be frequently compared with *Clinical Psychology* and other areas of specialization. Evaluation of the overlapping and differentiating features of these various areas of specialization is desirable.

If Counseling Psychology, or any other field of psychology, appears to be contributing to human welfare, this distinctive contribution should be defined from time to time and suggestions for strengthening it should be proposed.

THE EMERGENCE OF COUNSELING PSYCHOLOGY

In some ways counseling psychology is one of the newest psychological specialty areas; in other ways it is one of the oldest. The name *Counseling Psychology* was adopted by Division 17 in 1953, replacing its earlier name, *Counseling and Guidance.* The shift represented more than a mere change of name; it represented a change in direction, the meaning of which is gradually being clarified. So, although for several decades psychologists have been participating in some of the kinds of activity now considered to be within the province of counseling psychology, it is only recently that the identity of a *counseling psychologist* has taken shape.

The clearest available description of the new specialty can be found in the report of the Committee on Definition, Division of Counseling Psychology (APA, 1956). In a brief account of historical origins, the committee identified three trends that had merged in this specialty: vocational guidance, psychometrics, and personality development. The emphases now characteristic of counseling psychology were said to be: (a) the development of an individual's perception of self; (b) the individual's achievement of harmony with the environment; and (c) the influencing of society to recognize individual differences and to encourage the fullest development of all persons within it. Counseling psychology concerns itself with individuals' strengths rather than their weaknesses, with their utilization of environmental resources as well as with their self-perceptions.

Following upon this broadening of the concept of counseling psychology to cover more than had been covered by the vocational guidance concept was a decision of the Veterans Administration to establish a new kind of major psychological position in hospitals and clinics—to make use of psychologists who concentrate on helping patients to take their places in the world of work and community life rather than on attempting to cure their "illnesses." Similar trends are in evidence in various other medical settings.

Since 1952, the Division of Counseling Psychology has issued policy studies concerning the definition of the specialty (APA, 1956), the training of counseling psychologists (APA, 1952), practicum training (APA, 1952), internships (APA, 1960), the role of counseling psychology in the training of school counselors (APA, 1961), and the characteristics, attitudes, and expectations of its members (APA, 1959). Besides the formal studies that have led to official reports, the Division has sponsored symposia at conventions and a particularly fruitful series of local and regional discussions that have generated much valuable information for planning policies and activities.

In 1954, a new journal, the *Journal of Counseling Psychology,* was established by a group of members of the Division. In 1955 the American Board of Examiners in Professional Psychology changed the title of one of its specialty areas from *Counseling and Guidance* to *Counseling Psychology.*

The question of similarities and differences between counseling and clinical psychology has arisen again and again, and an increasing amount of clarity with regard to this issue has been attained.

STUDIES OF COUNSELING PSYCHOLOGISTS

We can form some impression of the nature of counseling psychology by analyzing data about Division 17, about training programs, about ABEPP, and about the authors who publish in the *Journal of Counseling Psychology.*

Let us first look at the Division. An examination of membership totals since 1955, the first year in which they are given in the Directory, shows that there has been a steady growth (see Table 1). Division 17 was one of the larger divisions to start with; it was third in size in 1955 and was third in 1961. It has gained membership regularly and has increased in size 38.6%. Eight of the 17 APA divisions in existence during the full six-year period show a higher rate of gain; eight show a lower rate.

In the 1959 report of the Committee on Divisional Functions referred to above, some concern was expressed at the finding that the median age of members at the time of the study, 1957, was 44, and that only 22% of the respondents indicated that counseling was their principal job function. It was also found, however, that about half of the members considered that their primary loyalty was to counseling psychology and that in this subgroup there was a larger proportion than in the division as a whole of persons with specialized training in the counseling area who reported counseling as their main function.

A study of the characteristics of persons who have joined Division 17 since it was constituted under its present name has recently been made by Tiedeman and Mastroianni (1961). It shows that these new members are somewhat younger, on the average, than those studied earlier and that they are more definitely committed to counseling psychology as a specialty. The median age for non-Fellows (called associates before 1958 and either associates or members since that time) is about 37. About 35% of this group of new members is under 35, 46% 35 through 44, and 19% 45 and over. The median age of persons elected to fellowship since 1952 is about 41. About 6% of the recent fellows are under 35, 56% 35 through 44, and 38% 45 or over.

About half of the new members belong to Division 17 only, and another quarter have affiliated with only one other division. Although Division 12, Clinical Psychology, is the one chosen with the greatest frequency, only about

Table 1. Divisional growth rates — 1955-1961

Divi-sion	1955 Member-ship	1957 Member-ship	1957 % In-crease	1959 Member-ship	1959 % In-crease	1960 Member-ship	1960 % In-crease	1961 Member-ship	1961 % In-crease	1955-61 % In-crease
1	490	493	.6	548	11.2	596	8.8	634	6.4	29.4
2	260	277	6.5	419	51.3	538	28.4	641	19.1	146.5
3	612	651	6.4	770	18.3	789	2.5	836	6.0	36.6
5	497	555	11.7	621	11.9	638	2.7	651	2.0	31.0
7	448	534	20.2	593	11.0	616	3.9	632	2.6	41.1
8	846	870	2.8	1151	32.3	1346	16.9	1509	12.1	78.4
9	672	697	3.7	797	14.3	806	1.1	850	5.4	26.5
10	75	101	34.7	114	12.9	118	3.5	126	6.8	68.0
12	1711	1907	10.9	2269	19.0	2376	4.7	2466	3.8	44.1
13	233	236	1.3	230	-2.5	232	.9	231	-.4	-.8
14	514	593	15.4	713	20.2	734	2.9	756	3.0	47.1
15	453	483	6.6	528	9.3	555	5.1	567	2.2	25.2
16	348	531	52.6	683	28.6	712	4.2	752	5.6	116.1
17	757	839	10.8	938	11.8	993	5.9	1049	5.6	38.6
18	177	214	20.9	218	1.9	227	4.1	267	17.6	50.8
19	249	249	0	271	8.8	276	1.8	292	5.8	17.3
20	204	216	5.9	222	2.8	238	7.2	238	0	16.7
21				229		273	19.2	298	9.2	—
22				181		246	35.9	749	304.5	

Note: 1955–57 and 1957–59 are two-year comparisons.

18% of the new members and 25% of the new fellows belong to it. Other divisions chosen fairly frequently are Division 5 (Evaluation and Measurement), Division 8 (Personality and Social), Division 15 (Educational), and Division 16 (School).

There is reason to believe that the overlap of Division 17 with Division 12 (which was 25% in 1957) will be less as the years pass. In the 1940s many APA members opted for charter membership in several divisions, some of which were not then or are not now their primary field; psychologists, however, tend to retain such memberships at the nominal cost of a few dollars a year. The younger members of divisions probably are less likely to seek or to be elected to many divisional memberships. It appears too that Division 8 is an increasingly important scientific base for counseling psychologists.

An analysis of the positions in which the persons recently joining the Division are employed indicates that, although there is a good deal of diversity, by far the most common setting is a college or university. The non-fellows are most likely to be working as counselors in college counseling centers and as teachers. The fellows tend to be concerned mainly with teaching and administration.

Another recent study (Peterson & Featherstone, 1962) also suggests that there is considerable uniformity in the positions held by counseling psychologists. This is a survey of what graduates of APA-approved counseling psychology programs are now doing. Information about position and job setting was obtained from 294 of the 337 graduates of 27 training programs. (Three of the 30 approved programs did not report.) Over three-fourths of the graduates are concentrated in four positions: counseling psychologist, faculty member, director of program, and psychologist (specialty not designated). Only 6% classify themselves as clinical psychologists. About half work in college and university settings, and the rest are distributed over a wide range of settings, most of them nonmedical in nature. About 4% work for public school systems. Very few are engaged in private practice.

Together, these two studies of recent entrants to the profession suggest that there is a fairly large core of positions and duties now being identified with this particular specialty.

Another source of data about the identity of counseling psychologists is the *Journal of Counseling Psychology*. During its first seven years, 1954-1960, inclusive, 384 authors were represented. Out of this number 312 are members of APA and 139 are members of Division 17. Sixty-three are members of Division 12. Only 25 are members of both Division 12 and Division 17. The 384 authors work in a wide variety of settings, including 98 different colleges and universities, 21 businesses and industries, and 25 government agencies and social institutions. Of the 312 who are APA members, 102 list counseling as their primary interest, and the stated interests of the others cover a wide variety of theoretical and applied fields. This suggests that counseling psychology is a specialty with a hard core of uniqueness but that ideas from many other areas are seen as relevant to this specialty.

If we examine the evidence provided in a National Science Foundation bulletin (NSF, 1960) with regard to doctorates awarded in 1958 and 1959, we have still another way of judging how this psychological specialty is faring in comparison with others. Table 2 gives these figures. Again we see that, although counseling is not one of the largest psychological specialties, it is certainly not one of the smallest. It is likely that the numbers given are underestimates, since some counseling psychologists may be included in the *Educational* category.

Table 2. Doctorates awarded in 1958 and 1959 in psychology

	1958	*1959*
Total	779	811
Experimental, Comparative, Physiological	151	204
Human Engineering	6	6
Social	74	71
Clinical	275	262
Counseling and Guidance	52	60
Developmental, Gerontological	17	27
Industrial and Personnel	28	43
Educational	82	65
Psychometrics	23	22
Psychology, General	63	35
Psychology, Other	8	16

Membership characteristics: Summary. One might safely suggest the following inferences from the foregoing information:

a. If Division growth rate is used as a criterion, then the state of health of counseling psychology resembles the state of health of psychology as a whole.

b. The newer members of the Division are reducing the average age of the Divisional membership and have a wide range of interests outside of their primary interest in counseling. It is apparent that they do not live in professional isolation.

c. Most counseling psychologists, whether new Division members, recent Ph.D.'s, or writers for the *Journal of Counseling Psychology,* are employed in educational institutions. Very few label themselves other than counseling psychologists, teachers, or, for the older ones, administrators. They do *not* call themselves clinical psychologists or school psychologists, and very few are in private practice.

d. Only a small proportion of the total securing doctorates in psychology do so in counseling. Far outnumbered by those in the experimental and clinical fields (perhaps they should be), they are numerically in the neighborhood of those taking degrees in social and educational psychology and considerably ahead of those taking the degree in industrial psychology. It is a "medium-sized" field which has good evidences of viability.

COMPARISONS OF COUNSELING AND CLINICAL PSYCHOLOGY

It is when one compares the development of counseling psychology with that of clinical psychology that one tends to become concerned about the counseling specialty. Although the growth *rates* of Division 12 and Division 17 shown in Table 1 are not very different, the absolute numbers of clinical doctorates are much higher than are the numbers for counseling. Training institutions report more difficulty in attracting first-rate students into their counseling programs than into their clinical programs.

A difference in the prestige of the two specialties apparently exists. Evidence for this has been presented in a study by Granger (1959). Groups of psychologists, chosen in various ways, were asked to rank for prestige 20 occupations within the field of psychology. All groups doing the ranking showed a considerable amount of agreement. Seven of the 12 groups assigned *Counseling Psychologist* the lowest rank of all the positions requiring the Ph.D. training.

Studies cited in the previous section indicate that there is a considerable amount of overlap between clinical and counseling psychology. The 1959 report of the Committee on Divisional Functions, to which reference has been made above, states that although 40% of the members belong only to Division 17 and that sizable numbers belong to Division 5 (Evaluation and Measurement), Division 15 (Educational), Division 14 (Industrial and Business), and Division 8 (Personality), the largest amount of overlapping membership is with Division 12 (Clinical). As of 1957, 25% of the members of Division 17 also belonged to Division 12. The Tiedeman and Mastroianni study showed that the overlap is somewhat lower for new members.

Paterson and Lofquist (1960) found that there is a large amount of overlap in training programs for clinical and counseling psychology. In view of this overlap and of the prestige differential favoring the clinical specialty, it is not strange that beginning graduate students are often attracted to the clinical rather than to the counseling major. The availability of some kinds of financial support, for clinical but not for counseling students, may also influence such decisions.

Counseling psychology also comes off badly in comparison with clinical so far as ABEPP certification is concerned. As of early 1960, 296 psychologists had earned the diploma by examination in clinical, only 28 in counseling. The facts mentioned above with regard to where counseling psychologists work may have a bearing on this situation, however. Since few work in medical settings or engage in private practice, counselors may see less need for certification.

THE DISTINCTIVE CHARACTERISTICS
OF COUNSELING PSYCHOLOGY

In spite of these indications that clinical psychology often looks more attractive to students than counseling does, and despite the fact that there is a large area of knowledge considered to be common to the two training programs, the kinds of evidence we have considered seem to indicate that there is an area peculiar to counseling, one not covered by clinical psychology as it is usually defined. One of the first attempts to delineate this was the report by Perry (1955) prepared for a conference on Psychotherapy and Counseling. Although the distinction here is between two functions or processes rather than between the clinical and counseling professional specialties, it is relevant to our purposes. Perry's view was that although counseling and psychotherapy cannot be sharply separated, counseling is primarily concerned with "role" problems such as education, vocation, marriage, and so forth, and psychotherapy with intra-personal conflicts.

In a recent study, Brigante, Haefner, and Woodson (1962) asked clinical and counseling psychologists in University and VA positions to indicate what they considered the similarities and differences between the two specialties to be. Both groups agreed that it is more characteristic of counseling psychologists to work with normal people and people having vocational and educational problems, to use interest and aptitude tests and paper and pencil personality tests rather than projective techniques, and to try to find environments compatible with clients' personality structures rather than to try to change their personalities. They agreed also that counseling psychologists are less likely than clinical psychologists to focus upon clients' past behavior, to discover and work through their major conflict areas, and to interpret their motives to them. There are several areas the respondents saw as equally characteristic of the two groups and several on which they disagreed.

When we consider these discussions and look at the contribution counseling psychologists are making and can make to society, we can summarize what is important about the specialty by saying that it focuses on *plans* individuals must make to play productive *roles* in their social environments. Whether the person being helped with such planning is sick or well, abnormal or normal, is really irrelevant. The focus is on assets, skills, strengths, possibilities for further development. Personality difficulties are dealt with only when they constitute obstacles to the individual's forward progress.

Regardless of how the lines are eventually drawn in applied psychology, it would seem that past and present demand for this special kind of service presents us as policy makers in psychology with a responsibility to plan for its development.

PLANS TO FURTHER THE DEVELOPMENT OF
COUNSELING PSYCHOLOGY

The preceding survey of various kinds of evidence suggests that, although the counseling psychology profession is flourishing, training for it in psychology departments perhaps is not. If we agree on the importance of the specialty, our responsibility becomes that of taking steps that will insure a continuous flow of able, well-trained persons into this type of work.

There would seem to be two principal directions the development of training for counseling psychology could take. The first would be *to view this specialty as a kind of subspecialty within the broad clinical area.* This would call for a merging of the present clinical and counseling training programs and for encouraging some graduate students to place more emphasis on mental health rather than on mental illness, on problems within the normal range rather than at the extremes of deviation, and on the relationships of individuals to their environment rather than on intra-psychic relationships.

The trouble with this proposal is that the distinctive counseling emphases may not be adequately taught in such joint training programs. It is too easy to assume that any clinical psychologist with a Ph.D. is competent to interpret a Strong or a DAT profile, to facilitate good vocational decisions, or to assess occupational assets in an inexperienced worker, even if he has never had any training at all in these special techniques. Examples of situations where this has occurred are not hard to find.

The opposite policy would be to attempt *to increase the distinctiveness of counseling psychology programs and to attempt to make them attractive to students.* It does not seem to matter whether the curriculum is placed in an arts and science psychology department or under a psychology staff in a school of education. It matters a great deal whether the curriculum is psychologically sound and whether the courses are taught by psychologists. The practice in some institutions of adding courses in group measurement and occupational information to a clinical psychology program or of adding courses in personality dynamics and clinical psychology to an educational psychology program or a pupil personnel program does not provide a counseling psychology program. Nor does it develop respect for the program.

The areas essential to a counseling psychology doctoral program have been stated and re-stated. We believe that these are essential areas, each to be offered by people qualified in that area. There has been quite enough gerrymandering of graduate counseling programs.

Counseling psychologists have never asked for completely independent training programs; they only insist that beyond a common core of scientific psychology and related disciplines for all doctorates and an additional common core of psychological training for all doctorates in the "helping" branches of psychology, there are some distinctive courses, seminars, and practica that fall under the rubric of counseling psychology.

What needs to be done?

1.   Publicize the need for properly qualified counseling psychologists. There is no lack of professional positions. We simply have not communicated what we know to be the demand in colleges, schools, business, hospitals, and government agencies generally. Among other things, we should make available to undergraduates more information about the nature of the counseling specialty so that more of them will be aware of it when they lay their plans for graduate work.

2.   Coordinate the best school counselor graduate programs at the two-year M.A. and doctoral levels with the doctoral level counseling psychology programs. In curricular requirements and in professional objectives, there is considerable overlap in these fields. Interdepartmental programs are functioning successfully in several institutions.

3.   Recognize that the roots of counseling psychology are as much in social psychology, personality theory, developmental psychology, the psychology of individual differences, and the psychology of learning as they are in abnormal psychology, if not more so, and on this premise encourage sound training in these fields as a basis for practice and research.

4.   Recognize and capitalize on the prevalence of many counseling assistant-ships in universities, schools, rehabilitation centers, and other public and private agencies, assistantships that provide good experience in counseling, as well as graduate support. They are almost as good as fellowships—better in some situations where the supervision on the job is a benefit not found in a fellowship. Publicize also the VA and OVR traineeships and fellowships. These are valuable and as good as any to be found.

5.   See that practicum facilities are distinctive for counseling psychology students. Clarify and insist upon the distinctiveness. Experience in hospitals or medical settings, no matter how good, is *not* a substitute for experience in school settings, college counseling bureaus, community agencies, placement settings, and so forth. These supervised experiences require qualified supervisors both in the agency and in the graduate school. No substitutes can be accepted.

6.   Seek to establish post-doctoral training programs in the counseling specialty, programs that will enable psychologists of all varieties to obtain the special kinds of knowledge and skill required for counseling at the time when they become interested in the counseling specialty.

7.   Make clear that the resources of the entire university are necessary to develop a good counseling psychologist—social sciences as well as behavioral sciences (and both of these in greater proportion than technique or applied courses). Rightly conceived and staffed, a counseling program can command as much respect in the university as any other applied psychology program.

8.   Require that counseling theory and counseling practice courses are taught by individuals who are not only qualified psychologists but have had substantial blocks of experience in the practice of counseling. Theory or practice courses in counseling psychology require experienced counselors, not merely psychologists.

CONCLUSIONS

The rate of growth of counseling psychology has been normal despite limited financial support for the development of graduate programs and the support of graduate students. In addition, this specialty has made progress in developing a concept of role and function that is broader than vocational guidance but different from clinical psychology in its emphasis upon development, assessment, plan, and role. In view of both growth and increased clarity of function, it seems clear that policies designed to maintain and strengthen these distinctive characteristics should be pursued. The social demand for well prepared counseling psychologists is great and continues to increase. The Division of Counseling Psychology has a deep professional obligation to meet this social need. This is an appropriate time to clarify and coordinate its goals and to develop a rigorous program.

REFERENCES

American Psychological Association. Division of Counseling and Guidance, Committee on Counseling Training. Recommended standards for training counseling psychologists to the doctorate level. Practicum training of counseling psychologists. *American Psychologist,* 1952, *7,* 175–188.

American Psychological Association. Division of Counseling Psychology, Committee on Definition. Counseling psychology as a specialty. *American Psychologist,* 1956, *11,* 282–285.

American Psychological Association. Division of Counseling Psychology, Committee on Divisional Functions. *The Division of Counseling Psychology studies its membership.* 1959. (Multilithed report)

American Psychological Association. Division of Counseling Psychology, Committee on Internship Standards. *Recommended standards for internships in counseling psychology.* 1960. (Multilithed report)

American Psychological Association. Division of Counseling Psychology. *The scope and standards of preparation in psychology for school counselors.* 1961. (Multilithed report).

Brigante, T. R., Haefner, D. P., & Woodson, W. B. Clinical and counseling psychologists' perceptions of their specialties. *Journal of Counseling Psychology,* 1962, *9,* 225–231.

Granger, S. G. Psychologists' prestige rankings of 20 psychological occupations. *Journal of Counseling Psychology,* 1959, *6,* 183–188.

National Science Foundation. *The science doctorates of 1958 and 1959.* Washington: U. S. Government Printing Office, 1960.

Paterson, D. G., & Lofquist, L. H. A note on the training of clinical and counseling psychologists. *American Psychologist,* 1960, *15,* 365–366.

Perry, W. G. The findings of the commission in counseling and guidance. *Annals of the New York Academy of Science,* 1955, *63,* 396–407.

Peterson, R., & Featherstone, F. Occupations of counseling psychologists. *Journal of Counseling Psychology,* 1962, *9,* 221–224.

Tiedeman, D. V., & Mastroianni, W. J. *Scuttle the Division of Counseling Psychology? Nonsense!* Unpublished paper, 1961.

Chapter 12
Status and Prospect in Counseling Psychology: 1962

DAVID V. TIEDEMAN

THE STATUS OF COUNSELING PSYCHOLOGY—1961

During 1960–61 I had the pleasure of collaborating with Professors Leona Tyler (chairman) and C. Gilbert Wrenn in preparing a report on the status of counseling psychology (1961). Although the Division of Counseling Psychology is itself solely responsible for preparation and circulation of that survey, the Education and Training Board of APA helped to stimulate the undertaking by questioning the distinctiveness, and ultimately the existence, of the Division. Should counseling psychology be perpetuated a bit longer as a unique form of psychological practice?

As you know, Tyler, Wrenn, and I offered justification for the continuing existence of the Division in terms of:

1. a distinguished history of responsible accomplishment;
2. a substantial and healthy rate of growth during the immediately preceding decade;
3. a lively journal, named after our Division, which provides a publication medium for our members;
4. existing specialized training programs;
5. the possibility of qualifying for a diploma, from the American Board of Examiners in Professional Psychology, which denotes special training in our field;
6. opportunity for employment which is reasonably specific as to the necessary training and certification; and,
7. goals, purposes, and techniques which are distinctly different from their counterparts in the field of clinical psychology.

Although we felt justified in urging continuation and improvement in counseling psychology on the above grounds, we also noted: (1) that the field

A paper prepared for "Symposium: The Future Development of Counseling Psychology," American Psychological Association, St. Louis, Missouri, 1 September 1962. The section on theory in this paper is from the paper *From the currently observed to the currently desired: A model for the science of purposeful action in guidance,* which I have prepared with my colleague, Frank L. Field. I am indebted to Mr. Field for letting me reuse the section here and for helping in developing this paper.

of clinical psychology presently enjoys a prestige above that of the field of counseling psychology; and, (2) that the fields of clinical and counseling psychology both stem from a common tradition in psychology.

Tyler, Wrenn, and I did not feel that those conditions—of prestige and similarity—invalidated our recommendation for the continuation and improvement of our practice, however. In fact, we suggested that the presently lower prestige of the counseling psychologist ought to challenge us, not disenchant us.

A DISSATISFIED PROFESSIONAL—1962

I trust that my participation in the framing of that latest "official" report on the status of counseling psychology makes my commitment to the field perfectly clear. I *am* a committed professional, one with a vested interest if you will. For me the question is not: Should we have a field of counseling psychology? Rather, the problem is: How can we best improve practice in counseling psychology?

However, the fact that I am committed to the practice of counseling psychology in no way binds me to a present condition of satisfaction with that practice. In fact, it is my present dissatisfaction with theory and practice in counseling psychology which I first want to specify today in order that I may later offer what may prove to be potentially useful opinions on the prospect in our field.

PROBLEMS IN THE PROFESSION OF COUNSELING PSYCHOLOGY—1962

My thesis today is that the field of counseling psychology, although successful in the past, presently has only a weak potential for growth because: (1) our espousal of "counseling," with the concurrent negation of "guidance," focused us upon a *single* technique without due regard for purpose, setting, and the arousal of motives; and, (2) our espousal of a mode of science typical of psychology in general has caused us usually to ignore the essential part of the object of our work, a person *becoming*. (I will delineate this concept later in order to avoid metaphysics.)

I shall devote the remainder of my time to consideration of these dual problems—technique in relation to purpose and setting, and science in relation to goal. In doing so, I shall attempt to develop a linguistic frame for guidance in which it is possible to consider purpose, theory, function, and authority, *simultaneously*. The major issue will then be discussed; namely, will the Division of Counseling Psychology embrace guidance as its area of concern or will it continue to embrace merely counseling as has been true since 1953?

GUIDANCE-IN-EDUCATION: A STATEMENT OF PURPOSE
AND OF ITS CONSEQUENCES

Guidance is practiced in an educational setting. The purpose of guidance is therefore to be found in education.

Education is arranged so that the dual processes of teaching and learning can take place efficiently. In teaching, an informed person attempts to empower a less informed person to act with his knowledge. Such knowledge is knowledge "that"—that is, "content." Of course, knowledge "that" is no more than the *beliefs,* and their bases, of a presumably respected person. Furthermore, implicit at all times, is the assumption that knowledge "that," as taught, is of functional value, and should be wanted by the student. At issue in my further argument shall be the origin of belief *in the student himself.* Is valu*ing* (perhaps adverse) deliberately incorporated as a part of teaching?

If the student is to become responsible and hence to "outlive his teachings," *he* must learn "how" as well as "that." In learning "how" a student must consider the *process* of education simultaneously with its content. The process of education as Heathers (1961) has noted consists of: (1) acquiring the power to assimilate through the framing and solving of problems; (2) exercising initiative for, and during the course of, problem solving; and, (3) evaluating one's efforts at problem solving using mastery as a criterion.

Since the process of education is hollow without a content, a fourth aspect of the process of education is the teacher's expectation of some previously impossible action by the student. The expectation of such skilled action, and training for it, is what a teacher ordinarily provides in education.

I contend that the purpose of guidance can be found only in the *simultaneous* consideration of content and process, the basic duality in education. If the student is to have benefit of expert help with *each* aspect of this duality in education, a *division* of responsibility between teacher and counselor is mandatory. The teacher should be primarily responsible for professing content, for "setting the stage" for a student's mastery of the process, and for training the student in the process. The counselor, for his part, should be responsible for the goal of process and should be a student of content only as needed for conduct of his primary responsibility. The three important consequences of this premise about a needed revision in the organization of responsibility for education are: (1) the purpose of our profession should be guidance-in-education, not just "counseling"; (2) the counselor should work in educational settings as an autonomous but collaborating professional with authority *equal* to that of the teacher and with primary responsibility for a student's mastery of the process of education; and, (3) to reach our ultimate goal of helping each citizen to a condition of responsible autonomy, we must advocate that guidance-in-education be professed in *all* aspects of the educational endeavor: school, college, education in industry, and education in adult life including life upon and after retirement.

GUIDANCE-IN-EDUCATION: A LINGUISTIC FRAME FOR THEORY

Purposeful Action

A goal, if defined as "desirable *future* state," certainly cannot exist prior to the means for its achievement. But a *concept* of this desirable future state can exist in the present. In these terms it is quite possible to compare the present state of X with the current concept of a future state of X, to note the difference, and to choose, develop, modify, and perform a series of actions designed to reduce this difference.

This process is what we mean by the term *purposeful action*. *Purpose* refers to the emerging pattern relating certain actions, specifically those actions that appear to decrease the difference between the currently observed and the currently desirable states.

The Origination of, and the Commitment to, Goals

A person moves *from* his currently observed condition *to* his currently desired condition in the transition necessary upon encountering a *discontinuity* in his life. For example, the transition from junior high school to high school is one such discontinuity.

The important point for guidance-in-education during the transition potentially inherent in a discontinuity is *the effect of that transition upon the person's attitude toward himself and his situation.* Some of the fundamental outcomes sought in guidance are: (1) personal satisfaction; (2) responsibility; (3) openness to subsequently needed modifications; and, (4) commitment to flexible, but not diffuse, goals.

Above all, the desired future state, once achieved, must continue to have a respected meaning for the person. The person cannot find his regard for himself greatly depleted because of the realized transition. Otherwise a once-valued objective can readily become an empty accomplishment.

Although I have great respect for the several technologies we have developed to deal with a number of life's discontinuities—the transitions from high school to college or work are good examples—I do not believe that any *one* of such technologies is sufficient for the goal I have suggested. I suspect that a person must both *practice* and *recognize* the achievement of purposeful action in the context of life's discontinuities before he can have any very meaningful experience which will help him control himself in his life situation. Practice with how many discontinuities is required? Four or five? Forty or fifty? I just do not know. I have not found any others who know either. Of course, the result of practice can be a function of the degree of recognition or consciousness involved, too.

Despite our present ignorance regarding the matter of *managing the origination of discontinuities* for the purpose of increasing satisfaction, responsibility, flexibility, and commitment, I suggest that we seriously consider setting this as the next challenge to those of us in counseling psychology. We have much to learn about discontinuities and how to intensify the awareness of ego process. How many trials are useful? When? In what sequence? With what potential consequences inherent in each discontinuity? With what help in which part of the sequence?

There are obviously sufficient problems in charting the relation of discontinuity to self-awareness, initiative, and object mastery to intrigue the "scientist" in each of us. It would be a real pleasure to begin reading articles, in "our" literature, dealing with the experiencing of *two* or more discontinuities, rather than one as is the current mode. We will first have to allay a doubt about freedom and the science of guidance, however. Let's now consider that doubt before going on with other implications.

GUIDANCE-IN-EDUCATION: FREEDOM AND THE APPLICATION OF THE SCIENCE OF GUIDANCE

Obviously, during the transition associated with the encountering of a discontinuity, a person may revise: (1) his opinion of his observed state; (2) what he wants; and/or (3) the basis on which his movement into the condition of discontinuity was founded.

Goals are inevitably in question continuously during such revisions. Because goals are at issue at such times, can a second party do something useful about the purposeful action of a person without thereby limiting the freedom of that person? I believe that a counselor can if he has *his* problem clearly in mind.

I have previously stated that the concern of the counselor during the transition potentially inherent in a discontinuity is the effect of that transition upon the person's attitude toward himself and his situation. Since the focus for guidance is therefore upon regard for self and others in a person's responsible practice of purposeful action, this is the only aspect of a person's freedom upon which the counselor brings his *scientific* knowledge to bear. It is literally true that the counselor must examine the currently observed state and desire and the plan for action *with his student* if the counselor is to accomplish that goal, however. This examination brings the counselor into direct consideration of the experience and means-ends sequences upon which the behavior of the student is probably founded. The counselor must limit *his* favoring of goals in direct relation to his science of managing self-regard and personal responsibility during the potential transition inherent in discontinuities. Otherwise the counselor will overstep the right for intervention ordinarily accorded those associated with education. The solution lies then in the fact that a student *and* the counselor consider the student's purpose as citizens but the counselor considers such data as a professional in relation to its potential effect upon the self-regard of the student. Furthermore, I hope it is obvious from this statement that the science of guidance *must* go more extensively into the *students'* consideration of their *commonly* considered data than is common in the behavioral sciences. Our regular techniques of investigation in experimental psychology are therefore insufficient for the goal of guidance.

To recapitulate, can we promulgate idiosyncratic purpose and related meaning without *loss* to the freedom of students?[1] For me the answer is negative only if we specify a particular *kind* of idiosyncrasy rather than *that* one develop idiosyncratic meaning for life. With specification of a *kind* of idiosyncrasy it is possible to favor, to require, and even to condition. Under such conditions guidance becomes noneducative, nondevelopmental. This is not true, at least of *the* idiosyncratic meaning actually achieved, if one specifies only *that* a person develop the convictions that can bind and support his life—that is, make it less random and more volitional. Hence we must bind an applied science of guidance only to the goal of fostering the responsible pursuit of idiosyncrasy. It is to this end that we must write the testable, and later, tested, propositions of a science which permit a practitioner to work with a little confidence.

GUIDANCE-IN-EDUCATION: PROSPECT IN COUNSELING PSYCHOLOGY

In this paper, I have noted my belief that the field of counseling psychology is *seemingly* in good health at the present time, but that it is without much potential for further advancement. Because I am committed to perpetuation of our interests, I then offered a statement of setting, purpose, theory, science, function, and authority, which, for me, are "of a piece." I purposely developed that statement to appeal to the "scholar" in each of us. There *is* a real problem in the science of behavioral *change*. The problem *is* worthy of our attention as scholars. If just the scientific problem I have outlined were to become the object of scholarly attention by members of the Division, the Division could enter a period of renaissance. Unfortunately, however, a renaissance so founded would not in my judgment strike to the *cause* of our present predicament. I believe that we are now floundering because we are *not* resolving our conflicts between: (1) profession and science; and, (2) guidance and counseling.

I think that we in counseling psychology should recognize that we *are* professionals who represent an aspect of professional practice in behavioral science. We *are* committed to *act*. Furthermore, I think we should commit

---

[1] If this seems paradoxical, remember that no living organism is entirely free; it must adapt or die. The freedom we seek for students of all ages is freedom from: 1) ignorance; 2) false information; and 3) conditioning for the achievement of goals that are not adaptive or not the students'.

ourselves to act in conjunction with *educators*. It is through education that we can advocate *managed* discontinuities, in fact a *series* of them. It is in education that we find responsibility for seeing that the goal, and the process of education become identical—as Bruner (1962) so gracefully puts the case. *Let's make guidance-in-education our professional problem again.*

Our present conflict with regard to our commitment is causing us to shirk responsibility for developments in education which are now possible. These developments include:

1. incorporation of the process of education as a goal of education;
2. establishing, for counselors in education, a position of authority equal to that of the teacher;
3. making the practice of guidance truly professional;
4. upgrading the status of personnel work in education;
5. spreading our membership from college to schools, to education in industry, and to other forms of adult education;
6. developing an integrated theory of behavioral *change* through the fostering of purposeful action; and,
7. describing a professional function which is attractive *after* qualification as well as before—that is, a source of satisfaction from *practice*, rather than the prospect of easy access to professional *status*.

I trust it is obvious that I want these developments to become a part of the goal of our field. Whether we realize it or not, we *are* professionals, not scholars. We *do* need a specific theory of behavioral change and we must do the needed research—since not many of our colleagues in psychology understand what we want. We *are* educators as well as psychologists. We *do* represent the liberation possible through education rather than the training which is so frequently obtained.

As I have indicated throughout my paper, if we are to lead in these developments, we must:

1. make our goal clearer;
2. give up our singular fascination with counseling as our only technique;
3. become more active in education of all kinds;
4. improve and expand our training; and,
5. settle our personal ambiguity about the value of a professional in psychology and of research on the development of purposeful action in which the subject participates in the formulation and review of information.

As I reflect upon the magnitude of this task, I do not consider our prospect for further development a certain one. In fact our prospect is quite precarious. We are currently a band of scholars, *not* of professionals. We are psychologists, *not* educators. We are envious of affiliation with medicine, *not* with education. We are misled by an inappropriate view of *applied* behavioral science.

The officers of our Division are now aware that we need a new basis for action. This is a condition presently in our favor. In addition, this symposium indicates that a number of us are disturbed by the current state of affairs and are desirous of clarifying what we currently desire so that our action in reaching it may become more purposeful. Finally, I do not personally despair. I *am* part of a training resource which I am trying to set on the course I have described.

But how about you? With each of you rests the fate of counseling psychology. What lies before us, consolidation or further differentiation? May we have the wisdom to elect further differentiation!

REFERENCES

Bruner, J. S. *On knowing.* Cambridge, Mass.: Harvard University Press, 1962.

Heathers, G. L. *Notes on the strategy of educational reform.* New York: The author, Experimental Teaching Center, School of Education, New York University, 1961. (Duplicated)

Tiedeman, D. V., & Field, F. L. Guidance: The science of purposeful action applied through education. *Harvard Educational Review,* 1962, *32,* 483–501.

Tyler, L., Wrenn, C. G., & Tiedeman, D. V. *The current status of counseling psychology.* New York: Dr. Dorothy M. Clendenen, Secretary, Division 17, The Psychological Corporation, 304 East 45th Street, December 5, 1961. (Multilith)

Chapter 13
Some Alternative Roads for
Counseling Psychology: 1962

IRWIN A. BERG

INTRODUCTION

In the present discussion, I shall talk of counseling psychology as a *psychological specialty;* that is, as a legitimately special area of psychology in the same sense that physiological, clinical, or social psychology are special fields. Thus I shall not consider counseling psychology as psychology useful for a special field in the sense that a school of law or a department of music might possibly find courses in psychology useful. This distinction, I think, is important because *counseling,* as an activity that certainly uses psychological knowledge, and *counseling psychology,* which is a specialty of psychology, are not necessarily the same thing.

The basis for my remarks is partially rooted in a report that Harold B. Pepinsky, E. J. Shoben, Jr., and I, as committee chairman, prepared in 1959. This committee was appointed by the Education and Training Board and asked to report on the status of Counseling Psychology. In 1960, the Education and Training Board requested that the report be published; however, contrary to the E & T Board request, the report was not published. The reasons for this are not entirely clear.

The title of my present report, "Alternative Roads for Counseling Psychology," implies that alternative roads are not only feasible but perhaps necessary. This may seem strange since membership in the APA Division of Counseling Psychology has increased, not in the numbers that clinical psychology has, but the increase is steady and definite. As accurately as I can judge, counseling as an activity is increasing very rapidly but *counseling psychology* is not.

Dr. Gilbert Wrenn reports that in 1959, 223 institutions of higher education had graduate programs in counseling. Virtually all of these programs were conducted by colleges of education. This is true of our most prestigeful programs of counseling psychology such as those at Columbia,

Read at American Psychological Association, Division 17 Symposium, St. Louis, 1962 Annual Convention.

Ohio State, and Minnesota. These programs all make heavy use of psychology courses but much in the same sense that schools of social work and law use psychology. Other very strong programs, such as that of the University of Illinois, have the same curriculum for both clinical and counseling psychology. Several reports from APA Division 17 (Counseling Psychology) have in the past pointed out that the scientific status of counseling psychology is far from satisfactory and that there is a dearth of systematized research. Similarly, the number of counseling psychologists who seek the ABEPP diploma in counseling has declined. In 1959, 114 psychologists registered to take the written examination (ABEPP) for clinical psychology, but only seven registered in counseling.

Be all that as it may, one may justifiably argue that this state does not necessarily indicate that alternative roads are essential. Yet, by the same token, one can indicate some *possible* alternative pathways that counseling *may* take in the future.

ALTERNATIVE ROADS FOR COUNSELING PSYCHOLOGY

Merger with Clinical Psychology

Some very strong programs have already done this—for example, the University of Illinois. The idea would be to have a fusion, not absorption, with a new field that would train for dealing with all sorts of both normal and seriously disturbed persons. Subspecialties of working with particular groups such as the aged, the handicapped, children, and so forth, would be feasible. This alternative would be a fulfillment of Super's (1955) prophecy that "the two fields will merge (into) a more broadly trained and oriented" kind of profession.

Development of a Genuinely Distinctive Program

This would be in accord with Danskin's (1959) idea that we should train counselors first and psychologists second. There are many broad areas that are increasingly important and for which a distinctive program in counseling psychology could be tailored; for example, problems of delinquency, racial strife, the gifted, preparation for retirement, preventive mental health, job and worker retraining in consequence of automation, rehabilitation, mental retardation, and so on. All of these areas could use specially trained counselors who are products of a genuinely distinctive program.

Development of a Technician Level of Counselor Functioning

This would be at the M.A. level and would be in harmony with the Miami Conference Report on graduate training in psychology. We need large numbers of vocational appraisers, counselors, guidance workers, and so forth. We already have a number of such programs in psychology, and the Miami Conference Report of such programs has been published. It is true that there are many activities that can be performed very adequately at a technician level. Also, most Ph.D.'s, after a few years post-doctoral experience, seem to seek broader professional activities and responsibilities. They become administrators or deal with personal problem counseling, and so on. Yet although there is a pressing social need for many M.A.-level technicians, I fear that using such programs at the M.A. level as an alternative road for counseling psychology would mean the disappearance of counseling psychology as *psychology.*

SUMMARY

If an alternative is necessary, and I think it is, I personally favor a program that would include both normal and seriously disturbed persons as a field for study. We do not know where the dividing lines are between normal and pathological states, and we already have clinical psychology extending its professional domain (particularly among private practitioners) to problems of normal persons. Furthermore, we already have solid programs which cover both specialties. Thus I should favor extending and formalizing a new program, preferably with some new name to avoid partisan semantic identifications.

In summary, I should say that *counseling* is a rapidly growing and important professional activity; however, *counseling psychology* as a special field of *psychology* does not seem to have experienced the same growth as a psychological specialty that it has as an educational specialty—that is, its growth has been under the aegis of colleges of education. Perhaps many of the tools and techniques we deal with are historically or by custom found more often in education. The same is largely true of the research; that is, the standardized test lists of vocational requirements (*Dictionary of Occupational Titles*), and so on, are perhaps found more often among professional educators than among psychologists. Whether such is the case or not, it is true that counseling is flourishing in colleges of education but not in departments of psychology. Thus counseling psychology as *psychology* should seriously consider some alternative roads.

REFERENCES

Danskin, D. G. Pavlov, Poe, and Division 17. *Counseling News and Views,* 1959, *12,* 4–6.
Super, D. E. Transition: From vocational guidance to counseling psychology. *Journal of Counseling Psychology,* 1955, *2*(1), 3–9.

THE GREYSTON CONFERENCE: THE PROFESSIONAL PREPARATION OF COUNSELING PSYCHOLOGISTS: 1964

5

Chapter 14
Counseling Psychology since the Northwestern Conference

FRANCIS P. ROBINSON

What has happened to us since the Northwestern Conference some 13 years ago? That conference worked on standards for Ph.D. training to provide for the first time a broad and unified view of our field. With one-third of our members lacking the doctorate (*Counseling News and Views,* November 1950, p. 10) and an evident need for better-trained counselors, the conference aimed to give direction to the then developing university programs. A subcommittee prepared a preliminary document, aided by an APA subsidy of $500. The working paper was reviewed in detail and approved by the conference; the conference report was discussed at the 1951 APA meeting, passed upon by the Divisional Executive Committee, and published as an official paper (APA, 1952).

This committee report has loomed large because of the impetus given by wide-spread collaboration in its development, by its direction-giving nature, and by its immediate application in the setting up of the Veterans Administration program in counseling psychology (Moore & Bouthilet, 1952). This subsidized training program helped set the Ph.D. standard for counseling psychologists, increased the number and subsidized the training of

From Albert S. Thompson and Donald E. Super (Eds.), *The Professional Preparation of Counseling Psychologists: Report of the 1964 Greyston Conference.* (New York: Teachers College Press, © 1964 by Teachers College, Columbia University.)

advanced graduate students in counseling, and lent support to depth and breadth in our conceptualization of professional education.

Our field has shown remarkable growth in the past 13 years. The division has always been one of the largest in APA, varying between second and fourth place in size. Between 1950 and 1960 our numbers increased 61%; the 1963 *Directory* lists 1211 fellows, members, and associates for Division 17 (APA, 1963). We work in an increasing variety of settings as counseling psychologists. Training programs in rehabilitation, school, and pastoral counseling have made use of personnel and ideas from our field.

Other signs of professional development also appeared (*CNV,* June 1960, pp. 4–11). Some early effort went into nomenclature. Division 17's first name of "Counseling and Guidance" was a hash of two common titles. Milton Hahn led in getting our name changed, in 1953, to that of Division of Counseling Psychology. To many of us then, this name did not sound right, but today it is commonly accepted and often borrowed by status seekers as we used to borrow the terms clinical and psychotherapy.

Other developments included the setting up of a Committee on Psychological Terminology in Counseling in 1953 and the starting of the *Journal of Counseling Psychology* in 1954. The success of this independent journal is in itself a sign of the development of the field. The year 1954–55 was a stocktaking and evaluative period. A Committee on the History of Division 17 was appointed so that the details of early developments would not be lost; a Committee on the Definition of Counseling Psychology was charged with noting changes since the Northwestern Conference and with projecting future developments (APA, 1956). In 1955 the setting aside of $1000 for a future conference of importance was a sign of reaching middle-aged security (*CNV,* November 1955, p. 2); eight years later this is the conference! Since 1955 a succession of ad hoc committees have studied the progress of our division— for example, the Committee on Divisional Functions and the Committee on the Current Status of Counseling Psychology (APA, 1961b).

Various events and conditions led to these committee ventures. The APA Policy and Planning Committee suggestion that the divisional structure be simplified stimulated self-studies (*CNV,* November 1954, p. 5; Sanford, 1955). Analyses were made of overlapping membership, of the size of the group belonging only to Division 17, and of answers to a forced-choice questionnaire asking about affiliation if one could belong to only one division. Factor, cluster, and similarity analyses were also carried out of patterns of affiliation within APA (Adkins, 1954; Sakoda, 1955; Sanford, 1955; Thorndike, 1954; and Wrigley, 1957). These varied studies generally showed that counseling psychology is an independent area and that it has a large core of members who feel primary loyalty to it. Even in 1950, early in APA divisional history when it was easy to belong to many divisions and people liked being broadly affiliated, over one-third of Division 17's members belonged only to it (*CNV,* 1950, No. 1); since then, as Samler's paper shows, the custom among new members of APA is more and more to belong to only one division (or, to *no* division) (APA, 1961a; Peterson & Featherstone, 1962).

Because in 1958 one quarter of our members belonged to Division 12 (APA, 1961a), because counseling has close working relationships with clinical psychology in VA hospitals, and perhaps as a result of the strength and wealth of clinical psychology, particular attention has been given over the years to our relationship to this latter field. It is generally agreed but equally generally ignored that we have affiliations with many divisions; actually we have greater *proportional* overlaps with the memberships of seven other divisions than with Division 12 (*CNV,* 1950, No. 1, p. 12; Hahn, 1955). The percentage affiliated with Division 12 is in part a function of its large size in the APA.

Happily the flurry of attempts to simplify APA structure seems to have died down; in turn we witness an avalanche of new divisions. Many of us have now cut the umbilical cords of earlier affiliations, and we stand now a more unified group, ready now to give attention to where we are going (APA, 1961b; *CNV* 1962–1963, No. 2, pp. 5–8; Berdie, 1964; editorials in the *Journal of Counseling Psychology*).

Although these data of growth in size and in unity of purpose indicate a healthy organization, indications of weakness also exist, and some people have viewed our field with gloom. During the 1947–1961 period "only" 32 persons passed the ABEPP examinations for the Diplomate in Counseling Psychology (Yamamoto, 1963). Other data suggest that this finding merely means that few counseling psychologists engage in private practice and so few feel a need for the diploma. Although we have gone into many new work settings, a large proportion continue to work in colleges and universities—for example, 50% in 1948 (Dreese, 1949), and 55% in 1961 (Yamamoto, 1963).

Since about 1958 various persons have commented on the small number of graduate students in counseling psychology and on the small number applying to read papers at APA meetings under Division 17 auspices. Both seem indicative of a drying up of the influx of members and of ideas (*CNV,* November 1958, pp. 5–6; August 1959, pp. 3, 6; 1960–1961, No. 2, pp. 4–11 and No. 3, pp. 10–11). The facts that some training programs attract large numbers of students and that our journal flourishes suggest this should not be looked at as a general trend, but rather that attempts should be made to find reasons for such variations.

One factor is the low status, among students and other psychologists, of counseling psychologists when compared to other Ph.D. psychologists (Granger, 1959; APA, 1961a; Porter & Cook, 1964). We need to give attention to educating our fellow psychologists concerning our contributions, and we need to improve our standards and our foundation in research.

Are we attracting nurturant individuals who make good counselors but poor research workers (Grater, Kell, & Morse, 1961)? The median age at which our members earn the Ph.D. is 36 (Yamamoto, 1963), but the median age for APA in general is 31.2. Thus productive years are lost (Pressey, 1962);

20% of Ph.D. graduates from APA-approved counselor-training programs do not join APA and 60% of the rest never bother to join any division (Peterson & Featherstone, 1962)!

Is the dominance of a few institutions another factor? Two studies, one in 1948 and the other in 1961, show that over half of our members obtained the Ph.D. from six universities (Dreese, 1949; Yamamoto, 1963). If our contribution is important, should we not have more missionary centers? Some progress may be being made here: Goodstein (1963) notes that in the first four volumes of the *Journal of Counseling Psychology* the top six universities contributed 27.5% of the articles, compared to only 23.4% in the next four volumes; furthermore, only two universities are in the top six for both periods.

Although VA support and Education and Training Board evaluation have increased and in some ways improved training facilities, they may also have been sources of difficulty. VA training is oriented toward hospital work, and its presently integrated psychology service has tended to blur distinctions. Paterson and Lofquist (1960) found that many approved university programs make little differentiation between clinical and counseling training. (Myers' paper brings us up-to-date on this point.) It may be that, in an attempt to orient toward hospital treatment, many of the 24 approved programs in counseling psychology fail to deal with the central core of our field. For instance, Yamamoto (1963) notes that, of the six universities awarding the most Ph.D.'s to Division 17 members, only half have APA-approved programs in counseling psychology. Paterson and Lofquist (1960) note that the topics covered in ABEPP examinations for the specialties of clinical and counseling differ little; the Division recently protested ABEPP oral examinations in counseling psychology conducted without adequate representation by our specialty (*CNV,* 1962–1963, No. 1, p. 4). Whereas we are often lumped with clinical psychology by APA agencies, we are excluded from opportunity to obtain certain important training and research grants (*CNV,* December 1960, p. 5). This feeling of the need for change by APA and other agencies was recently restated in the *Journal of Counseling Psychology* (Super, 1963, p. 412).

Various reports on divisional membership turn up another thought-provoking statistic. In 1948 the median age of Division 17 members was 39 (Dreese, 1949); successive reports show an increasing average age, and Yamamoto's (1963) tabulation of the 1961 *APA Directory* shows a median of 48 years. This increase in median age—9 years—represents seven-tenths of the time spanned—that is, 13 years! My own 17% sample of the 1963 *Directory* shows that our typical member is four years older than the median member of other divisions! Worried divisional officers have urged that we bring in young, new blood. However, two points help explain part of this gain in age. First, higher admission standards for the APA have generally raised the age of entrance. Furthermore, new movements tend to be started by young people; the median age of the Northwestern Conference's founding fathers was only 38 years. As older members have become grandfathers the median age has gone up, in spite of the young people coming in. In 1961 Tiedemann and Mastroianni found "that these new members are somewhat younger, on the average, than those studied earlier" (APA, 1961a, p. 3).

The question remains, are we getting enough young members? Two studies show that only 8% of our total membership is under 36 years of age (APA, 1961a; Yamamoto, 1963). My random sample of our divisional membership in 1963 shows 14.5% under 36 years of age, as compared with 19% in other divisions. It may be that the Ph.D. as an admission standard to APA, particularly in the case of our typically late Ph.D., prevents energetic young people from contributing to divisional activities (Pressey, 1962). Our problem is to get more young APA members to join and to be active. The 1963 Division 17 symposium on "Whither Counseling Psychology? Views of Neophytes" is one such step.

When young leaders start a movement, they tend to continue in control and so to prevent the normal entrance of new leaders. As a result the rising generation sometimes sets up new organizations to implement its ideas. This may be a useful means of development, but an organization should also fit changing situations. Hahn early warned of the danger of an inner circle preventing growth in our organization (*CNV*, November 1953); a 1958 constitutional amendment limited the number of terms for which certain Division offices could be held. Past officers have made a consistent effort to become informed about good, new people, but as a rule the known producer is the person appointed to a committee.

Governmental appropriations to increase the number of trained counselors usually designate some particular type of client. Although it can be argued that all such counselors should have the same basic training, the net effect is that the staff and trainees in each program feel that they need to band together to discuss their common problems. In the case of the VA training program this has worked out well within the framework of Division 17. In the case of the VRA, a separate division (Number 22) was set up in APA despite the work of a series of committees on rehabilitation training since 1953. Could Division 17 have been more flexible in working with developments in the rehabilitation field? NDEA appropriations to train secondary school counselors have been aimed at the master's degree level, at trainees who are not eligible for APA membership. But secondary school counselors will soon be expected to obtain sufficient training; those who qualify and who so desire should be welcomed to Division 17. In 1961 only 8% of our members worked in schools (Yamamoto, 1963). We should develop a program to attract and hold qualified school counselors rather than encouraging them, through neglect, to set up a separate division.

Division 17 has supported the NDEA counselor-training program and many of our members have served it as teachers, directors, and consultants. We have inherited one problem, however, from the traditional location of psychology and educational psychology in different colleges, a problem not only of inconvenience but of rivalry. The liberal arts college departments have jealously limited what the colleges of education might teach in psychology, and yet they themselves have not always offered what was needed. Because of this, colleges of education tend to offer technique courses and lack substantive offerings in psychological theory and principles. Because NDEA training programs have had difficulty in ensuring the offerings needed, a Committee on Training in Psychology for School Counselors was appointed in 1960 (APA, 1962). Committee members were selected from educational settings so as to escape the usual reaction to liberal arts college psychologists; the committee also took care to deal only with the psychological aspects of training, so as not to appear to prescribe the total program. The report was met with a storm of aggressive misinterpretation by some counselor trainers in education and by some school counselors who felt threatened by implicit criticisms of their programs and preparation. The danger in this type of reaction is the development of a nonpsychologically based orientation to counseling. Later developments have shown more integrative behavior, but it is obvious that we will have to attack problems occasioned by interdepartmental and interdisciplinary rivalries.

Although this account shows that counseling psychology has grown lustily and has come of age, and has no doubt reminded you of some other events along the way, it has also indicated some divisive elements. How to handle these and prepare for new stages of development is the subject of this conference.

REFERENCES

Adkins, Dorothy C. The simple structure of the American Psychological Association. *American Psychologist*, 1954, *9*, 175–180.

American Psychological Association. Division of Counseling and Guidance, Committee on Counselor Training. Recommended standards for training counseling psychologists at the doctorate level. *American Psychologist*, 1952, *7*, 175–181.

American Psychological Association. Division of Counseling Psychology, Committee on Definition. Counseling psychology as a specialty. *American Psychologist*, 1956, *11*, 282–285.

American Psychological Association. Division of Counseling Psychology, Committee on Divisional Functions. *The Division of Counseling Psychology studies its membership*. Multilithed, 1961. (a)

American Psychological Association. Division of Counseling Psychology, Committee on Current Status of Counseling Psychology. *The current status of counseling psychology*. Multilithed, 1961. (b)

American Psychological Association. Division of Counseling Psychology, Committee on School Counselors. The scope and standards of preparation in psychology of school counselors. *American Psychologist*, 1962, *17*, 149–152.

American Psychological Association. *American Psychological Association 1963 Directory*. Washington, D. C.: Author, 1963.

Berdie, R. F. The current status of counseling psychology. *Journal of Counseling Psychology*, 1964, *11*, 293–295.

Brigante, T. R., Haefner, D. P., & Woodson, W. B. Clinical and counseling psychologists' perceptions of their specialties. *Journal of Counseling Psychology,* 1962, *9,* 225–231.

Counseling News and Views (CNV). Official newsletter of Division of Counseling Psychology, American Psychological Association. Issued three times a year.

Dreese, M. A personnel study of the Division of Counseling and Guidance of the American Psychological Association. *Occupations,* 1949, *27,* 307–310.

Goodstein, L. D. The institutional sources of articles in the *Journal of Counseling Psychology. Journal of Counseling Psychology,* 1963, *10,* 94–95.

Granger, S. G. Psychologists' prestige ratings of twenty psychological occupations. *Journal of Counseling Psychology,* 1959, *6,* 183–188.

Grater, H. A., Kell, B. L., & Morse, J. The social service interest: Roadblock and road to creativity. *Journal of Counseling Psychology,* 1961, *8,* 9–12.

Hahn, M. E. Counseling psychology. *American Psychologist,* 1955, *10,* 279–282.

Moore, B. V., & Bouthilet, L. The Veterans Administration program for counseling psychologists. *American Psychologist,* 1952, *7,* 684–685.

Paterson, D. G., & Lofquist, L. G. A note on the training of clinical and counseling psychologists. *American Psychologist,* 1960, *15,* 365–366.

Peterson, R., & Featherstone, F. Occupations of counseling psychologists. *Journal of Counseling Psychology,* 1962, *9,* 221–224.

Porter, T. L., & Cook, T. E. A comparison of student and professional prestige rankings of jobs in psychology. *Journal of Counseling Psychology,* 1964, *11,* 385–387.

Pressey, S. L. Age and the doctorate—then and now. *Journal of Higher Education,* 1962, *33,* 153–160.

Sakoda, J. M. Comments of factor analysis of the APA structure. *American Psychologist,* 1955, *10,* 90–92.

Sanford, F. H. Annual report of the Executive Secretary: 1955. *American Psychologist,* 1955, *10,* 778–792.

Super, D. E. Comments on current books and the passing scene. *Journal of Counseling Psychology,* 1963, *10,* 409–412.

Thorndike, R. L. The psychological value systems of psychologists. *American Psychologist,* 1954, *9,* 787–789.

Wrigley, C. Cluster analysis or factor analysis? The divisional structure of the American Psychological Association. *Psychological Reports,* 1957, *3,* 497–506.

Yamamoto, K. Counseling psychologists—who are they? *Journal of Counseling Psychology,* 1963, *10,* 211–221.

Chapter 15
Where Do Counseling Psychologists Work? What Do They Do? What Should They Do?

JOSEPH SAMLER

When, finally, we create our long-sought-for identity, soul-searching will deserve an honorable place in it. In this almost constant self-questioning, enough data have emerged on where we work and perhaps on what we do to lead to acceptable inferences on who we are. The data are part of a literature of some size on what we should do instead; why we are more deserving, if not so well-placed, as our cousins of a lower number; why we are so scattered and why it is a very good and even necessary thing to be scattered; and why perhaps the best thing for us to do is to go away and not come back. From this considerable writing the impression is gained that here are the colors, if not the actual lineaments, of a picture of who we are.

The first such investigation on work and setting is Dreese's (1949) "Personnel Study of the Division of Counseling and Guidance of the American Psychological Association." The year following, Winifred Scott (1950–1951) presented her report on the characteristics of Division 17 members. The age, income, and professional characteristics of the Division were reported to the APA Convention in 1951 and appeared in print in 1952 (Berg, Pepinsky, Arsenian, & Heston, 1952). In 1954, a Division 17 Committee on Counseling Psychology and Relations with Public Schools (APA, 1954) presented a preliminary analysis of the employment of members of Division 17. In an ambitious 1957 membership study the Committee on Divisional functions (APA, 1959) analyzed various characteristics of Divisional membership. Two of the analyses offer data on function and, therefore, are of particular interest to us. In the circumscribed area of employment of civilian psychologists by the Federal government, a 1962

The assistance of Alfred E. Acey, Graduate Assistant, College of Education, the University of Maryland, with the data collection for this report is gladly acknowledged.
From Albert S. Thompson and Donald E. Super (Eds.), *The Professional Preparation of Counseling Psychologists: Report of the 1964 Greyston Conference.* (New York: Teachers College Press, ©1964 by Teachers College, Columbia University.)

study released by APA (undated) includes a limited amount of information on counseling psychologists. Studying the graduates of APA-approved counseling psychology training programs, Peterson and Featherstone (1962) presented useful data on the "job positions and settings" of such graduates. As part of his treatment of the history of Division 17, C. W. Scott (1979) analyzed 1961 *APA Directory* data. Yamamoto's (1963) thoroughgoing analysis of Division 17 membership is also based on 1961 data.

SETTING AND WORK

Where do counseling psychologists work? The first two columns of Table 1 present the work settings of a 20% sample of Division 17 membership—fellows, members, and associates—from the listing in the 1963 *APA Directory.*

Although most counseling psychologists work in higher education, the scatter of settings is noteworthy. This is a constant finding and other observers have noted it. In addition to educational institutions, the Committee on

Table 1. Work settings: Counseling psychologists[a]

Setting	Members of Division 17		Members of Divisions 17 and 12	Members of Division 17, not 12	
	no.	percent	no.	no.	percent
Colleges and universities	141	58	14	127	62
Federal government (VA)	21	9	5	16	8
Community counseling agencies	13	5	2	11	5
Private practice	12	5	5	7	3
Public schools	12	5	1	11	5
Business and industry (management consulting)	12	5	2	10	5
State and city government	9	4	3	6	3
Test publishers and services	5	2	1	4	2
Federal government (other than VA)	4	2	1	3	1
Hospitals (other than VA)	4	2	2	2	1
Private schools and institutions	3	1	1	2	1
Professional associations	3	1		3	1
Personnel work in industry	1	b		1	b
Research groups	1	b		1	b
Other	1	b		1	b
Total	242		37	205	

[a]Based on 20% sample of Division 17 members, *APA Directory,* 1963.
[b]Less than 1%.

Counselor Training (APA, 1952, p. 175) noted that "settings in which counseling psychologists function are business and industry, hospitals, and community agencies such as churches, youth organizations, marital clinics, parenthood foundations, vocational guidance centers, and rehabilitation agencies." The same point is made by the Committee on Definition (APA, 1956) and by Doleys (1962–1963).

Somewhat earlier Super noted that while counseling psychologists work in a variety of settings:

> Wherever they work, they share one common treatment philosophy, one common collection of methods, and they acquire various situational orientations according to the nature of the setting in which they are to work with people [Super, 1955, p. 5].

This, of course, is the critical point—whether there is in fact this identity of function regardless of setting.

Our constant peering over our shoulders at our sometime clinical friends is too well known to need documentation. Therefore it is of some interest to see what we look like if we doff the white coat. This information is provided in Table 1.

The incidental finding that only 15% of the Division 17 sample are members also of Division 12 was unexpected enough to require checking the entire Division 17 population against Division 12 membership. Actually, 18% of all Division 17 members belong to Division 12. As Robinson points out, as recently as 1961 Yamamoto found this proportion to be 24%; in 1957 the Committee on Divisional Functions (APA, 1959) reported it as 25%; and in 1950 Scott noted that it was 29.5%. The natural projection of this trend leads to the estimate that by 1984 the proportion of counseling psychologists who belong to Division 12 will be minus 4.73%.

Table 2 compares the findings of seven studies on where counseling psychologists work. Since different investigators use different categories, a few clumsinesses, as in partial repetition of work setting rubrics, are inevitable.

Comparison of work settings over time reveals two main points. For 14 years colleges and universities have been the major work setting of counseling psychologists. For the same period, the variety of work settings has been reasonably consistent. Also, for small but notable proportions, some work settings appear in later studies only; for instance, community counseling agencies and management consulting firms. This is logical, however, since both types of work are recent developments. By extension can it not be expected that as new work situations come into being new demands for the services of counseling psychologists will be felt? As half-way-house approaches for psychiatric patients are greatly extended and as more community mental health facilities come into being, it is certain that they will be added to the already extensive list of work settings. In the meanwhile, the breadth of work settings of those who identify themselves as counseling

Table 2. Counseling psychologists' work settings: Seven studies compared: Percent[a]

Setting	Samler 1963	Yamamoto 1961 (1963)[e]	C. W. Scott[b] 1961	Peterson & Featherstone[c] 1960 (1962)[e]	Division 17 Committee 1954	W. S. Scott 1950	Dreese[d] 1949
Colleges and universities	58	55	53	53	59	53	50
Federal government (VA)	9	9	9	15		12	19
Community counseling agencies	5		5[f]			7[g]	
Private practice	5	5	4		7	3	5
Public schools	5	8[h]	8	4	7	5	9
Business and industry (management consulting)	5	3	3	8			
Business and industry		3	3		7	4	7
State and city government	4						
State/national agencies and armed services				6		3	5
Federal government (other than VA)	2		3			1[j]	
Government (USOE, USES, USPH, State Department, etc.)		5					

Table 2. (Continued)

Setting	Samler 1963	Yamamoto 1961 (1963)e	C. W. Scottb 1961	Peterson & Featherstonec 1960 (1962)e	Division 17 Committee 1954	W. S. Scott 1950	Dreesed 1949
Armed forces (including schools and hospitals)		1					
Test publishers and services	2	7k	2				
Hospitals (other than VA)	2	2	3	5		2l	
Private schools and institutions	1						
Professional associations	1	1		-			
Research groups	i						
Public service			4		4		
Welfare agencies						2	
Other and unknown	i	3	4		16	7	5

a .5 and above raised to next highest percent; .4 and lower dropped.
b Adapted from C. W. Scott (unpublished).
c Authors state "These are the six most prominent settings."
d Adapted from Dreese (1949).
e Date within parentheses is publication year; other is year when data were gathered.
f Entry reads "Counseling or psychological service, private."
g Entry reads "Counseling or psychological agency."
h Entry reads "Schools (incl. Jr. Colleges)."
i Less than 1%.
j Entry reads "State Department of Education, including vocational rehabilitation."
k Entry reads "Private psychological firms (including test publishers)."
l Entry reads "Hospital and clinic (non VA); Prison."

psychologists seems urgent material for inference. The suspicion grows that here is material that, because of its diversity, paradoxically reveals identity. Different work settings should pull apart. Since they do not, there may be a stronger counterforce that maintains the bond.

Table 3 presents the positions (as differentiated from work setting) held by the sample group of counseling psychologists, again separating out those who are also members of Division 12. The issues raised in discussing the data on variety of work settings are perhaps more pertinent here. After all, it is not where counseling psychologists work but what they do that should provide answers to questions of identity. Position titles do not, of course, provide the essential answers, but they bring us closer to the data from which the answers must come. The positions which counseling psychologists hold are most varied, and no considerable difference emerges when those who hold membership in Division 12 are isolated. (It is not possible to relate these findings to the results of other studies, which vary in their classification schemes.)

Table 3. Positions held by counseling psychologists[a]

Position	Members in Division 17		Members in Divisions 17 and 12	Members in Division 17, not 12	
	no.	percent	no.	no.	percent
Colleges and universities— professor: psychology, education	56	23	5	51	25
Director: psychological service, clinic, counseling center	29	12	2	27	13
Counselor, counseling psychologist, psychologist	22	9	2	20	10
Dean, academic	7	3	1	6	3
Chairman/head: psychology department	9	4	3	6	3
Dean/director: student personnel	5	2		5	2
Vice-chancellor	2	1		2	1
Dean: men, women	2	1		2	1
Head: guidance and counseling	2	1		2	1
Director: management center	1	b		1	b
Public and private schools— psychologist, counselor	8	3	1	7	3
Director: guidance, pupil-personnel	6	2	1	5	2
Consultant	2	1		2	1
Counselor, counseling psychologist	21	9	5	16	8
Consulting psychologist	10	4	3	7	3
Supervisor, consultant, coordinator, project director: vocational rehabilitation	10	4		10	5
Clinical psychologist	9	4	7	2	1

Table 3. (Continued)

Position	Members in Division 17		Members in Divisions 17 and 12	Members in Division 17, not 12	
	no.	percent	no.	no.	percent
Director: community counseling service	8	3	1	7	3
Psychotherapist	7	3	1	6	3
Management consultant: industry	6	2	1	5	2
Officer, staff, test publishers and services	5	2		5	2
Rehabilitation counselor	3	1	1	2	1
Consultant	2	1	2		
Research consultant	1	b		1	b
Marriage counselor	1	b		1	b
Staff: professional association	1	b		1	b
Director: special school	1	b		1	b
Employment manager: SES	1	b		1	b
Personnel director: industry	1	b		1	b
Director: mental health education	1	b		1	b
Parole director	1	b	1		b
Director: YMCA youth project	1	b		1	b
Not classified	1	b		1	b
Total	242		37	205	

[a]Based on 20% sample of Division 17 members, *APA Directory*, 1963.
[b]Less than 1%.

The data reveal that at least 36% of the sample are engaged in counseling, in closely related activities, and in their supervision and direction. The data on positions in Table 3 are reasonably consistent. Even if clinical psychologists and psychotherapists are left out, about 39% of the sample may be said to be engaged in "direct labor" in counseling psychology.

Based on responses from 709 out of the then 840 members in 1957, the Division 17 Committee on Divisional Functions (APA, 1959) presented considerable information on members' characteristics. Tables 6 and 7 in that study are of particular interest. The report states that "The largest single group of Division 17 members perceive themselves primarily as administrators with two groups of approximately equal size reporting they are counselors and teachers. No other single function claims many members." Twenty-two percent stated that counseling was their major job function. However, if research, consulting, psychotherapy, testing, and private practice are included, the proportion engaged in "direct labor" increases to 37%. And yet we know this is a common pattern. The 37%, therefore, must be regarded as a minimum figure. In a way, this point is borne out by data in the same study on the proportion of time devoted to counseling: while only 20% reported that they spent more than half their time in such work, almost half stated that they spent some time, though less than 20%, in counseling.

Three years later Peterson and Featherstone (1962) found a not dissimilar situation in studying the graduates of APA-approved counseling-psychology programs. Twenty-eight percent were engaged directly in counseling, but to this group may be added those who are in research (7%), a part of those who do not designate a specialty (total, 8%), consultants (3%), to a total of perhaps 40% engaging in "direct labor." Presumably this is why, in his comments on the study, Super (1962, p. 235) says:

> Do counseling psychologists counsel? Yes, more than a quarter do this as their main activity. With those who teach and direct (and who, in many situations we know, give some time to counseling) they account for nearly three-quarters of the counseling psychologists sampled.

A reminder seems necessary, however. These are people who are at the beginning of their careers in counseling psychology. They may present a somewhat different picture than does the membership as a whole. In part, Table 3 reflects these differences.

The final bit of information it was possible to dredge from the biographical entries deals with interests. For each person in the sample, the first (presumably major) interest was classified under one of 34 categories in Table 4. These are professional interests. They may be regarded as expressions of what a person prefers to do at work. There is not necessarily a strong relationship of interests with work duties, but to dismiss interests as having a questionable relationship with work might be an even greater error. A

Table 4. Interests of counseling psychologists[a]

Type of Interest	Members of Division 17		Members of Divisions 17 and 12	Members of Division 17, not 12	
	no.	percent	no.	no.	percent
Counseling psychology	39	16.4	2	37	18.5
Vocational counseling	27	11.4		27	13.5
Psychotherapy	25	10.5	6	19	9.5
Psychological measurement, individual diagnosis, aptitude and performance testing	18	7.6	1	17	8.5
Personality, infancy, adolescence, old age, adjustment dynamics	16	6.7	5	11	5.5
Guidance and counseling, school case work	13	5.3	1	12	6.0

Table 4. *(Continued)*

Type of Interest	Members of Division 17		Members of Divisions 17 and 12	Members of Division 17, not 12	
	no.	percent	no.	no.	percent
Rehabilitation, rehabilitation counselor training	13	5.3	4	9	4.5
Executive selection, management development, personnel selection	13	5.3	1	12	6.0
Teaching, teaching psychology	7	2.8	2	5	2.5
Personality measurement	6	2.4	1	5	2.5
Clinical psychology, projective techniques	6	2.4	3	3	1.5
Group counseling, group dynamics, leadership training	6	2.4		6	3.0
Prediction of counseling readiness	5	2.0	2	3	1.5
Learning theory	4	1.6		4	2.0
Counselor training	3	1.2		3	1.5
Coordination of counseling and instruction	3	1.2		3	1.5
Gifted college student, college achievement	3	1.2		3	1.5
Self-concept	3	1.2		3	1.5
Educational psychology	3	1.2	1	2	1.0
Vocational interests	2	1.8		2	1.0
Pastoral counseling	2	b		2	1.0
Marriage counseling	2	b		2	1.0
Vocational adjustment, job satisfaction	2	b		2	1.0
Typology of behavior patterns	2	b	1	1	b
Perceptual defense	2	b	1	1	b
Predicting behavior	2	b	2		b
Antisocial behavior, juvenile delinquency	2	b	1	1	b
Hypnodiagnosis	1	b	1		b
Schizophrenia	1	b	1		b
Market research	1	b		1	b
Reading and study skills	1	b		1	b
Industrial psychology	1	b		1	b
Research design	1	b		1	b
Administration	1	b		1	b
No interest listed	6	2.4	1	5	2.4
Total	242		37	205	

[a]Based on 20% sample of Division 17 members, *APA Directory*, 1963.
[b]Less than 1%.

discipline in the process of becoming provides greater than usual freedom to its practitioners, and the job market for counseling psychologists is such that the person dissatisfied with his work tasks can move easily enough, other factors being equal, to another job. As a direct indication of what counseling psychologists want to do, and of what they may actually be doing, these data are worth examining.

It is to be noted that 60.7% of Division 17 members are interested in problems and concerns that are at the heart of counseling psychology. These interests include counseling psychology, vocational counseling, psychological measurement, individual diagnosis, aptitude and performance testing, guidance and counseling, school case work, rehabilitation, rehabilitation counselor training, executive and personnel selection, personality measurement, prediction of counseling readiness, counselor training, self-concept, vocational interests, and vocational adjustment and job satisfaction. For the same interest categories, and with those who are members also of Division 12 excluded (in this case not an unfair procedure), the proportion rises to 66.5%. The 6% increase may provide food for thought. The issue can be seen quite the other way, of course: that about 40% of Division 17 members are interested in problems and concerns that are at some distance from the core of counseling psychology. Although some of the excluded interests, such as teaching psychology, clinical psychology, projective techniques, learning theory, and educational psychology, seem to fall outside our direct area of work and interest, some are arguable—for example, psychotherapy, group dynamics, coordination of counseling and instruction, and adjustment dynamics. If admitted, these would increase the proportion of those interested directly in counseling psychology.

We have been wearing a hair shirt because a number of us are not engaged in counseling. Guilt feelings here seem unjustified as well as unproductive. In other professions, a certain proportion of practitioners leave the substantive content of their discipline, do other work, and yet maintain an interest in and some commitment to it. Thus teachers become school principals and administrators in education, working on budget, personnel, curricula, buildings, and public relations. Lawyers become executives, administrators, legislators, political figures. Physicians become hospital administrators and psychoanalysts, and so on. We are not exceptional.

From the data presented thus far I believe we can conclude that:

1. We work in a wide variety of work settings. In this we have been consistent over the years.
2. Most of us work in colleges and universities.
3. Administration, teaching, and counseling are our main activities.
4. As new situations for providing counseling develop we find our way into them.
5. The presence of clinically oriented psychologists in the Division does not change the essential pattern of work settings, positions, or expressed interests.

6. The proportion of Counseling Division members who hold membership also in the Clinical Division has gone down over the years.
7. Most counseling psychologists appear to be primarily interested in aspects of counseling psychology.

There is a certain satisfaction in pinning these points down, but in truth we do not know very much more about what counseling psychologists do than we knew before. Clearly, what is needed is an actual survey of counselor activities.

FROM THE OFFICIAL REPORTS

Publications on counselor functions encompass all that counseling psychologists do, how they do it, and all they are concerned with professionally. Analysis of this material is not an impossible task, but it is impracticable; selection is necessary, with its attendant biases.

The initial materials reviewed are the documents issued by Division 17 in its institutional character. The first of these are the reports prepared for and following the Northwestern Conference in 1951 (APA, 1952). The stress on counselor mission in these reports is large and global and, I suppose, represents inevitable compromise. In the "Recommended Standards for Training Counseling Psychologists at the Doctoral Level" appear these formulations: "The professional goal of the counseling psychologist is to foster the psychological development of the individual" (APA, 1952, p. 175). Although most of the time the counseling psychologist will work with normal persons, he will work with others also. We are told that "counseling stresses the positive and preventive" (p. 175). Group situations are included among the counselor's concerns. The counseling psychologist, the report notes, "should be acquainted with community resources for meeting educational, employment, health, social, and marital needs, and with socioeconomic and occupational trends" (p. 178). The references to methods are quite general. The earlier 12-member, Ann Arbor Conference (Bordin, 1950) had taken a basically similar position.

In analyzing the implications at the 1955 Stanford Conference for counseling psychology, a committee chaired by Seeman identified "at least three aspects which make counseling psychology at home with the concepts of the conference" (APA, undated): consistent interest in working with the normal person, a sensitivity to sociological and environmental factors in adjustment, and an interest in measurement and quantification. In helping provide psychological services to the community, the committee called to attention that the counseling psychologist might play any or all of three roles: as a direct participant, as a resource person or consultant, in research.

In his presidential address in 1954, Hahn urged that identification of counseling psychology's role demands "a comparison with other professional groups and a statement of a relatively unique pattern of practice" (Hahn,

1955, p. 279), and he suggested four hypothetical differences between counseling psychologists and other psychologists. Hahn saw counseling psychologists concentrating "on the problems of interfering value systems and judgments and the changing of attitudes." He noted, as have a number of other observers, that the "clinical psychologist appears to work more in the medically related areas of reorganizing basic personality structure." Four relatively unique functions of the counseling psychologist are notable: We usually deal with anxiety states at the frustrating, interfering levels; we appraise human traits for educational-vocational-social living; we follow our clients beyond the office door; and we stress positive psychological strength as against a process of diagnosing and remedying psychopathies.

The counseling psychologist, the Committee on Definition (APA, 1956) urged, is "a psychologist who uses varying combinations of exploratory experiences, psychometric techniques, and psychotherapeutic interviewing to assist people to grow and develop" (APA, 1956, p. 283). In whatever setting he works, and they may be very diverse, the committee considered that "the counseling psychologist may help individuals in their personal development while they are progressing through school, suffering effects of illness or physical disability, or attempting to cope with marital situations or problems of parent-child relationships" (pp. 283–289). In any of these settings the client is helped to increase his resources for coping with the environment. On the individual's behalf, the counselor will work with persons and groups with whom the individual has to deal. Therefore, in the committee's words, in the schools "the counseling psychologist plays a role in shaping admissions procedures, curriculum development, and extracurricular activities. In industry he collaborates in training programs for supervision, influences selection and placement procedures, and consults on personnel policies" (p. 284). Parallel activities exist in other settings, such as in hospitals and rehabilitation programs. A few references to methodology are comprehended in a summary sentence that the counseling psychologist "has unique resources—for example, tests and other methods of psychological evaluation—for helping individuals to achieve harmonious relationships with their environments" (p. 285). The counselor's goal, the committee stated "is to further the fullest possible self-realization of those who live in a particular social setting" (p. 285).

The Tyler-Tiedeman-Wrenn report (APA, 1961) reiterates the central point that "counseling psychology concerns itself with the individual's strengths rather than his weakness, with his utilization of environmental resources as well as with his self-perceptions" (APA, 1961, p. 2). Counseling psychology "focuses on *plans* individuals must make to play productive *roles* in their social environments. Whether the person being helped with such planning is sick or well, abnormal or normal, is really irrelevant. The focus is on assets, skills, strengths, possibilities for further development. Personality difficulties are dealt with only when they constitute obstacles to the individual's forward progress" (pp. 6–7).

The central themes are now familiar. The counselor assists people to grow and develop. Clients may be well or ill, within the so-called normal range or not. Client anxiety is dealt with at the frustrating and interfering level rather than when it is incapacitating. Client strength rather than weakness is stressed. The client is helped to increase his resources for coping with the environment. The counselor must therefore know community resources for meeting various client needs and play a role in influencing the environment. He utilizes various assessment devices in appraising client traits for educational, vocational, and social functioning. The counselor is a direct participant, a resource person, or a researcher.

This is the mission, and if enough is read into it, it is acceptable as such. Philosophy is less distinct, but there are indications of a role that is more active than the therapist's, of "advisory" functions, of involvement in and direct influence on the client's environment, and implications of a value system aiming at optimum functioning of the individual.

The emphasis on client strength and health, on "hygiology" in Super's (1955) formulation, is well placed and persuasive. However, the working counselor sees the battle as not yet completely won. Our diagnostic instruments too often present pathological variables rather than asset variables, and even when we use the hygiological CPI or Edwards, some of us tend to translate the results into the language of pathology. Illness is more prestigeful than health, if vocabularies reveal values, even in counseling circles. Perhaps it all stems from the fact that so much of personality theory is grounded in clinical experience. Although there are signs of attention to this problem, a great deal more work is necessary if talking of assets and strength is to have meaning.

UNOFFICIAL REPORTS ON ROLE AND FUNCTION

Seeking to learn what various campus groups perceived as the domain of the university counseling center, Warman (1960) administered a hundred-item questionnaire to 250 people. One general factor ("acceptance of counseling") and three specific factors ("college routine," "vocational choice," and "adjustment to self and others") emerged from the data. All subgroups except the counseling psychologists considered "vocational choice" most appropriate as an activity of the counseling center. The counseling center group felt that "adjustment to self and others" was more appropriate—and to a significantly greater degree than did any other groups. Warman concludes that counselors "must better orient and educate other people to the kinds of problems with which counselors feel they can be helpful and that are actually discussed with them by counselees" (p. 274), but somewhat different inferences could be drawn from the same data.

Thrush's (1957) study three years earlier was a harbinger of Warman's investigation. A comparison shows that, from 1952 to 1956, the counseling staff at the Ohio State University moved from emphasis on vocational guidance to a concern with personality adjustment counseling. A later study by Warman casts an interesting light on his own previous work. He tested the hypothesis "that differences exist among counseling centers as to the appropriateness of various problems for discussion with counselors" (Warman, 1961, p. 233). The hypothesis was confirmed for each of these problem areas: "college routine," "vocational adjustment," "adjustment to self and others." "Vocational choice" was considered appropriate by all centers. However, the study revealed a significant difference between the training and nontraining centers concerning "vocational choice," with the latter rating it more appropriate than did the training centers.

In a frequently cited study, Brigante, Haefner, and Woodson reported on perception of their specialties by clinical and counseling psychologists. Their data were consistent with Hahn's hypotheses that "counseling psychologists are less concerned with reorganizing basic personality structure than are clinicians, that counselors have greater concern with a positive approach to trait strength and are less concerned with medically diagnosed personality deviations requiring psychotherapy than clinicians, and that counselors resemble industrial psychologists in their general orientation more than they do psychotherapists" (Brigante, Haefner, & Woodson, 1962, p. 230). Counseling and clinical psychologists agreed that it is more characteristic of counseling psychologists to work with normal people and those having educational and vocational problems, to use paper and pencil personality, interest, and aptitude tests, to find an environment compatible with the individual's personality rather than attempt to alter his personality structure, and to have and give educational and vocational information.

More recently a different note has been struck. In an all-but-bitter fantasy Brayfield (1961a) notes that counseling psychology is a specialty in search of an identity. In Brayfield's curious twitting, three synergetic specialties will emerge in 1984: (1) counseling psychology-vocational, (2) counseling psychology-therapeutic, and (3) counseling psychology-psychopharmacology. Specialists in the first field will be few in number. Specialists in the last field will all be M.D.'s. Brayfield feels that counseling psychology will then indeed have found its identity, only it will have lost control!

It is disconcerting that university counseling center staffs see their primary function as personal adjustment counseling whereas others in the university see it as vocational counseling. Why not both functions? It is equally disturbing that a long established center discards its respectable vocational clothes for fancy therapeutic dress. Again, are two suits too many for a man to own? Perhaps the most significant finding in Warman's second study is that counseling centers in APA-approved training program settings do not feel that vocational counseling is as appropriate for their programs as do other centers. Has APA accreditation by clinically dominated committees led to a dilution of counseling psychology? The work by Brigante and others does suggest some presumably unique characteristics of the counselor that are visible not only to him but to the clinician as well.

One cannot make much of the de-emphasis of vocational counseling as the Divisional papers cited do not themselves offer this as a specific charter. But one might ask, in Brayfield's vein, whether the committees drafting Divisional papers during the 1950s were not themselves clinically oriented.

COUNSELING PSYCHOLOGY IN JOB DESCRIPTIONS AND REPORTS

What the counseling psychologist should do, and perhaps does do, is now somewhat clearer. However, we can bring it into sharper focus by examining job descriptions and interviewing a limited number of counselors. There are two limitations other than those of numbers: only four settings are considered, and although some of the people whose job descriptions I read are known to be counseling psychologists, others are not members of Division 17.

VA Hospitals

The work of the counseling psychologist in the VA hospitals and clinics should be viewed against the background of Wolford's (1956) article reviewing generally the first decade of psychology in VA hospitals. The specifics of the counseling program are presented in the *Program guide for vocational counseling* (VA, 1960). Cecil Peck and Elton Ash helped greatly in making available files of area supervision reports and annual hospital reports as well as job descriptions.

Three points stand out in review of these reports and job descriptions: First, there is the very considerable range of activities. The two-person counseling situation is there, and there are interesting related activities—for example, writing an employment handbook for psychiatric patients, running a group job problems clinic, and expansion of the psychological testing admissions program beyond its present focus on pathology by including assessment devices for uncovering patient's assets and resources that might be utilized for enhancing therapy and rehabilitation efforts. But also there is a congeries of other activities—for example, increase in the participation of public relations activities of the hospital, both on and off the grounds, career planning for candidates in station's program of high school graduate recruitment for supervisory manpower pool, total ward resocialization, setting up a course in rapid reading under the management development program. In interviews these activities were described as peripheral rather than central.

Second is the ongoing research activity. Considering the pervasive emphasis on research in hospital reports, it is surprising to find that the actual job descriptions now and again state "research activity occupies 10% of my time."

Third is the counseling psychologist's involvement in the community. There is reiteration of contact with employers and employment agencies on behalf of patients. Constant reference is made to the many variations in sheltered workshop operation in and out of the hospital, all requiring community contact. Employers in the community visit hospitals monthly and meet professional staff and selected patients. Counseling psychologists work out of the different types of half-way houses, talks are given to school, church, civic, and professional groups, and so on. The spread of interest and confidence in the NP (neuropsychiatric) patient among community employers is reflected (Sanders, 1963). But for the story of counseling progress in depth it is necessary to go to the case work-up, excellently related, for example, in Stubbins and Napoli's presentation (1958) of the counseling experience with Fred, including as it does the interrelationship with and parts played by other hospital services.

Rehabilitation Agencies

Counseling psychologists in VA hospitals and clinics of course do rehabilitation counseling. So do the counselors in the VA's Vocational Rehabilitation and Education Program. So does any counselor with any client who is handicapped as a result of disease, injury, emotional conditions, or degenerative aging process. Working with the mentally retarded may be called "habilitation," but the process has the same essential features. One can also include in rehabilitation's purview work with illiterates, delinquents, dropouts, criminals, and the culturally and economically disadvantaged. There is complete agreement that the general class is vocational counseling and that rehabilitation counseling is a specific under it. Thus the VA description applies to rehabilitation counselors. I will not recapitulate the dated arguments about whether such workers are coordinators or counselors, whether the para-medical emphases warrant the identification of a unique specialty, or, more currently, discuss the influence that considerable funds and extensive programs exert toward the creation of separate identity.

Although the Federal-State program dates back to 1920, the big push began as recently as ten years ago with the passage of Public Law 565, the Vocational Rehabilitation Act of 1954. Yet the development of services and the production of theory, research, and operational descriptions have been considerable.

The review of a number of job descriptions in one state program provides a close-up of counselor activities. About 25% of the counselor's time is devoted to securing information about the applicant, prescribing and interpreting results of psychological tests, and counseling and planning the individual rehabilitation program. An additional 20% of time is taken up by arrangements for and coordination of necessary rehabilitation services. These may range from corrective surgery and work therapy, through vocational training and providing tools and equipment, to placement on the job. The rehabilitation counselor is often away from his desk two days a week in the case of one person interviewed. He is in touch with personnel in schools, hospitals, clinics, welfare agencies, and other groups, consulting on rehabilitation services, helping in case finding, and facilitating referral of new clients. He is also out surveying and developing employment and training opportunities, and analyzing specific jobs for their suitability for handicapped clients.

Minor portions of the counselor's time are taken up with determination of rehabilitation potential of applicants for disability benefits under the Old Age and Survivors Insurance program and the preparation of reports on applicants with no rehabilitation potential. He determines client resources and need for maintenance or transportation. An agency may also provide services to individuals who function primarily as home-makers in their own homes. With some of these clients it may be necessary to provide help in rebuilding kitchens and arranging for special equipment so that the person can function properly.

The rehabilitation counselor works under supervision, but this appears to be more nominal than real because little or nothing is turned back. There is little consultation with co-workers or consultants other than in related specialties.

Community Guidance Services

The compensating feature for the limited number of job descriptions relative to the work in community counseling centers is that the Vocational Advisory Service in New York and the Psychological Service of Pittsburgh are excellent models.

In these agencies the counselor counsels individuals, building on information supplied by a skillful intake worker or, alternatively, by himself from the initial interview. He uses test results, school records, work history, biographical, and medical information. He may limit service to vocational counseling or provide other services, such as marital and family counseling, retirement counseling, therapeutic counseling, and clinical evaluations.

He determines the tests and other diagnostic devices the client is to take; he develops and selects informational materials (special schools, occupations, employment opportunities, colleges) appropriate to the client's problem; he decides on the need for medical or psychiatric referral or consultation; he prepares reports to counselees, parents, referring person, or other interested professionals; and he interprets test and interview findings.

Internal procedures vary. The admirable but expensive practice may be followed of holding a case conference on every client. Additional information is called for at discretion; additional interviews beyond the first few are held as needed. There are phone calls and visits with school people, agency workers, and resource persons. Employment contacts are made. Client progress is followed up, sometimes routinely and briefly, but in some instances it is a very serious concern. The usual supportive activities go on, such as talks to schools and civic groups, assistance in research, internship supervision, and help in training conferences.

University Counseling Centers

The best data we have are for counselors in educational settings. In response to a request from the Study Commission of the Council of Guidance and Personnel Associations (undated), the USES in 1952 made a considerable number of job analyses of educational personnel workers. The analyses follow the familiar format and present eight sets of duties for the position "counselor":

1. to collect, arrange, and analyze information about the individual
2. to assemble and disseminate occupational information
3. to assist the individual to make a better adjustment and intelligent educational and vocational plans
4. to provide group guidance
5. to maintain records
6. to provide a placement service
7. to engage in research
8. to perform related duties

The sets are as specific as one could please. For instance, under the first rubric is the statement, among a number of others, that the counselor "compares school grades and records against results of achievement and intelligence tests to ascertain those students in particular need of counseling, and arranges for interviews."

In his doctoral study Reeves (1963) developed a method for analyzing costs of student counseling services. In the process he established a category of functions, counseling, testing, and so on, in the Student Counseling Bureau at the University of Minnesota and secured detailed time study data for staff members. Reeves' findings, costs aside, are of interest. The Bureau's functions were grouped into broad areas of responsibility: counseling; educational skills; testing; test scoring; coordination; clearance and reporting; administration; public relations; teaching; group education; and public service.

The average counselor (if there *is* an average counselor at Minnesota) spends his work time as follows: 40% in counseling, 17% in teaching and training, 9% in staff development, 10% in public relations (contacts with student and faculty), and 24% in various related activities—for example, group education and administration.

A troublesome question remains. What demands are made upon the university vocational counselor for understanding of the working world? If, as at some institutions, the study body constitutes the top 10 or 15% of the state's high school graduates, how broad and deep is the counselor's knowledge of other than the high level professional occupations? Even within this limited area, how does he insure that he gets a feeling for, as well as information about, an occupation; for instance, how the architect secures and relates to his client, the concerns of the politically minded lawyer, or the technical demands upon and the specific working conditions of the ceramics engineer?

Counseling Psychology's Common Core

As far as the data go, they support the idea that *there is a common methodology.* The methodology embraces a two-person counseling relationship, supplemented by group methods, the utilization of assessment devices peculiarly appropriate for the study of vocational potential, assumption of a measure of responsibility by the counselor for the client, involvement with the client's environment (family, school, work), and considerable activity by the counselor on behalf of his client outside of counseling sessions. Evidence on research involvement is equivocal. Service demands on counselors are very great and seem to preclude any considerable time to be spent on research except in a few university centers. For what it is worth, I asked a number of my interviewees whether they felt they could move with comfort into and function in a different counseling setting—to a university counseling center from a rehabilitation service, for example. In each case the response was positive, and I am inclined to agree. The point is made in support of the existence of a common methodology.

WHAT SHOULD COUNSELING PSYCHOLOGISTS DO?

Avoid Premature Stabilization

Counseling psychology has been so long engaged in self-study that now that we are inclined to act on our self-knowledge, the temptation is very strong to say "This is who we are, this is what we do, this is where we stop."

I do not want to set up a straw man, to argue against freezing our identity; no one really advocates that. Rather we need a special awareness of the forces that affect and change our society, moving from that awareness to anticipation and from anticipation to considering what our function as counseling psychologists might be in a changed situation.

Two specifics may help to bring me down from this generalization. As Tilgher (1962) points out, the meaning of work has undergone successive change. Its values, mostly derived from the various religious movements, have moved so that the sanctity of work is now open to question. What will take its place? In what will we invest ourselves? How will needs beyond security be satisfied? How will creative urges be met? Will the investment be in a wiser and more active citizenship, recreational activities that do more than fill the hours of the day, and in reaching deeper and deeper levels of self-understanding?

Related to this is the reality of automation and, in the visible future, the reduction of the working week. With security needs met, how will self-satisfactions come about? How will we live in more than humdrum ways, perhaps even zestfully? Counseling psychology has no option on the problem and its solutions, but since we are centrally concerned with work and its use in self-fulfillment, what will be the outlines of our task?

In a way, this is not a new problem. If Wilensky's (1961) findings are sound, what should be done on behalf of, or with, those of our clients who will constitute the 70% of the labor force who cannot look forward to any kind of orderly career? Thus far, we have done little or nothing with or for them.

Restore Vocational Counseling to Its Central Place

Counseling psychologists, in informal discussions, recognize that vocational counseling is their "bread and butter."

I join Brayfield (1961b) and others in the conviction that vocational counseling is a major element in establishing the unique identity of counseling psychology. We might be closer to reality, however, if we said that vocational counseling *could be* a major element; it is not necessarily one now. The reasons for failure to grasp its potential social contribution and its promise for the counseling psychologist and for psychology generally, must include an impoverished theory of the human being at work, an inadequate focus on the pertinent data, an oversimplified view of what is really quite complex, and the effect of style and status in the working role we adopt. The reasons for derogation are understandable enough, and there is no great profit in lamenting them.

We need a viable vocational counseling to be adopted as the core of counseling psychology. This will happen only, however, when its true complexity is accepted. Three points must be made in this context.

First, although counselors talk glibly of work, occupations, and careers, how much they really know of and appreciate them is an open question. Even when occupational information resources are used, the major reference is likely to be the economically presented *Occupational Outlook Handbook*. The inadequacies of even an ambitious occupational information reference file based on standard occupational information resources are explicated in the literature, yet the needed material is available and is extensively documented—for example, by Brayfield (1961b).

Second, accepting Brayfield's thesis, I find it easier to confess that I must be one of the tender-minded who feel that personality needs are to be considered in vocational counseling. This is a process which should start with the individual who is a psychological as well as an economic entity who must function in industry. As Brayfield indicates, industry is organized on a competence and performance basis. Contrary to what some counselors appear to believe, the employer's mission is not to provide satisfaction and happiness for his workers. However, that does not mean that competence and anticipation cannot be jointed; they are not incompatible. For many who are troubled with themselves, meeting job requirements may be a road to self-acceptance. The firm requirements of work situations can promote emotional health. The vocational counselor thus is or can be a therapist of a very particular kind. Despite Freud's remark about the reality-binding nature of work, and despite much therapy-oriented work activity, very little has been done systematically to investigate work as therapy.

Third, the vocational psychologist, the counseling psychologist, is in a position not only to use personality theory in his work but, as a result of his work, to make rich contributions to it. Among others, Bordin (1957) and Brayfield (1961b) have called our attention to this situation, the latter citing as an example the work on vocational interest as constituting "the most substantial and significant work on personality in the history of psychology" (p. 32).

Change Our Approach to Personality Change

The prevailing philosophy in therapy is characterized by a thoroughgoing acceptance of the client. The communication is made and repeated that his feelings and behavior, considering his unhappy history, could not be different. When this communication is integrated by the counseling client, self-acceptance is favorably affected and personality change becomes possible. Since this is perhaps the sine qua non of mental health, reservations about any procedure that leads to it must be made in discomfort, yet they must be made.

The limitations of worker time are against it, as is also the notion that although this classic approach works (when it works), it is not necessarily the only one with promise of success. Perhaps particularly because of his relatively short-term contact with the client, the counseling psychologist should consider the possible place and function of nonacceptance (except it is not that at all, it is accepting the client as he should be, in terms of what he can become), the imposition of limits, and the requirement to hew to standards.

We are undeniably in the realm of values here, but in this instance we are safe enough; the values are reasonably well accepted. No common mold or procrustean bed is urged, but rather the assumption of minimum responsibility. The impact of investigations such as *The Mental Patient Comes Home* (Freeman & Simmons, 1963) is to underscore what we all know very well, the prime importance of role and role expectations when properly put before the person.

Define Relationships with Other Counselors

Beyond a given point, the data presented early in this paper are unrealistic; they are all limited to counseling psychologists who are members of Division 17. Other major groups also are centrally concerned with our goals and missions; school counselors, rehabilitation counselors in the Federal-State rehabilitation programs, employment counselors in the state employment services, and counselors who work in the increasing number of community counseling centers are generally, but not always, nonpsychologists (Super, 1964). On the face of it, we are up against highly sensitive role and status problems.

Two points at least are for consideration. First, whether workers in these various meetings regard us respectfully or defensively, they are trying to do a job of their own. Second, if we are, as we should be, sensitive to what is done in the schools, community agencies, and other settings, we have to state clearly what it is we ourselves do and seek to do.

As Super (1964) notes, the potential contribution of counseling psychologists to vocational counseling in the schools, community agencies, rehabilitation settings, and colleges and universities is indubitable. But how are we to make it? The general goal of greater psychological sophistication for other counselors is clear and is embodied—for example, in Division 17's report, "Scope and Standards of Preparation in Psychology for School Counselors" (APA, 1962). We have recognized, as a Division, the need for two levels in counselor preparation. One is our own—the doctoral level. The other is characterized by a recommended two years of professional preparation, a safe and even stylish requirement favored by the American Personnel and Guidance Association.

But there are other problems; for example, Winfield Scott writes (personal note) that only 19% of the personnel responsible for counselor education are members of Division 17, an additional 11% are members of other divisions, and 14% more are associates in APA. Fifty-six percent have no APA status. What do we do about this type of situation? Should we be discreet missionaries? Should we take a very much more active role?

Become Involved in Social Action

I make my last point hesitantly. All helping occupations are concerned with cultural and economic conditions that affect the individual. Some, however, attempt to affect and change the environment in the client's interest. In counseling this may involve finding an on-the-job training opportunity, influencing the establishment of still another curriculum in the secondary school, or helping father and mother to reconcile their differences so that the client will not be torn apart. The general outline of such environmental intervention is well established.

It is easy enough to say that this is as far as the professional should go. In his role as a citizen he can address himself to those social issues that in the particular affect his clients inimically. Perhaps this is quite the correct attitude.

We do not know how much of this environmental intervention by the counselor, as well as by the social worker, clinician, teacher, or perhaps also the physician, is to redress inimical social and economic conditions which block or endanger the client's progress economically or psychologically. It seems likely that a good many such actions might be so characterized.

Therefore, the nagging and troubling question remains: Should not counseling psychologists include in their role an involvement in social movements that seek the achievement of their professional objectives? It sounds embarrassingly pious to say that the social and economic movements are those that have to do with the security and dignity of man, but I think this is the fundamental issue.

Again, uncomfortably, we enter a values domain, but here also a disclaimer may help. It is not that all counselors should vote Democratic or Republican but that they should become consciously involved in the larger scene of what they are in any case involved in. There are difficult problems here relative to our scientific commitments. It is more comfortable, but perhaps less effective, to be involved in cases than in causes.

I must descend from these heights. I mean by social and economic movements those that have to do with desegregation, voting rights, employment practices, housing, and minimum wages. There is no getting away from it; the movements are all those that have to do with the dignity and security of man.

Our situation is not quite that of the physicists, aghast at the destructive power they have brought into being, nor, closer to home, of the experimental psychologists, at ease in the second Walden, but I submit nevertheless, that we cannot divorce ourselves from what we confront, that as a defininte part of our professional task we should set out to affect it.

REFERENCES

American Psychological Association. Division of Counseling Psychology. *An analysis of Stanford Conference proceedings.* Mimeographed, undated.

American Psychological Association. Manpower Resources Division. *A survey of civilian psychologists in the federal government.* Mimeographed, undated.

American Psychological Association. Division of Counseling and Guidance, Committee on Counselor Training. Recommended standards for training counseling psychologists at the doctorate level. *American Psychologist,* 1952, *7*, 175–181.

American Psychological Association. Division of Counseling Psychology, Committee on Counseling Psychology and Relations with Public Schools. *Counseling News and Views,* 1954, *7*, 19–20.

American Psychological Association. Division of Counseling Psychology, Committee on Definition. Counseling psychology as a specialty. *American Psychologist,* 1956, *11*, 282–285.

American Psychological Association. Division of Counseling Psychology, Committee on Divisional Functions. *The Division of Counseling Psychology studies its membership.* Multilithed, 1959.

American Psychological Association. Division of Counseling Psychology, Committee on Current Status. *The current status of counseling psychology.* Multilithed, 1961.

American Psychological Association. Division of Counseling Psychology, Committee on School Counselors. The scope and standards of preparation in psychology for school counselors. *American Psychologist,* 1962, *17*, 149–152.

Berg, I. A., Pepinsky, H. B., Arsenian, S., & Heston, J. C. Age, income and professional characteristics of members of the APA's Division of Counseling and Guidance. *American Psychologist,* 1952, *7*, 125–127.

Bordin, E. S. (Ed). *The training of psychological counselors.* Ann Arbor: University of Michigan Press, 1950.

Bordin, E. S. A counseling psychologist views personality development. *Journal of Counseling Psychology,* 1957, *4,* 3–8.

Brayfield, A. H. Counseling psychology: Some dilemmas in the graduate school. *Journal of Counseling Psychology,* 1961, *8,* 17–19. (a)

Brayfield, A. H. Vocational counseling today. In E. G. Williamson (Ed.), *Vocational counseling, a reappraisal in honor of Donald G. Paterson.* Minnesota Studies in Student Personnel Work. No. 11. Minneapolis: University of Minnesota Press, 1961, 22–58. (b)

Brigante, T. R., Haefner, D. P., & Woodson, W. B. Clinical and counseling psychologists' perceptions of their specialties. *Journal of Counseling Psychology,* 1962, *9,* 225–231.

Doleys, E. J. Counseling psychology: A profession in search of identity. *Counseling News and Views,* 1962–1963, *15,* 5–8.

Dreese, M. A. A personnel study of the Division of Counseling and Guidance of the American Psychological Association. *Occupations,* 1949, *27,* 307–310.

Freeman, H. E., & Simmons, O. G. *The mental patient comes home.* New York: Wiley, 1963.

Hahn, M. E. Counseling psychology. *American Psychologist,* 1955, *10,* 279–282.

Peterson, R., & Featherstone, F. Occupations of counseling psychologists. *Journal of Counseling Psychology,* 1962, *9,* 221–224.

Reeves, J. H., Jr. *Analyzing student counseling service costs.* Unpublished manuscript, University of Minnesota, 1963.

Sanders, J. F. Impact of the employed hospitalized and discharged mental patient on community attitudes. *Rehabilitation Counseling Bulletin,* 1963, *7,* 17–20.

Scott, C. W. Division 17 emerges: History of the origin, function, achievements, and issues of the Division of Counseling Psychology of the American Psychological Association, 1945–1963. In J. M. Whiteley (Ed.), *History of counseling psychology,* Monterey, Calif.: Brooks/Cole, 1980.

Scott, Winifred. Characteristics of Division 17 members, 1950. *Counseling News and Views,* 1950–1951, *3,* 9–14.

Stubbins, J., & Napoli, P. Counseling with neuropsychiatric patient: A case study. *Journal of Counseling Psychology,* 1958, *5,* 295–300.

Study Commission of the Council of Guidance and Personnel Associations. *Job analyses of educational personnel workers.* Undated.

Super, D. E. Transition from vocational guidance to counseling psychology. *Journal of Counseling Psychology,* 1955, *2,* 3–9.

Super, D. E. Comments on Peterson, R., & Featherstone, F., Occupations of counseling psychologists. *Journal of Counseling Psychology,* 1962, *9,* 221–224; 235–237.

Super, D. E. Professional status and affiliations of vocational counselors. In H. Borow (Ed.), *Man in a world of work.* Boston: Houghton Mifflin, 1964.

Thrush, R. S. An agency in transition: The case study of a counseling center. *Journal of Counseling Psychology,* 1957, *4,* 183–190.

Tilgher, A. Work through the ages. In S. Noscow & W. H. Form (Eds.), *Man, work, and society.* New York: Basic Books, 1962.

Veterans Administration. *Program guide: Vocational counseling.* Washington: D. C.: Author, 1960.

Warman, R. E. Differential perceptions of counseling role. *Journal of Counseling Psychology,* 1960, *7,* 269–274.

Warman, R. E. The counseling role of college and university counseling centers. *Journal of Counseling Psychology*, 1961, *8*, 231–237.

Wilensky, H. L. Orderly careers and social participation. *American Sociological Review*, 1961, *26*, 521–539.

Wolford, R. A. A review of psychology in VA hospitals. *Journal of Counseling Psychology*, 1956, *3*, 243–248.

Yamamoto, K. Counseling psychologists—who are they? *Journal of Counseling Psychology*, 1963, *10*, 211–221.

Chapter 16
The Substantive Bases
of Counseling Psychology

JOHN G. DARLEY

Three rather general observations should help to provide a setting for this paper. First, curricular planning and curricular revision represent the orgiastic, tribal ceremony of that strange primitive culture known as the faculty. Periodically, under malign or benign heavenly forces, we are gripped by the need to plan or replan a curriculum; we thrash through the arguments and compromises involved in establishing a training program and fall back pleasantly exhausted and surfeited from the ceremonial task. Whether the new curriculum is better than the old, at what point cyclic erosions will start within it, or when the frenzy will grip us again, we do not know and cannot know, since we do not have clear means-ends evidence in the fields of education and training, even at the professional level.

Second, within the total field of psychology, the published materials show that counseling psychology as a special application does not appear to be in high repute among psychologists. With few exceptions our APA-approved doctoral training programs are not sought out by students; the number of people seeking ABEPP certification in the field remains small; the field is low on the status scale among psychological specialties requiring the doctorate; members of Division 17 show interesting patterns of overlapping membership in other APA divisions; and external financing is not clearly focussed, even though it is more extensive than we may realize. These observations, I believe, are correct, even though among nonpsychologists our status may be higher, for as Brayfield has clearly pointed out, "vocational counseling today is an officially recognized instrument of our national policy in social welfare and national security. By federal legislative enactment, administrative action, and operational example our government has extended recognition and support to vocational counseling" (Brayfield, 1961, p. 23). He refers here to developments in state and federal employment services, counseling programs in the Veterans Administration, the work of the

From Albert S. Thompson and Donald E. Super (Eds.), *The Professional Preparation of Counseling Psychologists: Report of the 1964 Greyston Conference.* (New York: Teachers College Press, ©1964 by Teachers College, Columbia University.)

Vocational Rehabilitation Administration, and the counselor training programs of NDEA.

Third, in the house of counseling there are not only many mansions but quite a few tenements, redevelopment projects, and real estate operators. This figure of speech does some violence to its original Biblical source, but it does convey the idea that nobody really owns the property, is responsible for keeping it up, or can control the architectonic harmony of its development. We here may wish to speak to the importance of the counselor with the Ph.D. and full training in psychology—a psychologist first and then a counselor. The APGA, with equal integrity and comparable concern for society's needs, appears about to promulgate standards of professional preparation based on training programs requiring two graduate years (Wrenn, 1962). Federal and state agencies may promote and regulate practices at various educational levels, resulting in the existence of professional personnel widely variant from APA or APGA standards. Yet the generic term *counseling* must serve to cover this broad spectrum; society's needs may not be ill-served by the spectrum, and society can only be confused in the absence of clear guidelines or buying guides when it seeks to purchase services to meet its needs. All this has been referred to as our "identity problem"—we have no clear identity. In connection with our identity problem, the report on "Counseling Psychology as a Specialty" by Division 17's Committee on Definition (APA, 1956) makes all the correct sounds but seems to have gone unheard. It may be that our identity is unidentifiable and that our specialization has inadequate boundary lines and fences.

What solutions have we proposed? They may be briefly listed: a fusion of training at the doctoral level between clinical and counseling programs; a core program at the doctoral level for the "helping professions" in psychology, from which specialties could emerge; the development of clearly distinctive programs, including the establishment of new kinds of specializations in the field; the restriction of counseling psychology to a particular age range and setting, such as student personnel service at the college level; the allocation of counseling functions to a lower level of training, as in a two-year M.A. program. Each of these possibilities, be it noted, made certain assumptions about curriculum planning and revision, though these were not clearly spelled out.

Brayfield's excellent review of the field, quoted earlier in another context, makes this proposal: "I see two opportunities confronting us: (1) to fulfill our responsibilities as psychologists to establish and develop a body of scientific knowledge as the basis for the psychological service called vocational counseling, and (2) to stimulate the general development of psychology as a science through such endeavors. We need, I believe, to re-establish or reaffirm our roots in basic psychology . . . we should be psychologists first and foremost . . . I propose that we commit ourselves to the development, as an enterprise with the highest priority, of a science of the psychology of occupational behavior" (Brayfield, 1961, pp. 50–51). I like the sound of this, but a doubt intrudes: I'm not sure whether those of us who are old counselors will be much good as old scientists in developing a psychology of occupational behavior.

Assuming now that this paper should focus on curricular content at the graduate level, a look at our own statements on this matter will be pertinent. In our 1952 statement on practicum training (APA, 1952a) the following words appear: "The basic core recommended by the APA as background for graduate study in clinical psychology is in general considered desirable background for psychologists" (p. 166). The citation is to the 1947 report of a special APA committee on training in clinical psychology, the Shakow Report (APA, 1947), which says that undergraduate training should involve 20 semester hours in psychology and approximately 20 semester hours of biological and physical sciences, nine in mathematics and statistics, six in educational philosophy and—it is to be hoped—practice teaching, twelve in social sciences, nine in cultural history, and six in the area of "psychology as revealed in literature," as well as reading knowledge of two foreign languages.

In our 1952 statement on standards for training in counseling (APA, 1952b), we said that "The counseling psychologist should be given opportunity to acquire a core of basic concepts, tools, and techniques that should be common to all psychologists" (p. 177). We did not, however, specify what this common core was; this task was as difficult in 1952 as it was at the Miami conference on graduate training in 1958 (Roe, Gustad, Moore, Ross, & Skodak, 1959). Beyond the common core, we wanted counseling psychologists to learn about personality organization and development, the social environment, appraisal of the individual, didactic aspects of counseling, doing research, and professional responsibilities, broadly defined. This same report of course stresses practicum experiences and slips in an "area of diversification" as a means of broadening the training experience. Another sentence appears in our own statement (APA, 1952b): "We feel strongly that research must continue as a basic job of the counseling psychologist and that he must be trained accordingly" (p. 176). This same statement has appeared from time to time in the definition of training for clinical psychology; whether it has been more honored in the breach or in the observance in either field is an open question.

Still on the track of the elusive core, I went back to the original report (APA, 1947) on graduate training in clinical psychology. Within *general* psychology it recommended content in general, physiological, and comparative psychology, as well as work in the history of psychology and contemporary schools of thought, and work in developmental and social psychology. Within the area of *psychodynamics of behavior* would be found work in fundamental theories of personality and motivation in both normal and abnormal behavior, plus work in experimental psychodynamics and psychopathology. We may skip the recommendations in diagnostic methods and therapy, though I should point out that these encompass and go beyond what we believe is the content of appraisal and counseling in our field. In the area of *research,* we find course work in experimental psychology, advanced statistics and quantitative methods, and research in dynamic psychology. From related disciplines, the committee wants the clinical psychologist to know something of physiological sciences, social organization and pathology, and cultural impacts on personality development, in addition to some elementary consideration of clinical medicine.

This 1947 report is an interesting and significant historic document. While no one identified primarily as a counseling psychologist participated in its preparation, I believe we in counseling psychology would have cheerfully concurred in its recommendations. Certainly I find nowhere else in my search a statement from counseling psychology about doctoral training that does not implicitly or explicitly stem from, and accept the assumptions of, the report.

Having studied the 1947 report in some detail, I can more easily understand the Paterson-Lofquist (1960) findings on similarities in training programs for counseling and clinical psychologists. Since we have always held to the ideal of creating a psychologist first and a specialist second in our graduate training programs, any recommendations about training will have high communality of definitions about general psychology; furthermore, the training programs *in action* will tend toward convergence on a substantial proportion of their subject matter.

Historically, as the forces of professionalization begin their work, idealized statements of graduate training programs come under practical translation in procedures for accreditation and institutional approval. Since accreditation in turn becomes the basis for certain kinds of financial support, more institutions seek it. As more institutions seek it, standards imperceptibly shift to allow greater participation in the training task by larger numbers of institutions. This is inevitable, since the standards are judgmental and consensual, rather than external or clearly objective. Psychology, unlike the older professions, also finds it hard to give up its skepticism, its individuality, and its commitment to variety in means-end formulations for graduate work. This adds to the difficulty of achieving consensus and occasionally erupts into soul-searching or actual revolt about our status as a professional field. We are presently, within the APA, witnessing another period of soul-searching about our past and future in this respect, including our legislative thrusts, our accreditation activities, and our professional aspirations versus our scientific roles.

At this point, I submit that we have a pragmatic or workable consensus about the substantive bases of counseling psychology and that further word games about it are both futile and unnecessary. It will approximate the 1947 statement I have already mentioned. The institutions carrying APA approval for training in counseling psychology represent tolerable limits of faculty strength, student selectivity, course offerings, and practicum facilities interacting together to produce adequately trained individuals. Needed improvements—and there are such—in these programs will come about under internal pressures and local soul-searching. In saying this, I may still reserve personal convictions that some are doing a better job than others, that I would be discriminating in sending children or adolescents to some individuals rather than others, and that I would want my daughter to marry the graduate of a particular approved program. But then I would be equally discriminating in choosing a physician, a psychiatrist, or even a clinical psychologist!

My point here is, quite simply, that we tend to reflect in our Ph.D. programs our commitment that, so far as possible, counselors will be well-grounded in psychology *and* will be given general minimum competence in the specialty of counseling *and* will then learn more on the job *and* will later have access to post-doctoral experiences of value in enhancing their competencies.

Any attempt to spell out course titles, areas of knowledge, proportional time distribution, or other details of training—to the goal of greater standardization—will not significantly reduce the variance in our Ph.D. programs, nor will it bring about any greater degree of compliance among those institutions carrying the training burden. Graduate schools have accepted about all the external social controls they are likely to accept, either in the form of accreditation, or meeting standards set forth in laws governing psychology, or responding to professional demands for extensively and minutely differentiated majors at the Ph.D. level. My position here is that of a conservative old department chairman, of course!

The discussions that follow will indicate whether or not my position that a tolerable consensus about the training of counseling psychologists exists is accepted. Let me assume for a moment that it is accepted. What then shall we say needs to be done about counseling psychology? Must we attract more students; if so, how? Must we attract better students; if so, how? Must we change our name and image; if so, how? The psychiatrist may feel that he can do anything better than the clinical psychologist, and he certainly knows he can do more things than the clinical psychologist. Our colleagues in clinical psychology may cherish the same set of perceptions about those of us who are in counseling psychology, and we probably perceive similar elements of superiority as we look at some of our colleagues in related subdoctoral specialties. Is this pecking order immutable? Or valid? Should we seek to establish research as the major contribution of the Ph.D. in counseling psychology? If so, do our graduate programs stress research and are our students likely to find appropriate models among us?

Alternatively, are we different in some way from other professional fields in psychology—less entrepreneurial, more service oriented, more educational, more committed to a kind of institutional practice—and are these differences sufficiently fundamental so that we shall remain essentially as we now are, with an acceptance of this self and a maturity about our contributions that will permit us to do our job without feeling insecure and without constant breast-beating? Since we have not successfully exhorted ourselves into visibility and distinctiveness, it is comforting to recall that the meek shall inherit the earth and that other applied fields of psychology are being driven back to greater concern with our research substrate and the need to synthesize the range of empiric studies available to us.

REFERENCES

American Psychological Association, Committee on Training in Clinical Psychology. Recommended graduate training program in clinical psychology. *American Psychologist*, 1947, *2*, 539–558.

American Psychological Association. Division of Counseling and Guidance, Committee on Counselor Training. The practicum training of counseling psychologists. *American Psychologist*, 1952, *7*, 182–188. (a)

American Psychological Association. Division of Counseling and Guidance, Committee on Counselor Training. Recommended standards for training counseling psychologists at the doctorate level. *American Psychologist*, 1952, *7*, 175–181. (b)

American Psychological Association. Division of Counseling Psychology, Committee on Definition. Counseling psychology as a specialty. *American Psychologist*, 1956, *11*, 282–285.

Brayfield, A. H. Vocational counseling today. In E. G. Williamson (Ed.), *Vocational counseling, a reappraisal in honor of Donald G. Paterson*. Minnesota Studies in Student Personnel Work, No. 11, Minneapolis: University of Minnesota Press, 1961, 22–58.

Paterson, D. G., & Lofquist, L. H. A note on the training of clinical and counseling psychologists. *American Psychologist*, 1960, *15*, 365–366.

Roe, A., Gustad, J. W., Moore, B. V., Ross, S., & Skodak, M. (Eds.). *Graduate education in psychology*. Report of the Conference on Graduate Education in Psychology held at Miami Beach, Florida. Washington, D. C.: The American Psychological Association, 1959.

Wrenn, C. *The counselor in a changing world.* Washington, D. C.: American Personnel and Guidance Association, 1962. (See also *Report of the committee on professional preparation and standards,* American Personnel and Guidance Association, Washington, D. C.: August 1963. Mimeograph, 13 pp.)

Chapter 17
Recommendations of
the 1964 Greyston Conference

ALBERT S. THOMPSON
DONALD E. SUPER

INTRODUCTION TO THE RECOMMENDATIONS

Counseling psychology is organized to facilitate the development of the potential of all persons. The attainment of this goal requires that counseling psychologists be prepared to understand and to work with persons at all age levels in all stages of ability or disability and in all types of settings. The emphasis in this specialty has been and will no doubt continue to be on adolescence and adulthood. It is recognized that counseling psychology must concern itself actively with social and economic issues affecting the contexts in which people develop and for which they must acquire appropriate repertoires of adaptive behavior.

This conference endorses the historic statements of the Division of Counseling Psychology on the roles and preparation of counseling psychologists, statements that are reproduced in the Appendices of this report. With these statements we agree.

The conferees further recognize that counseling psychology has significant overlapping interests with the related specialties of clinical, educational, industrial or personnel, and school psychology. The great majority, but not all, subscribe to the statement that counseling psychology has a special substance and emphases requiring preparation in a number of didactic as well as practicum courses that are not necessarily included in the preparation of other psychologists. This special substance consists of the educational and vocational and, less distinctively, the familial and community environments of the individual, of the psychology of normal development, and of the psychology of the physically, emotionally, and mentally

This chapter brings together specific recommendations prepared by the commissions of the conference and discussed at the final plenary session. The recommendations are presented separately in order to make them easily available but are best understood in the light of the rest of the report.

From Albert S. Thompson and Donald E. Super (Eds.), *The Professional Preparation of Counseling Psychologists: Report of the 1964 Greyston Conference*. (New York: Teachers College Press, © 1964 by Teachers College, Columbia University.)

handicapped; the special emphases are on the appraisal and use of assets for furthering individual development in the existing or changing environment.

With these basic argreements, the following recommendations are made by the conference and are herewith transmitted to the appropriate boards, organizations, agencies, institutions, and interested individuals.

It is recommended to counseling psychologists that they:

1. seek ABEPP certification, as well as professional approval, as psychologists within the states in which they are employed as soon as eligibility requirements are met;
2. seek identification with and actively participate in the appropriate division of the APA, in state psychological associations, and in local or state counseling or student personnel associations;
3. work with other appropriate groups and institutions in support of collaborative efforts to promote the realization of the potential of all persons.

It is recommended to the division of counseling psychology that:

1. a study be made of methods and criteria for the selection of doctoral students in counseling psychology to provide universities with better guidelines for admitting appropriate students to the field;
2. a brochure describing the field of counseling psychology be prepared for dissemination in undergraduate departments and high schools to help overcome the lack of awareness at those levels of the existence and nature of counseling psychology as a specialty. The brochure should include information concerning the availability of various types of financial support for training in counseling psychology;
3. more active steps be taken to increase the number and variety of training grants to students, universities, and internship facilities with APA Central Office and Education and Training Board cooperation, in order to strengthen the support and the appeal of training in counseling psychology;
4. information on social and economic problems affecting student and client development and adjustment be more effectively made available to counseling psychologists, by means such as bibliographies and conferences on the problems of technological change, college characteristics, and so forth.

It is recommended to the APA, together with its appropriate boards, that it:

1. analyze *convergent* and *divergent* trends in programs for the preparation of counseling and of clinical psychologists, evaluating the effects of these trends on the numbers, functions, and roles of psychologists receiving degrees in these more and less differentiated programs, in order to provide guidelines for future development;
2. organize for dissemination and make available through appropriate channels, data on hand on approved programs in counseling psychology, to clarify alternative types of training for the guidance of departments

studying their programs and as an aid to students in the selection of institutions offering the type of program and emphasis desired;

3. support the university departments in keeping requirements within reasonable limits, despite the conflicting demands of maintaining close ties with the basic core of scientific psychology, the more common requirements of training in all the psychological services, and the special needs of counseling psychology, in order to enable students to complete training in a reasonable period of time;

4. develop explicit criteria for evaluating internships in counseling psychology (making use of materials already prepared by the Division of Counseling Psychology), evaluate internship centers applying for evaluation after the publicizing of the program, and publish an approved list of internship facilities (coordinating internship evaluation procedures with those developed for related specialties), in order to improve and stabilize the utilization of such facilities;

5. analyze the roles in producing counseling psychologists played by a few departments of psychology that do not announce specialties, by departments of educational psychology, and by departments of guidance in schools of education with programs that have developed without the cognizance of the Education and Training Board, and consider the implications of the findings of such an analysis for its advisory and accrediting activities;

6. plan and conduct a conference of appropriate persons, in view of the role of counseling psychology in meeting the mental health needs of college students, adolescents in transition from school to work, technologically displaced adults, the handicapped and disabled, and older persons in a rapidly changing and complex society, to consider ways of increasing the financial support necessary to the training of more counseling psychologists. The conference took special action on a resolution to this effect, transmitted on February 7 to the Executive Officer of the APA, as follows:

Whereas four million students in American colleges, preparing for leadership positions, cope daily with questions of roles and values in a world that is increasingly complex; six million adults, adrift in a rapidly automated economy, face aggravated problems of placement in the world of work while uncounted others are concerned with changing and sometimes conflicting roles; more than a million adolescents leaving high school with diplomas but not going on to college flounder and are uncertain because they, too, do not seem to fit in; and additional millions of Americans of various ages, handicapped by years of cultural disadvantage, stagnate in apathy or seethe in discontent; And whereas the mental health needs associated with these roles and conflicts are those with which counseling psychologists are peculiarly prepared to deal;

Be it resolved, by this Conference on the Professional Preparation of Counseling Psychologists, this 26th day of January, 1964, that the National Institute of Mental Health be asked to support a conference of directors of counseling psychology training programs and of appropriate representatives of the American Psychological Association, to consider the need for more adequate support of such programs, leading to the strengthening of their capacity to produce psychologists of a type and in the numbers required to meet these social needs.

It is recommended to universities offering graduate degrees in psychology that:

1. information on the nature and functions of counseling psychology and on training and employment opportunities in this specialty be covered in appropriate courses and in other ways, to help overcome the relative ignorance of counseling psychology among potential students;

2. counseling psychology programs not be developed unless with full participation by psychologists with clear competence in, and a career commitment to, counseling psychology, so that appropriate faculty as well as internship role models may be available to students in this specialty;

3. subject matter prerequisites for admission in counseling psychology programs (when such are offered) be flexible in view of the varied backgrounds and ages from which this specialty draws, even while encouragement is given for the early choice of the specialty;

4. counseling psychology programs provide supervised professional experience beginning with the first year, even while ensuring the study of basic courses as early in the program as possible. Increasing professional responsibility can be given in the three or four year planned sequence of full-time study;

5. counseling psychology programs permit the development of breadth of competence and of ability to work in the variety of settings in which services are needed (vocational psychology has been and is an appropriate area of special strength and competence requiring depth of experience in at least one type of setting);

6. attempt to facilitate exchanges of interns among institutions with captive internship facilities, leading to the publishing of a list of such exchanges, to help overcome parochial tendencies;

7. early and continuing research experience be provided for students of counseling psychology to develop habits of basing decisions on data and of seeking the data (in research or in case studies) on which to base decisions;

8. the bases for university evaluation of faculty in the service fields be restudied with the possibility that professional advancement may properly be based on various kinds of service contributions that are legitimate alternatives to the traditional research and publication requirement;

9. responsibility for the preparation of counselors at the master's level be assumed in cooperation with other departments to meet rising demands for competent counselors that far exceed the potential number of doctorally trained psychologists;

10. for doctoral candidates in counseling psychology, the existing doctorates of philosophy and education, with the research requirement, be continued for the foreseeable future. This conference is not prepared to substitute a professional degree in psychology. This recommendation is not intended to discourage experimental programs in strong departments;

11. the foreign language requirement for the doctorate be dropped, in recognition of the fact that its original intent was the development of skills needed in research only in certain fields.

It is recommended to practicum agencies and internship centers that:

1. the key figure (generally a coordinator or supervisor but not necessarily all

supervisors) of the practicum experience of students of counseling psychology be clearly identifiable as a counseling psychologist to provide an appropriate role model;

2. practicum experience be a progressive sequence designed to provide early contact with real situations and persons, the handling of problems with which a degree of success is likely at the student's stage of professional development, familiarity with a variety of clients and settings, and the understanding and skill in working with one type of client in one kind of setting that will provide a sound basis for further professional development (it is recognized that this may mean an internship experience in a second type of setting; variety of client is probably more important than variety of setting);

3. the internship be organized to provide experience in appraisal, individual and group counseling, consultation with other professional persons, supervision of less advanced practicum students or less trained counselors, experience in dealing with other community agencies and with administrators, and first-hand contact with, if not actual experience in, research, all in association with appropriate role models;

4. the effects of internship experiences on students be evaluated, both for the guidance of individuals involved and for the planning of university and of internship programs;

5. the present pattern of predoctoral internships be continued as the standard program but that experimentation with postdoctoral internships be approved when the university assumes responsibility for exercising appropriate control over the student's plans.

It is recommended to agencies employing counseling psychologists that:

1. the establishment of increasing numbers of internships in counseling psychology by agencies that need the services of counseling psychologists be continued;

2. the provision of adequate stipends for interns and of qualified supervisors with scheduled time for internship supervision is a legitimate use of regular agency funds as well as of special training grants, as it ensures both a supply of candidates for regular employment and a flow of new ideas and hence the improvement of services in the agency.

It is recommended to agencies supporting training and services in psychology, guidance, and rehabilitation that:

1. consideration be given to the full and direct support of the professional preparation of counseling psychologists, as an effective means of meeting the developmental (educational, vocational, mental health) needs of large numbers of persons at all ages and in a variety of settings, through the direct service of the counseling psychologists themselves and through their contribution in training, supervising, and consulting with workers in related specialties and in conducting research.

CONCEPTIONS OF COUNSELING PSYCHOLOGY: 1968-1976

6

Chapter 18
The Counseling Psychologist:
A Definition in 1968

JEAN-PIERRE JORDAAN
ROGER A. MYERS
WILBUR L. LAYTON
HENRY H. MORGAN

A Project of the Professional Affairs Committee
Division of Counseling Psychology
American Psychological Association

PSYCHOLOGIST, COUNSELING. Provides individual and group guidance and counseling services in schools, colleges and universities, hospitals, clinics, rehabilitation centers, and industry, to assist individuals in achieving more effective personal, social, educational, and vocational development and achievement. Collects data about the individual through use of interview, case history, and observational techniques. Selects, administers, scores, and interprets psychological tests designed to assess individual's intelligence, aptitudes, abilities, and interests, applying knowledge of statistical analysis.

From J. P. Jordaan, R. A. Myers, W. L. Layton, and H. H. Morgan (Eds.), *The Counseling Psychologist*. Division of Counseling Psychology, American Psychological Association. ©1968 by the American Psychological Association. (New York: Teachers College Press, 1968). Reprinted by permission.

Evaluates data to identify cause of problem and to determine advisability of counseling or referral to other specialists or institutions. Conducts counseling or therapeutic interviews to assist individual to gain insight into personal problems, define goals, and plan action reflecting his interests, abilities, and needs. Provides occupational, educational, and other information to enable individual to formulate realistic educational and vocational plans. Follows up results of counseling to determine reliability and validity of treatment used. May engage in research to develop and improve diagnostic and counseling techniques.[1]

THE COUNSELING PSYCHOLOGIST

Have you ever been concerned about whether a step or decision that you were contemplating was the right one? Felt that the information that you had about yourself or some situation was inadequate? Wondered how you might use your interests, abilities, and personal assets to the best advantage? Felt the need to take stock of your goals and values or to evaluate your plans for achieving them? Been compelled by some experience that you have had to question or revise your self-image? Become aware of an inadequacy in yourself that you felt you should do something about? Been disturbed by your inability to live up to your own or others' expectations? Been concerned about your relationships with other people? Had the desire to embark on a program of self-development?

If you have, you will know that unaided introspection and trial and error are not always the best or most economical ways of dealing with such situations and that a knowledgeable and understanding person can often be very helpful in arriving at a workable plan or solution.

There are professionally trained persons who specialize in helping individuals with these kinds of problems and needs. This booklet is about one such group of persons, counseling psychologists. Having read it, you may wish to include counseling psychology among the career possibilities which you intend to explore further. Or, if you are already considering it, this booklet may help you to become better acquainted with the field of counseling psychology.

Above is a definition of counseling psychologist taken from the Dictionary of Occupational Titles, a sourcebook frequently used by counseling psychologists. It is suggested that you read it carefully because it helps to set the stage for the discussion that follows.

WHAT A COUNSELING PSYCHOLOGIST DOES

Three Roles

Counseling psychologists play three different but complementary roles when engaging in practice, as contrasted with related research, teaching, or

---

[1] Adapted, with slight modifications, from the *Dictionary of Occupational Titles. Volume I: Definitions of Titles.* U. S. Department of Labor, Washington, D. C.: 1965.

administration. One is to help persons who are presently experiencing difficulty. This is the *remedial* or *rehabilitative role*. Another is to anticipate, circumvent, and, if possible, forestall difficulties that may arise in the future. This is the *preventive role*. A third role is to help individuals to plan, obtain, and derive maximum benefit from educational, social, avocational, vocational, and other kinds of experiences that will enable them to discover and develop their potentials. This is the *educative and developmental role*.

The counseling psychologist is therefore as concerned with facilitating optimum development as he is with remedying faulty development, as interested in cultivating assets and potentials as he is in correcting and overcoming deficits and shortcomings.

Clientele

Counseling psychologists work in many different settings and with many kinds of persons. The *setting* may be a college counseling center, a mental or general hospital, a rehabilitation center, a mental hygiene clinic, a community vocational guidance center, a high school, the personnel department of a business or factory, a project for retraining displaced workers, or a training camp for underprivileged and undereducated youth who lack job skills. His *clients* may be high school students, mental patients, older persons facing retirement, college students, outpatients of a mental health clinic, physically handicapped persons, delinquents, unemployed, underemployed or displaced workers, or normal adults in need of educational, vocational, or personal guidance.

What these clients need in the way of help will vary considerably. If the client's problem stems from lack of information ("How does one get to be a surveyor?" or "Which colleges have good art departments?"), the counselor may not need to do much more than supply accurate information or to direct him to an appropriate source. However, if the client's problem stems from an unclear or unrealistic self-concept, lack or loss of skill, lack of direction, feelings of inadequacy, unrealistic aspirations, distortion or denial of feelings and experiences or inability to hold or perform satisfactorily on a job, much more than information is needed. Identifying the source of a client's difficulty and devising appropriate strategies for dealing with it are among the most difficult and important of a psychologist's tasks.

How He/She Helps

To these problems the counseling psychologist brings a point of view that holds that individuals can change, can lead satisfying lives, can be self-directing, and can find ways of using their resources, even though these may have been impaired by incapacitating attitudes and feelings, slow maturation, cultural deprivation, lack of opportunity, illness, injury, or old age.

To achieve these goals, the counseling psychologist uses a variety of techniques. One of these is the use of *exploratory* experiences. He may, for example, get the individual to try himself out in certain tasks or situations in order to build confidence, to discover or develop his interests and abilities, or to practice new and more constructive ways of handling situations that are giving him trouble. For example, he may encourage a would-be trial lawyer to join a debating club in order to test the wisdom of his choice or to develop certain useful verbal skills. Or he may arrange for a convalescing mental patient to work several hours a day in the hospital cafeteria in order to accustom him to the kind of work routines he will face when he is discharged. Or he may get a person who loses his temper whenever he thinks he is being criticized to formulate and practice more constructive responses, either alone, in counseling interviews, or in role playing situations such as psychodramas.

Another commonly used technique is *environmental intervention.* Since a person's behavior is determined not only by what goes on inside of him but also by what goes on about him, there are obvious limits to what can be accomplished within the four walls of a consulting room. The gains made in counseling can be dissipated very quickly if, for example, a delinquent, an addict, or a discharged mental patient returns to an unfavorable situation that caused or contributed to his problem. These are, of course, extreme examples. More often the problem is not how to separate a person from a patently unsatisfactory situation but how to modify certain features of his environment in ways that will enhance his chances of making a successful adjustment.

Thus a counseling psychologist may explore with the prospective employer of a physically disabled person, or of a mental patient who is about to be discharged, ways of restructuring the patient's job so as to maximize his chances of success. Or he may confer with the patient's wife about the kinds of demands that she should, or should not, make of him upon his return. Or, if he works in a college setting, he may investigate the stresses and strains to which students are subjected and suggest ways in which student unions, student government, residential arrangements, and the like may be modified or used to create not only a less destructively stressful campus milieu, but also one which will make a positive contribution to the students' intellectual, personal, and social development.

As his job title suggests, the counseling psychologist's primary tool is *counseling.* Counseling, whether it is performed with individuals or groups, is a special kind of interchange between a professionally trained counselor and a person who has sought or might benefit from his services—special because it is based on unconditional acceptance of the client and is usually free of blame, criticism, recrimination, and reproof. Its major premise is that guided self-examination, self-discovery, and self-generated decisions are more likely to lead to constructive action and personal growth than persuasion, exhortation, prescription, or advice. As some of the newer techniques for modifying client behavior (for example, modelling, desensitization, operant reinforcement, computer assisted counseling, and practice in role-taking and self-regulation) become better understood, present conceptions of counseling may change considerably. The prevailing emphasis, however, is still on using interviews to create the kind of atmosphere in which the individual can examine his feelings and experiences without being defensive and can be helped to put his views about himself and the world to the test by trying himself out in new roles and situations, by taking tests that provide objective data about his interests, abilities, and personality, and by reading books and other materials that describe the nature and requirements of important aspects of his environment such as occupations, colleges, and various types of training programs and work-settings. Having developed a clearer picture of himself and of these and other aspects of his environment, he is in a better position to change, or to come to terms with, the realities as he now sees them.

The counselor serves as a guide, facilitator, informant, question-raiser, commentator, and, above all, as a person on whom the counselee can try out ideas and ways of behaving. The expectation is that the client will emerge from this experience not only with a solution to his present problem, but also with knowledge and strategies that he can apply to the solution of future problems.

The Psychologist as a Data-Oriented Problem-Solver

To achieve these objectives the counselor must be able to integrate two rather different roles. The one requires that he place himself in the client's shoes, adopt *his* frame of reference, see the world through *his* eyes. The premise is that subjective reality (what the client believes to be so) is often as important and objective reality (what actually is so). The other role involves looking at things, not through the client's eyes, but through a psychologist's eyes.

When he lays aside the client's frame of reference and adopts his own, the counselor substitutes the scientific role for the empathic role. He turns his attention to collecting, analyzing, and integrating pertinent facts about the individual and his situation. He administers tests, accumulates biographical data, studies and evaluates the client's behavior, and, where appropriate, solicits reports from teachers, employers, and other persons who know the individual and his situation. These data help him to understand the client's present behavior, to evaluate his readiness for counseling, to formulate and test hypotheses about the source of his difficulty, to determine what the goals of counseling should be, to decide on à strategy for bringing the client's perceptions into line with reality, and to identify feasible alternatives.

Consequently, counselors learn not only to be empathic (to enter into another person's world) but also to be scientific (to seek and be guided by data). They have to be familiar with research findings regarding the predictive validity of various types of tests, the ways in which people differ, the practical significance of these differences, the nature and etiology of various types of malfunctioning, the relative merits of various counseling strategies, social and economic factors which influence a person's prospects, the distinguishing characteristics of colleges and occupations, occupational and industrial trends, the state of the labor market, and the availability of various kinds of community resources. They use this knowledge to decide what additional information is needed about a person and his situation and how to obtain it. They also use it to generate hypotheses about the nature of the client's difficulty and to decide on possible solutions.

Because in formulating and testing hypotheses he tries to be guided by data and not by his own predilections and preconceptions, the counseling psychologist can lay claim to being a scientific practitioner. As we shall see later, the counseling psychologist is expected not only to have a scientist's respect for existing knowledge, but he is also expected to add to it. He is encouraged, in other words, to be both a producer and a consumer of research.

Differences between Counseling Psychology and Clinical Psychology

There are those who hold that clinical and counseling psychologists are "kissing cousins" rather than blood brothers. They contend that there are important differences between the two kindred specialties that should be recognized and nurtured. There are others who say that the differences have become blurred and are no longer valid or useful. It is true that there are training programs that minimize the distinction between clinical and counseling psychology. It is also true that there are positions that enable or require the counseling psychologist to perform many or all of the functions usually performed by clinical psychologists and vice versa. How a counseling psychologist will function on the job is usually a matter of the kind of training he received, the role he himself aspires to, and his employer's expectations.

A recent conference on the preparation of counseling psychologists (Thompson & Super, 1964) indicates what a group of leaders in this field perceived to be the distinguishing characteristics of their specialty:

First, the counseling psychologist tends to work with normal, convalescent or recovered persons whose problems are neither so severe nor so deep-seated that they require intensive long-term treatment. Severely incapacitated persons whose personalities will have to undergo radical change before they can be helped or rehabilitated are generally referred to other practitioners who specialize in intensive, long-term treatment.

Second, the emphasis is on the more typical and, in that sense, more normal needs and problems of people that can be dealt with, after some initial exploration and clarification, on a relatively cognitive level.

Third, the focus is not on reconstructing personalities but on drawing out and developing what is already there and on helping people to recognize, develop, and use the resources that they have within themselves or in their environment. This holds even for the counseling psychologist who works in a mental hospital. He usually sees himself as doing his most useful work when the patient has improved to a point where vocational planning and possible re-entry into the community become feasible, perhaps with exploratory employment in the hospital as a first step. Although he cannot ignore the patient's pathology and will need to utilize therapeutic insights and procedures, he will tend to focus on helping him capitalize on residual, partially restored, or newly developed social and vocational skills, rather than on reshaping his personality.

Fourth, although he uses psychotherapeutic techniques in his work with clients, he does not limit himself to these. Exploratory experiences and environmental intervention using community resources and tests of personality, interest, aptitudes, and values are utilized much more frequently than they are by psychologists who function primarily as psychotherapists.

Fifth, counseling psychologists attach particular importance to the role of education and work in a person's life. They hold that our lives and even our personalities are shaped by what we learn and by how we earn our living. Education and occupation, they say, are not only the most important determinants of social status but, along with marriage, perhaps the most important sources of satisfaction and frustration in a person's life. Consequently, the counseling psychologist who is interested in facilitating self-development and self-realization is likely to feel that anything he can do to help individuals make thoughtful educational and vocational decisions, to improve their performance at school, in training, or on the job, or to find a more congenial or stimulating position, curriculum or training program will yield important, long-term dividends. It is therefore no accident that many counseling psychology training programs place heavy emphasis on the study of educational and vocational development.

Finally, as the Greyston report emphasizes, the counseling psychologist's role is essentially educational, developmental, and preventive rather than medical or remedial. In connection with his preventive role, it might be pointed out that even cities with good fire prevention programs maintain fire-fighting crews and equipment. Counseling psychologists will no doubt continue to be engaged in putting out fires as well as in preventing them. But as they become more adept, not only at identifying, removing, or circumventing obstacles to *normal* development but also at helping individuals to achieve *optimal* development (that is, not just to become or remain adjusted, but to fulfill their potential for growth), it is likely that this developmental rather than the preventive or remedial role will become the over-riding concern of many counseling psychologists, particularly those who work in educational settings.

WORK SETTINGS AND DUTIES

We have stated that counseling psychologists work in a variety of settings. Although there are certain activities in which all counseling psychologists engage, the clientele they serve and the services they provide can vary considerably from one setting to another. These similarities and differences will become clearer as we examine the various settings in which counseling psychologists work and the roles they play.

Where Counseling Psychologists Work

There are at least a dozen different agencies and institutions that employ counseling psychologists, including colleges and universities, schools, hospitals, community agencies, state and city governments, and business and industry. The following table (Table 1) summarizes the findings of a recent study (Thompson & Super, 1964, p. 44) and indicates the percentage of counseling psychologists employed in five broad areas.

Table 1. Settings in which counseling psychologists work

	%
Educational settings (colleges and universities, private and public schools)	64
Health-related settings (hospitals, rehabilitation agencies, mental health clinics)	11
Industry and government (excluding hospitals and schools)	13
Community counseling agencies	5
Private practice	5
Other	2

Most counseling psychologists work in educational settings. Of these, approximately nine out of every ten are employed by colleges and universities. Several developments are under way which are likely to increase the demand for counseling psychologists in certain of the areas listed above, and in another ten years the figures cited in Table 1 may look quite different from what they do today. What these anticipated developments are will be discussed a little later when we come to the topic of current employment opportunities and future trends.

What Counseling Psychologists Do

One way to get a picture of a profession is to ask where the people who practice it work. Another is to ask what they do. The table that follows (Table 2; Thompson & Super, 1964, p. 48) shows the percentage of counseling psychologists holding various positions.

Table 2. Positions held by counseling psychologists

	%
Primarily teaching: Professor, department head, other academic positions	32
Primarily service administration: Director or coordinator of a university counseling center, psychological clinic, counseling service, community agency, rehabilitation project, student personnel services	23
Primarily service: Counselor, psychologist, psychotherapist, consultant in colleges, universities, schools, private practice	38
Miscellaneous	7

The five activities in which counseling psychologists engage most frequently are teaching, research, administration, consulting, and counseling. Usually they engage in more than one of these. Thus the teacher and administrator may do some counseling or supervision. About 20% of all counseling psychologists devote more than half of their time to counseling; 70% devote at least some time to it.

How the Setting in Which Counseling Psychologists Work Determines Their Role

Although certain skills, interests, and activities are common to all counseling psychologists, there is room for considerable variation in what counseling psychologists do and how they do it. The key to these differences is of course the particular setting in which they happen to be working. The setting determines the clientele with which counseling psychologists work, their goals, and to some extent also their procedures.

Let us take three settings in which counseling psychologists work and see how what they do is affected by where they work.

The professor of counseling psychology. Like other professors he will advise students, teach, serve on committees, study, write, and do research. But he will also differ from them in several important ways. The courses that he teaches are likely to carry such labels as: "Principles and Practices of Guidance," "Tests and Measurements," "Methods of Appraisal and Diagnosis," "Sources and Uses of Occupational Information," "Theories of Counseling," "Techniques of Counseling," "Counseling the Culturally Disadvantaged," "Physical and Psychological Aspects of Disability." His research is likely to take him into such areas as determinants of vocational choice, behavior modification, the outcomes of counseling, the prediction of job satisfaction, and group counseling. By doing some counseling himself, or by supervising the work of learner-counselors, or through his teaching and research, he keeps close to the substance and procedures of counseling. This is only to be expected since his primary function is to train counselors.

The counseling psychologist in a college counseling center. Although he may teach some courses and hold professorial rank, his principal function is to counsel. He spends a considerable part of his day counseling students and whomever else the counseling center is designed or prepared to serve. The kinds of problems that are brought to him include vocational indecision, lack of satisfaction with college or social life, poor grades, doubts about the wisdom of continuing in college, feelings of depression, lack of a sense of direction or fulfillment.

In order to decide what kind of help the student needs, the counseling psychologist may confer with his colleagues in the center and with psychiatric consultants. In these staff conferences the decision arrived at may be to have a senior and more experienced staff member work with the client, to assign him to a junior counselor or intern, or to refer him to a more appropriate source of help. Promising techniques for helping the client with his problems may be explored and periodic case conferences scheduled to evaluate his progress.

If the decision is to assign the client to a junior member of the staff or to an intern or student-trainee, the counseling psychologist may supervise the counselor's work. The decision arrived at in a case conference may be to modify some aspect of the client's environment (his course load, his parents' expectations of him, his living arrangements, and so on), in which case the counseling psychologist will confer with those who are in a position to effect these changes.

As a member of a profession that prides itself on the fact that its members are not only practitioners but also scientists, he is likely also to have research interests that lead him to undertake investigations concerning the effectiveness of the service that he and his colleagues render and the most promising means of realizing certain desired counseling outcomes. The most effective and sought-after college counselors are those who can contribute to, as well as apply, existing psychological knowledge. These are the ones who feel most at home in an academic environment.

Mindful of the important influence that the environment can have on behavior, he may also become involved, either as a consultant or a participant, in curriculum revision, orientation programs, residence halls work, and the like.

A counseling psychologist in a Veterans' Administration hospital. Because of the setting in which he works, his clientele differs in important ways from that of clinical psychologists. His clientele includes persons who have been emotionally or physically incapacitated and have now reached a point in their convalescence when they can begin to think about re-entering the community. Where disability has been alleviated rather than removed, the patient may have to be helped to accept his disability and to consider and prepare for another occupation.

Because his work involves identifying and developing remaining strengths and locating situations in which these might profitably be utilized, the counseling psychologist in a hospital performs a wide variety of functions. These include individual and group counseling, visiting employment agencies and potential employers, follow-up after discharge, close collaboration with medical specialists, occupational therapists, shop instructors and the like, and planning helpful social and work experiences in the hospital as the patient's confidence and condition improve. He also attends case conferences and, if there are psychologist-interns or junior level psychologists on the staff, a substantial portion of his time may be devoted to supervision and training. Like his colleagues who work in other settings he will, if his interests tend in this direction, also find opportunities to engage in research, if not directly, then at least as a consultant to interns who are in the process of developing or executing a dissertation proposal.

Differing Satisfactions and Rewards

The ideal that is held up to psychologists in training is that they should be scientists as well as practitioners. To do justice to both these roles is not easy and most psychologists end up emphasizing one or the other. A counseling psychologist will usually select a work setting with this in mind. If he is attracted to a scholarly life in which the emphasis is on teaching, research and the professional preparation of future counseling psychologists, he is likely to seek a professorial appointment in a university; if he prefers to be an active practitioner, he is more likely to be attracted to counseling centers, community agencies, and rehabilitation centers, where he will be encouraged and expected to carry a fairly heavy case load.

However, these need not be "all or none" choices. Psychologists whose primary responsibility is teaching and research can still find time to engage in counseling; those who work in counseling centers, hospitals, or community agencies have opportunities to engage in research, training, and teaching in addition to providing direct service to clients.

The satisfactions that people seek and get from their work are both a matter of their particular psychological make-up and of what their work-setting demands, allows, encourages, and rewards. The important thing to remember is that because of the multiplicity of settings in which counseling psychologists work and the variety of functions that they perform, the occupation can accommodate persons with differing interests, values, talents, and aspirations.

HOW ONE BECOMES A COUNSELING PSYCHOLOGIST

According to the *Occupational Outlook Handbook,* there are approximately 27,000 psychologists in the United States. By no means all of these possess the Ph.D. or Ed.D. For example, almost half of all psychologists who work in mental health establishments lack the doctorate. Although sub-doctorally trained persons will continue to be in demand, the emphasis in many training programs is on doctoral level training. There are several reasons for this: the skills that today's psychologist must master are not only more varied, but also more complex; the responsibilities that he is called upon to assume are much greater; the body of knowledge that he must master has grown so rapidly that it can no longer be acquired in a year or two; most important of all, there is the expectation that he will serve the profession not only as a highly skilled and unsupervised practitioner, but also as a competent and productive researcher.

Undergraduate Preparation

Some undergraduates develop an interest in psychology quite early and major in it. Others develop this interest later and consequently are not as well prepared in psychology when they enter graduate school. Most departments of psychology and schools of education allow for this. Although some require or prefer an undergraduate major in psychology, many do not. Undergraduate courses which a prospective psychologist will find helpful, in addition to psychology, are mathematics, statistics, computer science, foreign languages (especially French and German), courses in the humanities that deal with man in his culture, and courses in the biological, physical, and social sciences.

Doctoral or Subdoctoral, Ph.D. or Ed.D.?

Some graduate departments and schools of education admit only students who plan to obtain a doctorate. Others also accept students on the subdoctoral level. Subdoctoral programs are usually of one or two years' duration and lead to an M.A., M.Ed., or professional diploma in counseling. They prepare students for beginning and intermediate positions; more responsible, less supervised positions, particularly those requiring research competence and advanced clinical skills, are usually reserved for persons with the doctorate. Students who are not sure that they want to commit themselves to a long program, or who cannot qualify initially for admission to a doctoral program, often select a subdoctoral program and then transfer to the doctoral program if and when their grades or aspirations change.

Some graduate departments and schools of education offer only the Ph.D. (a doctorate in philosophy), others only the Ed.D. (a doctorate in education). Some offer both. The two programs may be quite similar, differing only in the foreign language requirement and in the distribution of courses outside the major field. Sometimes the distinguishing feature is a heavier concentration in the Ph.D. program on theory, research methods, and experimental design. The Ph.D. is conceived by some to be the more appropriate degree for those who intend to work in academic or research settings, while the Ed.D. is thought to be more appropriate for those who are more interested in the practical applications and the broader perspective that supporting work in education, anthropology, sociology, and other related disciplines can furnish.

The foregoing cannot be used as a rule of thumb, however. The Ed.D. and Ph.D. programs vary from one institution to another and the differences between the two programs may be quite negligible. Both types of programs produce competent, versatile, data-oriented practitioners who are able to apply and add to existing knowledge, and who meet all certification, licensing, and employment requirements.

Requirements for admission. In considering applicants, graduate departments usually review undergraduate attainment, references, performance on such tests as the *Miller Analogies* or the *Graduate Record Examination,* and relevant experience. These and other admission requirements, such as application deadlines, required references, and tests, vary with the specific institution. It is recommended that prospective applicants begin corresponding with institutions about admission approximately nine months in advance.

Differences in training programs. There are more than 40 institutions that offer advanced degrees in counseling psychology and such related areas as rehabilitation counseling, student personnel work, and guidance. Of these only about half have approved programs in counseling psychology. These are programs which meet the standards laid down by the American Psychological Association's Education and Training Board. It should be pointed out, however, that there are some good schools that have elected not to seek or to retain accreditation. For information about training programs and financial support consult *Graduate Study in Psychology,* published by the American Psychological Association.

Most universities that have accredited programs in counseling psychology also have approved programs in clinical psychology. In some institutions the two programs resemble each other very closely, differing perhaps only in the practicum and internship experiences of students. In others, the differences are more substantial. The distinguishing factor may be the greater emphasis in the counseling psychology program on the process involved in arriving at sound educational and vocational decisions and the ways in which this process may be facilitated. Where this is the case, the distinguishing courses may be ones bearing such titles as "The Sociology of Work," "Sources of Educational and Occupational Information," "The Psychology of Careers," "Characteristics of American Colleges," "Occupational Structure of the United States," "Vocational Rehabilitation of the Physically Disabled," "Psychological Aspects of Disabilities," "Vocational Testing," and "Techniques of Educational and Vocational Counseling."

In some institutions the counseling program is a cooperative undertaking between several departments. The cooperating departments are frequently the department of psychology, the department of guidance, and the department of educational psychology. Joint programs like these reflect counseling psychology's long standing interest in preparing counselors who will work in educational settings.

Which type of program? Although there are differences among the three types of programs described above, the similarities frequently outweigh the differences. To select a program appropriate to his needs the prospective student should obtain program descriptions from a variety of institutions and compare them. If he has difficulty deciding among them or has doubts about whether this is the right career for him, he should consult his adviser, a member of the psychology department at his college, or the nearest counseling center.

Students who are interested in vocational counseling and in work as an organizing and integrating factor in a person's life, will want to consider programs that reflect this particular emphasis. Students who plan to work in educational settings, and particularly in secondary schools and junior colleges, will want to look at programs that are administered jointly by schools or departments of education and psychology. Students who have not yet chosen between clinical and counseling psychology or who prefer a program that minimizes the distinction between the two specialties, will want to consider programs in which they can explore both types of offerings and can transfer from one to the other without difficulty.

Content of programs. Doctoral programs in counseling psychology usually encompass the following areas:

1. *Nature of the Social Environment:* structure of the world of work, occupational trends, social class structure, social mobility, community resources, culture and personality, characteristics of colleges and their student bodies, educational systems, and social and economic factors that affect development and adjustment
2. *Personality Organization and Development:* developmental psychology, theories of personality, theories of learning, the psychology of the physically, emotionally, and mentally handicapped, psychology of adjustment
3. *Development of Clinical Skills:* psychological tests, diagnostic procedures, counseling theory, approaches to community mental health, field work, supervised counseling practice and internship, group counseling, consultation skills
4. *Professional Orientation:* professional ethics, settings in which counseling psychologists work, relationships with members of other helping professions, techniques of supervision
5. *Development of Research Competence:* review and analysis of the research literature, measurement and evaluation, statistics, experimental design, planning and execution of a doctoral research project

To cover the areas listed above psychology departments may draw on courses offered in other departments of the university. Some require that the student complete a minor in one of the related disciplines. Others encourage students to take courses in several areas. Areas frequently drawn on include philosophy, sociology, anthropology, education, social work, economics, industrial relations, physical medicine and rehabilitation, computer science, and statistics.

How long does it take? A doctorate in counseling psychology can be completed in four years after the Bachelor's, but many students take five or six years. Why does it take so long? The most important reason is that in addition to mastering a body of knowledge, the prospective counseling psychologist must develop clinical skill and research competence. Clinical competence is developed by giving the student carefully graded experiences in an actual work setting such as a student counseling center, a mental health clinic, or the counseling service of an agency like the YMCA. These experiences are carefully supervised either by the faculty or by the staff of the agency involved.

In addition to the experiences a student may have early in his program, he is required, usually in his third or fourth year of study, to serve the equivalent of a one-year full-time internship in an agency providing counseling services, such as a college counseling center or a Veterans Administration Hospital. These are usually paid internships; the size of the stipend is a less important factor in the selection of an internship center than the quality of the services it provides and the quality and amount of supervision the intern will receive.

Research competence is provided through courses in statistics and experimental design, through seminars in which students review, analyze, and plan research studies in their field of interest, and through research assistantships. As in other fields, a doctorate in counseling psychology involves a dissertation, usually one involving the manipulation of experimental variables or a design in which the relationships between various variables can be explored statistically.

Beyond the doctorate. There are many opportunities for continued professional development beyond the doctorate. Active involvement in the affairs of the *American Psychological Association* and the *American Personnel and Guidance Association* and their regional and state organizations; participation in the programs that are presented at the annual conventions of these organizations; service on the editorial boards of professional journals like the *Journal of Counseling Psychology* and the *Personnel and Guidance Journal;* consultantships; research and scholarly writing; further study through post-doctoral fellowships: these are some of the ways in which counseling psychologists serve the profession and deepen and diversify their skills.

There are several ways in which the profession recognizes and rewards competence beyond that signified by the possession of a doctorate. Counseling psychologists with five years of experience are eligible for diplomate status which is conferred after an examination conducted by the *American Board of Examiners in Professional Psychology.* Counseling psychologists can also achieve the status of Fellow in the American Psychological Association, which requires a substantial contribution to psychology as a science. Potential fellows are nominated by an appropriate division of the Association, in the case of counseling psychologists Division 17, the Division of Counseling Psychology. Finally, both the American Psychological Association and the American Personnel and Guidance Association periodically make awards in recognition of outstanding research and service.

DEMAND FOR COUNSELING PSYCHOLOGISTS

One way to gauge the importance and future of a field is to ask how many people are engaged in it and to compare the present figures with past figures. According to this criterion, counseling psychology is both a strong field and a growing field. In membership, the Division of Counseling Psychology is one of the larger of the 26 divisions of the American Psychological Association, varying over the years between second and fourth place in size. Even more important is the fact that it increased membership by more than 60% between 1950 and 1960. The Division currently has approximately 1600 members.

In spite of the increase in the number of counseling psychologists, the demand for them continues to outstrip the supply. Although accurate figures on supply and demand are very difficult to ascertain, the following will serve to give a general picture of the need for counseling psychologists.

College and University Counseling Centers

At the time this is being written, the demand for doctoral-level counseling psychologists in well-established college and university counseling centers is reported to be approximately five times the available supply. That is to say, if all counseling psychologists who received the doctorate this year were to work in college and university counseling centers, they would fill only one-fifth of the present available positions. As established institutions expand and new institutions inaugurate counseling services, future demand will exceed the supply in even greater proportions.

Veterans Administration

Based on present staffing criteria, the Department of Medicine and Surgery of the Veterans Administration estimates its present need for psychologists at 1890. Against this need, 840 psychologists, mostly clinical and counseling psychologists, are employed in the Veterans Administration. In commenting on the need for counseling psychologists a Veterans Administration official has said "Because of the tremendous shortages in both clinical and counseling psychology, it has been futile for us to try to project specifically for either clinical or counseling psychologists." The need for counseling psychologists is, in his words, "overwhelming," not only in the Veterans Administration, but in other Federal agencies as well. For some years, counseling psychologists have been designated a critical shortage category.

Other Agencies

According to figures compiled (Hitchcock, 1965) by the Executive Director of the American Personnel and Guidance Association, there are between 50,000 and 60,000 full- and part-time counselors in the United States today. Simply to meet currently anticipated needs the number of full-time counselors will have to increase by more than 10,000 per year between now and 1970, and by about 12,500 a year between 1970 and 1975. This means that "the present program of education of counselors clearly must be more than tripled immediately. By 1970 the production of counselors must be expanded again, probably two-fold." By 1975 the number of counselors in elementary schools will need to have increased from 2500 in 1965 to 53,500, in secondary schools from 31,000 to 72,000, in junior colleges from 800 to 5000, in colleges and universities from 4000 to 7600, in employment services from 3000 to 8000, in rehabilitation programs from 3500 to 5700, and in Office of Economic Opportunity programs from 450 to more than 7000.

Although most of these positions will be filled by counselors with one or two years' training beyond the bachelor's degree, persons holding a doctorate in counseling psychology, guidance, or a related field who can fill or advance to supervisory and leadership positions will also be in great demand.

Future Trends

Although the demand for counseling psychologists is already far in excess of supply, there are several factors that are likely to increase that demand still further in the years ahead. The most important of these is society's growing concern for those who are physically, emotionally, mentally, and culturally handicapped, a concern that is reflected in such undertakings as the Job Corps, Operation Headstart, Youth Opportunity Centers, and the expansion of various types of rehabilitation programs.

Equally important are the changes that have been and still are taking place on the educational and occupational scene. These include the growing recognition by schools and colleges of the part they can and should play in helping students fulfil their potential for growth; the displacement of workers through automation and technological change; the decline in the number of jobs that can be filled by persons with limited education and training; the difficulties that many young work-seekers encounter in getting established occupationally; the increasing number of married women who are seeking to return to work after age 35; the rapidly growing number of young people who want or are finding it necessary to continue their education and training and need help in making sound educational and vocational decisions.

These are some of the developments that have created a demand for counselors who are skilled in identifying and developing outlets for human potential in all its different forms. This is the challenge—and the *raison-d'etre* of counseling psychology.

REFERENCES

Hitchcock, A. A. Counselors: Supply, demand, need. In *Counselor development in American society*—A report to the Office of Manpower, Automation and Training (U.S. Department of Labor) and the Office of Education (U.S. Department of Health, Education, and Welfare). Washington, D. C.: 1965, pp. 83–111.

Thompson, A. S., & Super, D. E. (Eds.). *The professional preparation of counseling psychologists. Report on the 1964 Greyston Conference.* New York: Bureau of Publications, Teachers College, Columbia University, 1964.

Chapter 19
Counseling Psychology, the Psychoeducator Model and the Future: A Definition in 1976

ALLEN E. IVEY
University of Massachusetts

Counseling psychology is what counseling psychologists do. Activities, however, are never sufficient to describe a profession or a psychological specialty. Constant reference to conceptual frames, goals, and specific methods and techniques of professional practice is needed to maintain counseling as a distinct professional grouping with a unique potential for contribution to society.

The Professional Affairs Committee of Division 17 (counseling psychology) was charged in 1974 with the task of (1) defining the current boundaries and relationships of counseling psychology with other specialties; (2) defining the role of counseling psychology as a preventive-developmental function; and (3) more specifically, to examine the policies counseling psychologists should adopt in "the teaching of skills to noncounselors. To what extent should we give our profession away?"

The thrust of these charges implicitly defines counseling psychology as a *unique* helping specialty that is deeply concerned with educative functions as well as traditional remedial roles. Further, the teaching function of the counseling psychologist has become clear enough that special attention now must be given to standards to be used when working in educational/preventive functions. Out of the charges and from the reports of the several subcommittees attacking issues of professional role and function has evolved a counseling psychologist who is envisioned as a *psychoeducator,* a person who uses many skills, theories, and methods to facilitate human growth. Counseling and psychotherapy remain as important skills of the counseling psychologist, but they are only one aspect of a broad new helping role . . . the counseling psychologist as psychoeducator.

This paper by Dr. Allen E. Ivey, Chairman of the Division 17 Professional Affairs Committee, 1974–1976, is intended to integrate the several papers of the Committee's long report into one brief statement.

"Counseling Psychology, the Psychoeducator Model and the Future," by A. E. Ivey, *The Counseling Psychologist,* 1976, 6(3), 72–75. Reprinted by permission.

At this point, it seems appropriate to turn to the several reports of the subcommittees of Division 17's Professional Affairs Committee and examine their determination of the future role definition of the counseling psychologist.

WHAT IS COUNSELING PSYCHOLOGY?

The counseling psychologist was defined in 1968 (Jordaan, Myers, Layton, & Morgan, 1968) as engaging in three primary roles. The first is the *remedial* or *rehabilitative* role, the second the *preventive,* and the third the *educative and developmental.* In essence, the report of the Professional Affairs Committee endorses this tripartite definition, but the ordering of primary roles has changed. It is believed that the educational/developmental role of the counseling psychologist must now be considered to be primary with the preventive role serving as the secondary function. The traditional remedial and rehabilitative role is not discarded, but it becomes subsumed under a clarified and enlarged definition of counseling psychology.

The psychoeducator model has been put forward by Authier, Gustafson, Guerney, and Kasdorf (1975) and provides an all-inclusive model for the functions of the counseling psychologist. The psychoeducator sees the helping function "not in terms of abnormality (or illness) → diagnosis → prescription → therapy → cure; but rather in terms of client dissatisfaction (or ambition) → goal setting → skill teaching → satisfaction or goal achievement. The person being served "is seen as analogous to a pupil, rather than a patient" (Authier et al., 1975, p. 31). Remedial and rehabilitative functions remain important in this model, but the mode of action for change becomes far broader. Prevention activities focus on attainable goals rather than vague descriptions of client or system "need." Most important, systematic educational programs are made available to teach people how to achieve their own uniqueness.

The counseling psychologist engages in all the functions of remediation, prevention, and education, but her or his role is no longer primarily *counseling*—that "special kind of interchange between a professionally trained counselor and a person who has sought or might benefit from his services" (Jordaan et al., 1968). Rather the counseling psychologist now considers counseling only one of a host of skills to educate people for life. Counseling and therapy, important though they may be, are now limited constructs that fail to take into account the broad new functions of the counseling psychologist.

Counseling psychologists work in educational settings, primarily in colleges or universities. Those who work in clinics or hospitals are often involved in educational functions. In contrast, clinical psychologists are more frequently employed in hospital or psychiatric settings and school psychologists in public schools (Cates, 1970). Manning and Cates (1972), in addition, found marked differences in work activities among the three groupings:

public schools, colleges and universities, and clinics or hospitals. Counseling psychologists were found to be working with vocational, educational, and personal adjustment problems as well as in student personnel areas and with counseling theory. Psychotherapy, as a work orientation of counseling psychologists, ranked low, whereas it was a primary activity, along with diagnostic testing, of clinicians. School psychologists were especially concerned with behavior problems and pupil assessment. Counseling psychologists do indeed do things other than those in closely related fields.

Thus, although overlap clearly exists with related specialties in psychology, counseling psychology does appear to have its own unique identity and function. The 1964 Greyston Conference (Thompson & Super, 1964) presented counseling psychology as a distinct discipline and was supported by the 1968 statement (Jordaan et al., 1968). The functions and work settings of the counseling psychologist do not appear to have changed markedly. However, the ordering of work functions seems to be changing markedly. Despite some arguments about the role of psychological education and the psychoeducator model (cf. Arbuckle, 1976a and b; Ivey, 1976), a new role and function building on traditional roles seem to be developing. The counseling psychologist is becoming a broadly based psychoeducator.

A CONCEPTUAL FRAME FOR PSYCHOEDUCATION

"Counseling" is but one of many intervention strategies we now have in our professional repertoire. We are now able to talk about training, consultation, media—such as films, videotapes, computer terminals, bio-feedback, and programmed manuals—to mention just a few intervention strategies. It was never intended that "counseling," which is a process, should become an outcome or be perceived as an end in itself [Hurst, 1976].

This statement of the subcommittee on skills dissemination sets the stage for a much-needed model of the counseling psychologist role. If the vaguely defined task of "counseling" is not to be the total role, how can one conceptualize a new model of helper functioning, one that gives special attention to psychoeducation? Four key aspects of psychoeducation in counseling practice have been identified (Morrill, Oetting, & Hurst, 1974):

1. *The product or content variable.* Psychoeducation is not just a concept, it is also a wide array of products with a substantial content. These products range from training in discrimination skills for effective helping, life-planning workshops, training in listening skills, videotapes for systematic desensitization, parent effectiveness training, couples workshops, interpersonal process recall, paraprofessional training guides, documents, films, family intervention strategies, and biofeedback training. These innovative methods and concepts are now very much part of counseling psychology practice. They are as much the *content* of counseling psychology as the Rogerian construct of empathic understanding, or the Gestalt hot-seat, or the psycho-dynamic free association technique.

The content of counseling psychology has broadened in the past several years to include psychological education, behavior modification training, family practice, community consultation, and many new skills. Although each of these products can be employed in a remedial sense, the psychoeducator function of teaching skills is becoming increasingly important.

2. *The target variable.* Counseling psychology even as recently as 1968 was conceived of primarily as an individually oriented profession. Although lip service was given to organizations and society, training and practice were primarily focused on single persons. Since 1968, this has changed markedly; although individual practice is still important, counseling psychologists are increasingly working with primary groups, associational groups, and the community or institution. The primary group of family or close friends is now recognized as a prime target for interventions. Although some members of a group may receive therapy, the bulk of group members is receiving psychoeducational work and training in goal achievement. No longer can the counseling psychologist rest comfortably in her or his office and do only individual counseling. The target population for professional helping has grown immensely.

3. *The method variable.* Although once counseling psychologists thought only in terms of working directly with clients, they now find themselves training others to provide service (for example, paraprofessionals) and thus find themselves in an indirect service function. Skill dissemination within the psychoeducational model may include the use of media, programmed texts, and computer terminals. Each change in method expands the ability of the skilled counseling psychologist to provide services. No longer is counseling psychology relegated to one-to-one helping.

4. *The purpose variable.* Simply put, this is the traditional counseling psychologist triad of education/development, prevention, and remediation. The Professional Affairs Committee as a whole and in its several subcommittees seemed to emphasize the point that psychoeducation as a counseling psychologist role would be best oriented toward educative rather than remedial functions.

In summary, the psychoeducational model provides a broad new content for counseling psychologist functioning; our clientele has broadened from individuals to include families, primary groups, associational groups, and larger community institutions. Our method can range from direct intervention to the more purposeful indirect interventions of teaching others how to help, and it can even include media approaches. The purpose of these new functions becomes primarily educational with remedial work clearly becoming a secondary function.

AN EXAMINATION OF SKILL DISSEMINATION

Assuming that the psychoeducational model is to become even more prominent in the role of the counseling psychologist, it seems appropriate that standards of skill dissemination and psychoeducation be developed. Prior ethical standards for professional practice in counseling are used as are standards for excellence in psychological tests. However, the following statement seems especially pertinent:

> Increasingly, counseling psychologists have become aware of the proliferating number of programs being developed to teach a variety of intervention skills to "paraprofessionals" as well as a number of programs being designed to teach life or coping skills directly to individuals (self-help programs). The proliferation of such programs has gone on without a clear statement by counseling psychologists concerning the standards by which to evaluate such programs, or, in the case of developers of such programs, the standards that should be maintained with regard to the development of these programs [Danish & Ginsberg, 1976].

The subcommittee on skill dissemination examined standards for skill-dissemination programs. If counseling psychology is to move to a psychoeducator model, then clear standards of professional competence need spelling out. It is not possible to detail all the recommendations of this subcommittee here, but a few relevant portions provide impetus for thinking through the professional role of the psychoeducator. Some of the key recommendations for standards of skill dissemination follow:

1. Manuals for skill dissemination should communicate information regarding the program clearly and succinctly. Data should be included on the theoretical-conceptual frame, and a summary of research data on effectiveness of the program should be presented.
2. Advertising for skill dissemination programs should maintain full professional standards of truthfulness.
3. The audience for the skill dissemination program should be clearly defined. The nature of the specific problems focused on by the program should be clear.
4. The necessary professional skills to begin a program should be clear. Specifically, what should be the competencies of the trainer? What is the recommended format for instruction (workshop, lecture, media, and so on)? What are the specific procedures for training?
5. What systematic evaluations have been conducted on the validity and effectiveness of the program? Are there specific groups where this program may not be effective? This may be supplemented by specific evaluation techniques whereby users of the program may determine their own effectiveness.

If one views the many training programs for the psychoeducator counseling psychologist that are available, it may be realized that few of them meet these minimum criteria. Advertisements are accepted in our professional journals, workshops are conducted with glowing promises . . . unless we police ourselves and our use of materials, the promise of skill dissemination will be lost.

THE ROLE OF PREVENTION

Prevention is only one of the major thrusts we emphasize. Perhaps an even greater emphasis should be placed upon giving psychology away so that the greatest number of persons achieve the best possible adjustment. In addition to focusing on the suffering of the sick, the profession should be enhancing the growth and development, the adjustment and satisfaction of all people. In other words, helping everyone use psychology to help themselves. This approach leads to a strengthening and broadening of individual self-reliance and interpersonal support. If people can be assisted in the use of cultural and societal resources, in making autonomous decisions, and to rely on themselves, we will be moving toward a psycho-sufficient society [Clack, 1975].

Prevention is too often thought of as a locating of sore spots in society or in an individual and the elimination of them. In this way, much of what is termed prevention in fact closely follows a traditional medical model of rehabilitation. Prevention as defined by the subcommittees examining this issue lies closer to the psychoeducation model of educative/development functioning. Exemplary prevention activities include educating families in better ways of bearing and raising children, educating and training people in interpersonal relations, having psychological education as a part of curricula at all education levels, giving special attention to the concerns of minority, disadvantaged, disenfranchised, and forgotten groups, sensitizing the public to the prevalence and effects of mental disorder, and involving counseling psychologists in career counseling.

These broad functions could be defined as any effort that makes a society richer and fuller for its inhabitants. Prevention, then, includes issues of socioeconomic injustice and unequal income distribution, examination of poor school facilities, study of health delivery systems, job development as well as job counseling . . . in the broadest dimension, the counseling psychologist in the psychoeducator model is interested in developing the health environment for its citizens. This, of course, is not new and simply reflects the ancient statement of Parsons (1894) that counseling must be concerned with institutions and society as well as the individual person.

Prevention at the College Level

Because many counseling psychologists work at the college level, special attention was given to the importance of prevention with this population. The parallels between conceptual frames in this report and the statement below should be evident:

Prevention aims to anticipate future problems and move to prevent them (1) by teaching individuals new skills that will help avoid problems and by supporting individuals' attempts to use their skills, (2) by modifying environments to prevent problems, and (3) by studying environments and populations (for example, total population, "high risk" populations, and populations at critical periods) to gather data on which (1) and (2) would be based. Prevention implies an essentially proactive role [Haskell, 1975].

Important in the above statement is the emphasis on environments. The statement begins with a strong educative model evocative of the remainder of this summary statement. In this statement, an additional emphasis is put on the importance of environmental intervention as an important psychoeducational role of the counseling psychologist.

The report of this committee is lengthy, but a few of their key recommendations for the future follow:

1. Counseling psychologists should involve themselves actively in policy-making boards of the institutions in which they serve. They can bring policy-making and decision-making skills to bear on broad institutional problems.

2. Problems of institutional racism are paramount on a university campus. Counseling alone on discrimination issues will be ineffective. Counseling psychologists must involve themselves in affirmative action programs, sponsor symposia and workshops on racism in society, and actively involve themselves in programs of cultural awareness.

3. Issues of alienation appear frequently in individual helping sessions. The institutional climate that helped produce alienation must be attacked as well as the individual problem. This may be done through increased use of small groups in classrooms, peer counseling programs, residence hall efforts to "humanize" living situations, and consultation with residence hall staff.

4. Student-faculty relationships should be facilitated through better classroom atmospheres, student-faculty informal interaction, training of faculty advisers in counseling and communication skills, and attempts to see that the university reward system recognizes interpersonal excellence among its faculty members.

5. The relationship among communities in the university and between university and state or city needs to be improved. The articulation between high school and college can be improved by a wide variety of organizational efforts. High school career days, meetings with state legislatures, peer counseling programs, freshman orientation programs, attention to special groups such as veterans, older students, and women are but a few of the many things counseling psychologists can do to enrich student life. Counseling psychologists must make themselves accessible and available to many groups, which may mean a major change in time schedules and life styles for some helpers.

6. Counselor role and function in colleges and universities must change. Advocacy models, use of peer counselors, new relationships with other professionals, inclusion of consumer populations (that is, students) in program planning, and new programs in staff development are essential.

7. Finally, evaluation of new programs and methods is essential if new

modes and models of counseling psychology are to flourish and grow. Systematic program evaluation should be part of every counseling psychologist's training and no program should be implemented without an adequate evaluation design.

It may be seen that this subcommittee, although operating within the framework of the term *prevention*, has expanded this concept to the psychoeducation model once again. The counseling psychologist can no longer be a passive individual sitting in an office waiting for someone with a "problem" to appear. The counseling psychologist, the psychoeducator of the future, must be ready with a wide array of techniques to promote effective development of clients in a nurturing and healthy environment.

CONCLUDING STATEMENT: THE EFFECTIVE COUNSELING PSYCHOLOGIST

Terms such as *effective* and *competent* are appearing increasingly in the literature. As our field becomes more precise, our ability to predict results from our efforts increases. We are now at the time when we can state quite precisely, in many cases, the anticipated results of our treatment, be it preventive, educative, or remedial.

In the past, the counseling psychologist who has been able to "talk a good story," in the jargon of the trade, has been considered professionally effective. We had little on which to base judgments of competence and effectiveness. However, as counseling and psychology have grown over the past decade, our ability to make significant changes in clients and in client situations (that is, environments) has increased manyfold, and counselor competence and effectiveness can be more adequately judged. (It was once thought that the psychologist who could manage a case load of clients was effective.)

Counseling and therapy skills remain as important as always, but they are no longer sufficient for the helper to be fully professional. The profession of counseling psychology is at long last at the place where it can deliver effective educative and preventive services that will make a difference in the lives of clients. The psychoeducator model, which is implicitly or explicitly mentioned in all reports of the Professional Affairs Committee, appears to be the direction of the future.

REFERENCES

Arbuckle, D. The school counselor: The voice of society? *Personnel and Guidance Journal,* 1976, *54,* 427–430. (a)

Arbuckle, D. Comment. *Personnel and Guidance Journal,* 1976, *54,* 434. (b)

Authier, J., Gustafson, K., Guerney, B., & Kasdorf, J. The psychological practitioner as teacher: A theoretical-historical and practical review. *The Counseling Psychologist,* 1975, *5*(2), 31–50.

Cates, J. Psychology's manpower: Report of the 1968 Register of Scientific and Technical Personnel. *American Psychologist,* 1970, *25,* 254-263.

Clack, J. *Report of the Midwest Subcommittee on Prevention.* Unpublished paper. Counseling Center, Illinois State University, Bloomington-Normal, 1975.

Danish, S., & Ginsberg, M. *Evaluating skill dissemination programs.* Unpublished paper, College of Human Development, The Pennsylvania State University, University Park, Pennsylvania, 1976.

Haskell, E. *Prevention: A program dimension for college and university counselors.* Report of the Western Subcommittee on Prevention. Unpublished paper, Counseling Center, San Francisco State College, 1975.

Hurst, J. *Skills dissemination: Guidelines for counseling psychologists.* Report of the subcommittee on skills dissemination. Counseling Center, Colorado State University, Fort Collins, 1976.

Ivey, A. Invited response: The counselor as teacher. *Personnel and Guidance Journal,* 1976, *54,* 431-434.

Jordaan, J. (Ed.), Myers, R., Layton, W., & Morgan, H. *The counseling psychologist.* Washington, D. C.: American Psychological Association, 1968.

Manning, T., & Cates, J. Specialization within psychology. *American Psychologist,* 1972, *27,* 462-467.

Morrill, W., Oetting, E., & Hurst, J. Dimensions of counseling functioning. *Personnel and Guidance Journal,* 1974, *52,* 354-359.

Parsons, F. The philosophy of mutualism. *The Arena,* 1894, May, 783-815.

Thompson, A., & Super, D. (Eds.). *The professional preparation of counseling psychologists.* New York: Bureau of Publications, Teachers College, Columbia University, 1964.

INDEX